SPEECHES IN ENGLISH

Consulting Editor   Don Geiger

UNIVERSITY OF CALIFORNIA, BERKELEY

SPEECHES
IN ENGLISH

Edited by *Bower Aly*,

PROFESSOR OF SPEECH
UNIVERSITY OF OREGON

and Lucile F. Aly,

ASSISTANT PROFESSOR OF ENGLISH
UNIVERSITY OF OREGON

 Random House · New York

In so far as a dedication may be thought necessary,
the editors gleefully dedicate this book to each other.

§ Preface

Some people choose to read poems; others prefer to read speeches. Poems are sometimes thought to be more universal in their appeal, more spiritual in their approach to mankind than are speeches that must often deal with problems seemingly temporary and mundane. Yet some speeches are doubtless closer to the human being than are some poems; as the wisest man who ever wrote about speeches observed long ago, deliberative speeches deal characteristically with the very human problems of ways and means, war and peace, national defense, imports and exports, and legislation.[1]

In the United States in recent years speeches have declined in popularity, even in the schools, where every form of discourse—including the detective story—seems to thrive somewhat better than the speech. This development is to be deplored because the Americans of today, more than any other people, need to understand (as their forefathers did) what speeches are for, what they are supposed to do, and, above all, how far a speechmaker can be trusted.

The editors offer this volume as a modest effort toward making the texts of some of the great speeches readily available in an attractive format. Each speech is provided with an introductory essay. The editors have also provided, following each speech, a Critical Analysis and Suggestions for Further Reading.

Of all the arts, oratory (speechmaking) is the most human, doubtless because a great speech is man talking to mankind, whereas all the other arts today appear more and more as artists talking to each other. A truly great speech is, as M. Lincoln Schuster observed, "literature on fire," and the fire warms—or burns—not only the sophisticates, the literati, the cognoscenti, but all who can hear. If it be said that a taste for the reading of speeches must be cultivated, a similar observation could doubtless be made concerning most of the endeavors of men. In a relatively open society, where men are generally free to make and to listen to speeches, perhaps no learning men can achieve is more useful socially and hence more worthy of

[1] Aristotle, *Rhetoric*, 1359b.

vii

cultivation than the understanding of the business of speechmaking.

The speeches here recommended as worthy of thoughtful reading have two common bonds: each speech is in English and thus exemplifies the tie that has existed and still exists among those for whom this language is the common tongue; and each of the speeches presented is certified, not only by the present editors but by the judgment of many other editors, scholars, and critics, to have been a great speech at its delivery and to remain as one of the treasures of discourse in the English language.

If one classifies extant texts of speeches by their faithfulness to what the orator actually said, there are two types to consider: corrupt and more corrupt. The editors have naturally favored the former type, so far as they were able and knowledgeable; but no attempt has been made to go beyond the documentation of the source of the text through the sometimes impenetrable thicket of its complete provenience. Every text provided is believed, however, to be taken without any abridgment from one of the better sources available.

Every book is the product of many minds and many hands. For assistance in the preparation of this book the editors are indebted to many persons, of whom it is possible to name the following: Professor Don Geiger, of the University of California, for editorial assistance and especially for indulgences granted; to David Dushkin of Random House, for patient forbearance toward somewhat opinionated editors; to Gregory and Mary Hutchison, of Washington, D.C., and to Frances Gray, of South Eugene High School, for criticism and counsel; and to Gwendolyn Diana and Velma Francisco, of the University of Hawaii, and to Gwen Clavadetscher, of the University of Oregon, for invaluable assistance with the manuscript.

For errors of omission or commission, the editors admit full responsibility.

Bower Aly

Eugene, Oregon, 1967   Lucile Folse Aly

Contents

§ *Contents*

SPEECHES IN ENGLISH

Introduction:
The Study of Speechmaking

☙❧

BACKGROUND

The art of speechmaking has long been studied in schools. Before the English or any other modern language existed, teachers taught and pupils learned in ancient Greece and Rome—even in the Egypt of the Pharaohs—how to make and to understand speeches. In schools of the Occident, perhaps music alone has a longer tradition than speechmaking. And in these thousands of years during which speechmaking has been studied systematically, it has been the subject of many theories. The theory presented here is chiefly that of the scientist-philosopher Aristotle, as supported by the Roman orator Cicero and modified by the ideas subsequently developed by scholars, teachers, and speechmakers.

One way to understand speechmaking is to suppose that there are two elemental forms of discourse: poems and speeches. This division of the arts of discourse, if followed blindly, can be misleading; and indeed some modern scholars prefer to think of *all* discourse as imbued with suasion—a term normally reserved for speeches and their counterparts. Nevertheless, most people most of the time will make a distinction between verse being read or chanted and a speech being delivered.

From the art of discourse employed by the poet has developed the short story, the novel, the drama—those forms of literature that are *about* life. They call upon fancy, upon imagination, in a special way to produce a work of art that stands removed from what men sometimes call "the real world." To be sure, a drama may include speeches, and if the drama is a good one, even some great speeches; but even the greatest speeches represented in drama are related to speeches delivered from the public platform only as are the battle scenes in the play to an actual field of combat. It is unlikely that an audience

3

observing Mark Antony speak his lines in Shakespeare's *Julius Caesar* will rush out, as the mob does in the play, and burn the city.

Just as certain literary forms have developed from the poem—perhaps in its earliest form the ballad, the saga, the epic—so other forms of discourse have developed from the art of speechmaking. Especially since the invention of printing, editorials, pamphlets, and propagandistic tracts have been designed to influence people and to move them to action. The development of mass media, particularly radio and television, has altered the problems of persuasion in some respects; and these media have sought and sometimes found new approaches. Yet the leading principle of sober discourse, that is, of influencing people in the world about us, appears today to be as old as the art of speechmaking.

VALUES AND DIFFICULTIES
Values

If men are interested, as Ralph Waldo Emerson observed them to be, in accounts of speechmaking, perhaps it is because in the annals of speechmaking, as in those of warfare, men can envision themselves as participants. As the stories, the anecdotes, the history of speechmaking provide one of the most interesting ways to view the past, so they are also one of the most highly educative. For speechmaking, the most pervasive of all the arts, reveals mankind in a uniquely human enterprise, one that other creatures cannot employ. If it be true, as Cicero observed, that not to know the past is always to remain a child, then those who wish to be adult must learn something of the past; and a significant part of man's past is to be found in his public discourse.

Admittedly, difficulties exist in discovering and understanding the history of speechmaking. But such difficulties exist wherever man turns toward understanding his past. Even a battlefield can be lost; and military historians may ponder, as they endeavor to re-create a battle scene, why Meade did not pursue Lee after the battle of Gettysburg or whether Lee should have ordered the charge on Little Round Top. The difficulties in studying the history of speechmaking are thus not altogether unique, and to a degree they can be circumvented. In any event, the values to be gained from learning what can be discovered about speeches of the past would seem to make the effort worthwhile for many people, particularly those who wish to enjoy a liberal education, that is, those who have decided not to remain children forever.

Difficulties

Three major difficulties in the study of historic speeches that should be recognized at once concern the *text*, the *utterance*, and the *hearers*.

THE TEXT

The thoughtful student must bear in mind that the paper held in his hand is not the speech: it is merely a report of the speech. Like any other document, this report has its provenience—its own history. The student must seek out the life story of the text purporting to represent what the orator said on a given occasion. As he studies the great speech attributed to Patrick Henry, for example, the student will find that the text now current was reconstructed by Patrick Henry's nephew, William Wirt, some years after the event; and that the text may not be accurate. A speech reconstructed from what men remember years later is likely to bear something less than a close resemblance to the speech as delivered. And the student will learn that Daniel Webster was given to revising his speeches—perhaps to make them read better—after they were spoken; thousands of copies of his revised speeches were printed and distributed throughout the country. Other speakers, less gifted than Webster, have so revised their speeches that the qualities of oral style have been largely removed.

THE UTTERANCE

Even if the text of the speech is beyond doubt—say an electronic transcription of a speech made in recent times, perhaps one by Winston Churchill—the student must remember that a text is at best only part of the speech. The written word does not reveal the

5

speaker's inflection, his gesture, his face, his eye, his movement. Although accurate in so far as the text is concerned, the transcript of the speech is limited in other ways.

THE HEARERS

Often what the student most wants to know about a speech is the way it affected the audience. Yet this information is exceedingly difficult to obtain, even for speeches of comparatively recent times. For example, newspaper accounts of the reception given speeches delivered by Thomas Hart Benton in Missouri before the Civil War vary according to the partisanship of the editor. One newspaper will declare that the senator spoke to a large and enthusiastic audience. Another, reporting the same occasion, will say that a small group of "Old Tom's" supporters gathered round to hear him. What members of an audience really thought about a speech, what they said about it, how they responded to it should be the object of cautious study.

Having confronted the difficulties of text, of utterance, and of audience, the student of speeches may find still other problems. He should take comfort, however, in the knowledge that the goal he pursues—an understanding of speechmaking—is worth the effort. And perhaps he may also take a perverse satisfaction in observing that his difficulties, though different in some respects, are really not greater than those of some other seekers after knowledge.

THE USES AND ABUSES OF SPEECHMAKING
The Uses

In a sense, speechmaking has no special subject matter, for speeches can presumably be made on any subject whatsoever. Yet in another sense, speechmaking does have its own specialty, namely, that part of any topic requiring explanation or persuasion. Speechmaking is concerned characteristically with questions of probability, with problems of doubt or belief that cannot be settled by inspection. The responsible orator values both fact and truth. If he is wise, he em-

6

ploys the facts available to him, and presumably he relies upon his own conception of truth and that attributed to his audience. But as he makes speeches, he is concerned to establish a policy that has not yet been concerted, to get men to see why they should act in a given way. This area of probability is the special province of persuasion, of speechmaking.

Speechmaking is thus one of the social forces. It is a way to influence policy. Indeed, some people would say that persuasion, as employed characteristically in speeches, is one of the three great social forces, the others being violence (police or military action) and money (fiscal or economic control). One who wishes to understand human events is wise to ignore neither the role of persuasion nor those of economic and military power.

The Abuses

Considered as a form of power, like wealth or generalship, speechmaking is apt to be abused. The knowledge of the uses of speechmaking is available to anyone who has the ability and the willingness to learn: to the informed and the uninformed, to the reasonable and the unreasonable, to honest men and shysters. It has been said that figures do not lie, but liars do figure. So also it may be said that speechmakers are not shysters, but shysters do make speeches. Cato's definition of the orator—"a good man speaking well"—is subject to the observation that in various times and places wicked men have made speeches that have been effective with many classes of hearers.

That men who are evil or ill-advised can and do make speeches provides still another reason for understanding the art of speechmaking; for only two remedies are available to counter the effects of demagoguery, deceit, and perversion in public discourse. One is to educate men and women to intelligent, responsible, and effective use of the public language. The other is to create audiences wise in the ways of speakers. In an open society, where ideas may compete in relative freedom, some advantage exists for the speaker urging sound policy: it is usually easier to prove a fact than a lie. Furthermore, if the dictum attributed to Lincoln be accepted ("You can fool all of the people some of the time, and some of the people all of the time, but you can't fool all the people all the time"), a measure of safety can be found in folk wisdom. The reliance on the wisdom of the people and on the natural superiority of truth over falsehood is hazardous, however, unless truth (or wise policy) is supported by those skilled in detecting sophistry and advancing sound courses of action. Truth crushed to earth does not rise again without assistance, and some of the assistance is likely to come from responsible speakers and audiences.

THE SPEAKER'S MATERIALS

What materials are available to the speaker who must defend a cause or urge an action? In the conventional analysis, the speaker may find his materials of proof in three sources: the reasons inherent in his proposition, the emotions of his audience to which he can appeal, and his reputation as judged by the audience.

Reasons

The basic proof consists of reasons why the proposition is sound, why the cause is just, why the action advocated is wise. Thus Wendell Phillips in his remarkable speech in defense of Lovejoy demonstrated that, contrary to the assertions of his adversary, the murderers of Lovejoy bore no resemblance to the founding fathers:

> Mr. Chairman:—We have met for the freest discussion of these resolutions, and the events which gave rise to them. I hope I shall be permitted to express my surprise at the sentiments of the last speaker,— surprise not only at such sentiments from such a man, but at the applause they have received within these walls. A comparison has been drawn between the events of the Revolution and the tragedy at Alton. We have heard it asserted here, in Faneuil Hall, that Great Britain had a right to tax the Colonies, and we have heard the mob at Alton, the drunken murderers of Lovejoy, compared to those patriot fathers who threw the tea overboard! Fellow-citizens, is this Faneuil Hall doctrine? The mob at Alton were met to wrest from a citizen his just

8

rights,—met to resist the laws. We have been told that our fathers did the same; and the glorious mantle of Revolutionary precedent has been thrown over the mobs of our day. To make out their title to such defence, the gentleman says that the British Parliament had a *right* to tax these Colonies. It is manifest that, without this, his parallel falls to the ground; for Lovejoy had stationed himself within constitutional bulwarks. He was not only defending the freedom of the press, but he was under his own roof, in arms with the sanction of the civil authority. The men who assailed him went against and over the laws. The *mob*, as the gentleman terms it,—mob, forsooth! certainly we sons of the tea-spillers are a marvellously patient generation!—the "orderly mob" which assembled in the Old South to destroy the tea were met to resist, not the laws, but illegal exactions. Shame on the American who calls the tea-tax and stamp-act *laws!* Our fathers resisted, not the King's prerogative, but the King's usurpation. To find any other account, you must read our Revolutionary history upside down. Our State archives are loaded with arguments of John Adams to prove the taxes laid by the British Parliament unconstitutional,—beyond its power. It was not till this was made out that the men of New England rushed to arms. The arguments of the Council Chamber and the House of Representatives preceded and sanctioned the contest. To draw the conduct of our ancestors into a precedent for mobs, for a right to resist laws we ourselves have enacted, is an insult to their memory. The difference between the excitements of those days and our own, which the gentleman in kindness to the latter has overlooked, is simply this: the men of that day went for the right, as secured by the laws. They were the people rising to sustain the laws and constitution of the Province. The rioters of our day go for their own wills, right or wrong.[1]

The foregoing chain of reasoning established by Phillips clearly discloses the lack of parallel between the Alton mob and the revolutionary fathers who spilled the tea in Boston harbor. Observe that Phillips does not depend on a single statement: he provides a cogent series to support his contention that the Boston patriots were engaged in a just, and the Alton mob in a riotous, action. Note some of the lines of proof:

---

[1] For the full text of the speech, see below, pp. 167–175. In this and the following excerpts, references to interruptions and applause are omitted.

1. Lovejoy was not only defending the freedom of the press, but he was under his own roof, in arms with the sanction of the civil authority.
2. Our State archives are loaded with arguments of John Adams to prove the taxes laid by the British Parliament unconstitutional.
3. The arguments of the Council Chamber and the House of Representatives preceded and sanctioned the contest.

And finally, summarizing the argument that no parallel exists, Phillips concludes this section of his speech:

> They [the patriot forefathers] were the people rising to sustain the laws and constitution of the Province. The rioters of our day go for their own wills, right or wrong.

Obviously, Phillips considered that his statements—on which the probative value of his reasoning depends—were so well known and accepted by his audience as to require no citation to chapter and verse. Doubtless he was correct. Sometimes, however, facts or claims must be supported by citation or by testimony; and the speaker should expect to substantiate his evidence if and as required. The audience, as the end and object of the speech, is the judge of the extent to which the speaker must go in providing citation to documents or corroborative testimony. In establishing his reasons, the speaker has two and only two instruments: the example and the enthymeme.

THE EXAMPLE

The example, employed in the inductive approach to the reasoned speech, suggests or fortifies a conclusion that what has happened once may happen or is likely to happen again. The example is often one of historical precedent, based on the principle of Patrick Henry:

> I have but one lamp by which my feet are guided, and that is the lamp of experience. I know of no way of judging the future but by the past.[2]

[2] Wayland Maxfield Parrish and Marie Hochmuth, eds., *American Speeches* (New York: Longmans, Green, 1954), p. 92.

In the search for historic examples, the speaker may look to ancient times: the founding fathers who debated the Constitution of the United States were given to quoting examples from the city-states of Greece. Or the speaker may choose examples from more recent experience. Miss Dorothy Thompson, speaking to the people of Canada, had no difficulty in finding recent examples of Hitler's perfidy:

> It seems that Germany has no quarrel with Great Britain. Hitler's quarrel is exclusively with this particular British Government, and especially with its head, Mr. Churchill. If Mr. Churchill will only resign and a government come in which is acceptable to Mr. Hitler, he will be glad to make peace immediately. He has no desire to destroy the British Empire. The man standing in the way of peace is Churchill, and the so-called fifth columnists are "only honest men, seeking peace." That is Hitler's argument.
>
> Now, of course, we have all become familiar with this. Mr. Hitler had no quarrel with Austria, only with Mr. Schuschnigg. So the moment Schuschnigg resigned he made peace with Austria by annexing it. He had no quarrel with Czechoslovakia, only with Mr. Beneš. So when Mr. Beneš resigned he made peace with Czechoslovakia by turning it into a Nazi Protectorate. He had no quarrel with any of the countries he has absorbed—only with those leaders who opposed the absorption. Mr. Hitler has no quarrel with traitors in any country on earth. They are his agents, and, as his agents, are honest men seeking peace. His quarrel is only with patriots.[3]

THE ENTHYMEME

The enthymeme, a way of reaching a tolerable conclusion in circumstances that do not permit a complete demonstration, is a kind of syllogism. The strict syllogism, often the product of the scientist's laboratory or the scholar's study, approaches certainty as a normal limit. For example, a physician may say, "Since the man's brain has been shattered, he must die," for in the present state of medical science, no way has been found to supply an artificial brain. The physician's syllogism could be stated categorically in its complete terms as follows:

[3] A. Craig Baird, ed., *Representative American Speeches: 1940–1941* (New York: H. W. Wilson, 1941), p. 139.

All men with shattered brains must die;
This man's brain has been shattered;
This man must die.

The responsible orator will not neglect the strict syllogism: indeed, he welcomes one whenever he can find it. The trouble is that in the kinds of questions that concern him and his audiences, the relative certainties from which strict syllogisms can be constructed are difficult or sometimes impossible to find. Hence he must employ the enthymeme, an instrument that should be known to every speaker as a way of thinking about those contingencies that do not permit complete proof.

In first-class speeches, the enthymemes will often appear as a chain, each link supporting the others. There is in fact nothing mysterious about the enthymeme: people use it every day—with greater or less success—to meet problems for which no certain answer is available. In normal pursuits, men and women have to decide whether to marry or remain single, whether to take a job with General Motors or with Chrysler, whether to move to California or to stay in Arkansas. In business, men must decide on the basis of judgment enforced by enthymemes whether to give the bonds of the state of New York a rating of AA or AAA, whether to support sterling or to devalue it, whether to buy life insurance or to invest in mutual funds.

The orator, the public man, must meet the same kind of problems, and he has no instruments to guide him other than those employed, perhaps crudely, by other citizens. The speechmaker, like the lowliest member of his audience, faces an inscrutable future. In dealing with matters affected with a public interest, he employs—as well as his talents and disposition permit—the enthymeme, the means everyone uses in coming to a conclusion about personal affairs. Hence, one of the best ways to study speeches is to seek out their enthymemes and to judge them in the brighter light supplied by time, by subsequent events.

In judging a speaker's enthymemes, the student should remember that the orator was speaking toward a future that had not yet appeared. The orators arousing South Carolina to secession, Woodrow Wilson refusing to compromise on the League of Nations, Hitler leading Germany to disaster—all might have made different speeches if they could have had a glimpse of things to come. Only to the greatest orators may be attributed the high quality of prescience, that is, not of prophecy exactly, but of a superior understanding of means at hand and of objects in view, with a wise assessment of what can be accomplished. Such an orator was Winston Churchill. A study of his speeches, with a special concern for his enthymemes, should prove rewarding.

Among other orators remarkable for their prescience may be named Edmund Burke and John Bright, among the British, and John C. Calhoun and Alexander Hamilton, among the Americans. The following excerpt from one of Hamilton's speeches before the convention called in New York to consider the proposed federal constitution will provide at once an example of the enthymeme and of Hamilton's use of it:

> But can we believe that one state will ever suffer itself to be used as an instrument of coercion? The thing is a dream. It is impossible. Then we are brought to this dilemma: Either a federal standing army is to enforce the requisitions, or the Federal Treasury is left without supplies, and the government without support. What, Sir, is the cure for this great evil? Nothing, but to enable the national laws to operate on individuals, in the same manner as those of the states do. This is the true reasoning upon the subject, Sir.[4]

In summary, anyone wishing to understand speechmaking should look to the speaker's materials, among which reasoning should normally be pre-eminent with a qualified audience; and the instruments available to the speechmaker's reasoning are the example and the enthymeme. One of the earliest considerations in judging a speech, therefore, should involve a series of questions: What were the examples? What were the enthymemes? Were they sound? Were they adequate to the purpose?

[4] Harold C. Syrett and Jacob E. Cooke, eds., *The Papers of Alexander Hamilton* (New York: Columbia University Press, 1962), Vol. V, pp. 19–20.

Appeals

If men had no passions, if they were creatures only of reason, then closely reasoned demonstration employing examples and enthymemes would constitute the speeches addressed to them. But men are not creatures of reason alone: they are subject to emotions and to loyalties that the speaker must consider as he constructs his speech. Perhaps no problem is more perplexing than that of determining the place of appeals to these emotions. No easy answer exists. Anyone can observe, however, two ways in which orators have dealt with the problem:

1. Those who can remember the speeches of Adolf Hitler, and those who hear the speeches of Fidel Castro, must be impressed with the emotional appeals to the baser passions of enmity and hatred.
2. Those who read the great speeches of Abraham Lincoln must be impressed with the appeals made, even in a terrible civil war, to the handsomer passions of human brotherhood and fellowship:

With malice toward none, with charity for all, with firmness in the right as God gives us to see the right, let us strive on to finish the work we are in, to bind up the nation's wounds, to care for him who shall have borne the battle and for his widow and his orphan, to do all which may achieve and cherish a just and lasting peace among ourselves and with all nations.[5]

The student of speechmaking is well advised, in the first place, to determine (if he can) whether the orator's appeals were to noble or to ignoble passions. Furthermore, he may apply this test: Were the emotional appeals employed in support of or in lieu of the enthymemes and examples that should be advanced in behalf of any serious proposal? The orator whose ranting appeals to the baser emotions are unsupported by evidence worthy of acceptance has found and will doubtless continue to find a hearing. If the human race

[5] Abraham Lincoln, "Second Inaugural Address," James D. Richardson, ed., *A Compilation of the Messages and Papers of the Presidents: 1789–1908* (Bureau of National Literature and Art, 1909), Vol. VI, p. 277.

is to prosper, however, a hearing must also be found for the orator whose appeals are based on reason and addressed to the healthier passions of mankind. One way to study speeches, then, is to examine the kind and quality of the orator's appeals to the emotions of his audience.

Reputation

In addition to his reasons and his appeals, the orator has another source of materials for advancing his cause. In some circumstances, the speaker's own reputation is the most powerful of all forces in behalf of his argument. Daniel Webster observed concerning true eloquence that it "does not consist in speech. Words and phrases may be marshalled in every way, but they cannot compass it. It must consist in the man, in the subject, and in the occasion." Concerning the man speaking, Ralph Waldo Emerson once declared: "The reason why anyone refuses his assent to your opinion, or his aid to your benevolent design, is in you. He refuses to accept you as a bringer of truth, because, though you think you have it, he feels that you have it not."

It is fair to say, in comment on the views of Webster and Emerson, that at the time the speech is being presented, the man, the subject, the occasion, and the speaker's character *as revealed* to his audience are so intricately mingled as to make separation difficult if not impossible. Yet the wisest criticism of speechmaking, and for that matter ordinary observation, leaves no doubt that what the speaker is, or is believed to be, often shouts to his audience in louder tones than does the message he conveys in words. In a free society, where the hearers are expected to decide, the issue they raise with the orator is often not "Is your counsel wise?" but "Can I trust you?" Hence the speaker is never far removed from at least three essential questions:

1. How can I make the hearers understand that I am a man of courage?
2. How can I make the hearers understand that I am a man of good common sense?

3. How can I make the hearers understand that I have their interests at heart?

In providing his answer to the foregoing questions, the speaker is aided enormously if the hearers know, or if he can demonstrate, that he is one of them—that he speaks their language, knows their thoughts, has a common heritage. Men will listen to a stranger and will sometimes listen with admiration; but in their great concerns, they are unlikely to follow the counsel of a man they do not trust, and they find it difficult to trust a man they do not know. Hence speakers normally seek common ground with their audience. The candidate for state's attorney will say, "You all know me: I was born and raised right here in Tompkins County." With similar technique, but in somewhat more impressive style and circumstances, Winston Churchill, addressing the Congress of the United States on December 26, 1941, remarked: "Here we are together." In his introduction he had already suggested that if his father had been an American, and his mother British, instead of the other way around, he might have got to Congress on his own! The introduction thus reminded the members of the Congress that Churchill's mother was Miss Jennie Jerome, of New York; that Churchill was, after all, part American; that he was not really a "foreigner."

The serious student of speechmaking observes that, even in a good society, audiences can sometimes be deceived by artful dodgers; for the first endeavor of the successful rogue engaged in speechmaking must be to appear as "a good man speaking well." And in a society where corruption is honored in high places, rogues are likely to have an advantage. Nevertheless, any group is apparently more likely to respond to the speaker who demonstrates courage, common sense, and good will toward his audience. One of the ways to study speechmaking is thus to discover the reputation of the orator with his audience and especially to find out what means he employed to make his virtues apparent.

Assumptions Underlying the Speaker's Materials

If the speaker is forthright, the best way to discover what he really believes is to look not solely to what he seeks to prove but also to what he assumes to be true. For when a speaker endeavors to prove a proposition, he admits that some doubt concerning it must exist, else his effort would be silly. The assumptions on which he rests his argument indicate what he considers to be a common ground of belief on which he—and presumably his audience—can rely.

Hence the student would do well to give double attention to every speech: once to discover what is being proved and again to discover what is assumed. The second listening (or reading) can be amazing as well as fruitful, for speakers—like audiences—are sometimes capable of believing egregious doctrines and, correctly or incorrectly, of attributing a belief in such doctrines to others. Furthermore, an assessment of the speaker's assumptions is necessary fully to understand his reasons, his appeals, and his attempt to establish himself as a person worthy to give counsel. In the choice of his examples and in the construction of his enthymemes, the speaker must be guided in part by their acceptability to his audience. Indeed, the speaker would like to be able to count on his hearers—or at least on some of them—to assist him in the construction of his chain of reasons; for a truly effective speech is likely to be a special kind of dialogue in which the speaker and the hearers work together to supply the proof. Similarly, the speaker should know what he can assume about the emotional state of the hearers and about their attitude toward himself as speaker. In short, a complete understanding of the speech requires a reading (or hearing) between the lines to determine the assumptions on which the speech materials—reasons, appeals, reputation—have been grounded.

THE KINDS OF SPEECHES

Because man is a classifying animal, and because he has found the classifying of speeches helpful in understanding them, he has instituted categories of speeches. One of the oldest and most convenient categories is by function: the deliberative speech, looking toward the future, is concerned with making policy; the forensic speech, looking toward the past, is concerned with rendering justice under law or equity; the ceremonial speech, looking at the present, is concerned chiefly with delineating honor and dishonor, praise and blame. Although the categories are illuminating when wisely employed, they can mislead the student who endeavors to put each speech neatly into one pigeonhole; for a speaker rarely if ever says to himself, "I will now construct a deliberative speech," or "I will deliver a ceremonial address." He is more likely to say, "I have to give a speech on the new tax policy," or "I am going to pay tribute to Thomas Jefferson." One who observes the speech after the event may discover the leading tendency to deliberate a policy, to plead a case, or to dedicate a shrine; but the speaker himself, preoccupied with the immediate task, is not circumscribed by categories.

In fact, to make a sharp division of all speeches by function is doubtless impossible: the President of the United States who goes to the Tennessee Valley to dedicate a dam may be concerned with the dedication; but he may also wish to influence opinion toward public power and toward the next election. The prosecutor who has one eye on the jury in a trial of great public interest may have the other eye on public opinion. The deliberative speeches in the House of Commons are ceremonial in the sense that they observe customs, rituals, and language fixed by the precedents of centuries. The categorizing of speeches should thus be employed in the light of the presumed chief function of the speech and its main tendency. One interesting approach is to look for the deliberative qualities in a presumably ceremonial speech or to discover those elements of a forensic speech that may influence future policy.

Deliberative Speeches

The best place to find deliberative speeches is in bodies that make rules, laws, or policies for their constituents. The Parliament of Great Britain, the Congress of the United States, and the legislatures of the several states are the obvious but by no means the only examples of such bodies. In a free society, voluntary organizations bring together persons of like mind or interest. The committee, the association, the club, and the society are found everywhere at all levels throughout the United States. Millions of Americans belong to one or more groups empowered to legislate as far as their writ runs. Thus the House of Delegates of the American Medical Association promulgates certain legislation for physicians. The American Bar Association develops policy for lawyers. Delegates to the Democratic or the Republican Party conventions make decisions of a quasi-legal status for their adherents.

Similarly, rules, laws, and policies are determined for a host of less well known but sometimes influential organizations: the National Association for the Advancement of Colored People; the Missouri State Teachers Association; the faculty of Cornell University; the American Cancer Society; the School Board of Portland, Oregon; the First Baptist Church of Dallas, Texas; the American Legion Post No. 221; and innumerable others sharing common purposes or loyalties. Normally these groups, governed by customs derived from the rich experience of the British and American peoples in the procedures of legislative bodies, prefer constitutions, bylaws, and standing rules, that is, provisions for protecting the right to debate, to deliberate policy. Doubtless the deliberation of such groups sometimes concerns trivia—or what would appear as trivia to outsiders. Yet in sum the deliberations of voluntary groups in free conclave show a democratic society at work in some of its better moments.

In the tradition of speechmaking, the place of honor has been given to deliberative speaking, since it is likely to concern public or quasi-public rather than private affairs. And in deliberative oratory first place has been reserved for the great speeches of great men delivered in times of dramatic crisis. Alexander Hamilton and Melancton Smith in New York and Patrick Henry and James Madison in Virginia debating the ratification of the new constitution for the American commonwealths illustrate deliberative speaking at a high level. Some of the speeches included in this volume are notable examples of deliberative speaking. They will repay an examination of their reasoning, their appeals, and their assumptions. Perhaps no better way can be found to understand the American people than to study their public deliberations—or such elements of them as have been preserved.

Forensic Speeches

The best place to find forensic speeches is in a courtroom where a trial is taking place and lawyers must plead before judge or jury. Forensic eloquence concerns justice and injustice, legality or illegality, as well as equity, between persons and between persons and their government. In certain instances, as in the Supreme Court of the United States, forensic speaking may concern matters litigated between states; in the World Court, it concerns issues presented by sovereign powers. To be sure, the essentials of forensic speechmaking may be found elsewhere, as when a medical society hears charges that would deny a physician the right to practice or a school board hears charges preferred against a teacher. The spirit of the laws may be observed in the protection of the defendant's rights and in the due process employed. Still, the easiest way to learn how men speak in matters of law and equity is to attend public trials and to read accounts of trials, including the texts of speeches delivered in open court. An outstanding example and one of the landmarks in defense of the freedom of the press—so often safeguarded by lawyers and jurisconsults—is the speech by Andrew Hamilton, the great Philadelphia lawyer, in the Zenger case.

Ceremonial Speeches

Speeches of ceremony, designed to commemorate a great occasion, to praise a living person or a dead hero, or to congratulate a group for a notable accomplishment, can be observed by anyone who wishes to hear them. Among the common occasions for ceremonial speaking are the dedication of a public enterprise or a building, often in the laying of the cornerstone; the anniversary celebration; and the presentation of an award. No matter what the form or immediate purpose, the ceremonial speech should always be and sometimes is notable for its felicity. Its object is in part to observe the amenities, to add dignity to a life or an occasion, and to contribute to good feeling.

Since ceremonial speeches make a strong demand on the speaker, they are often delivered by one who has a reputation as a speechmaker, who has presumably some special grace of manner or of style, as well as good judgment in choosing what to say. Ceremonial speeches, though ostensibly not directed toward policy, may be powerfully persuasive in their effects, partly because they offer people landmarks of patriotic devotion or dedication to dearly held causes or traditions. Abraham Lincoln's "Gettysburg Address," perhaps the most widely known speech in the United States, suggests policy; but it also represents to some Americans their finest experience with literature. Like some other ceremonial speeches, it exemplifies speechmaking at a level of dignity not always attained. Such speeches may be studied with profit.

THE PROCESSES OF SPEECHMAKING

Whether a speech be deemed deliberative, forensic, or ceremonial, if it is well prepared, it will be subject to five processes: *invention, adaptation, style, preparation,* and *delivery.* An experienced speaker, or any speaker in the heat of debate, may forget the processes, as a great pianist may no longer give thought to the scales; but even in an impromptu speech, the five processes may be considered in theory to be involved. With reference to historic speeches, the five processes may perhaps best be considered as topics for inquiry.

Invention

How did the speaker invent, discover, or come upon the materials for his speech? A part of the answer to the question will always be available in a sound text. Anyone who reads the text of Wendell Phillips' "The Murder of Lovejoy," for example, will be struck by Phillips' reference to the state archives, to "Faneuil Hall Doctrine," to the arguments of the Council Chamber, and to the laws and constitution of the province of Massachusetts. Perhaps even more striking is the orator's pressing into service the portraits of the heroes: Otis, Hancock, Quincy, and Adams. Nor does Phillips neglect to support his argument by the testimony of an eyewitness to the events leading to the murder. Throughout the speech, he envelops the whole of his argument in a profound emotional appeal—subtle rather than crass—to the sentiments dear to citizens of Massachusetts. He calls to his aid the memories of the revolutionary fathers, the spirit of independence celebrated on the Fourth of July, the dedication to liberty and to republican institutions, the doctrines of the New England hills. In so doing, Phillips tends to establish his own character as a Massachusetts, a New England, man of ardent beliefs and right principles. His high-minded reference to "immortal beings" doubtless served still further to suggest to his Boston audience that he was a man worthy to be heard:

> As much as *thought* is better than money, so much is the cause in which Lovejoy died nobler than a mere question of taxes. James Otis thundered in this Hall when the King did but touch his *pocket*. Imagine, if you can, his indignant eloquence, had England offered to put a gag upon his lips.
>
> The question that stirred the Revolution touched our civil interests. *This* concerns us not only as citizens, but as immortal beings. Wrapped up in its fate, saved or lost with it, are not only the voice of the statesman, but the instructions of the pulpit, and the progress of our faith.[6]

Certain of Phillips' assumptions, although unstated, can also be found within the text of the speech. For example, Phillips obviously assumed that his hearers were Americans and Christians, or believers in Christian principles; that they believed in freedom of the press and in republican institutions generally; that they revered their revolutionary forefathers.

Beyond the text of a speech, a student may go to other sources to learn something of a speaker's resourcefulness, of his opportunity to discover and of his aptitude in finding the materials of his speech. Wendell Phillips was not speaking out of an empty head or heart when he came to the defense of freedom in his address in Faneuil Hall. A graduate of Harvard College, Phillips had spent a year of his college life in a systematic study of the English Revolution of 1640. He made a point of reading everything he could find about it: memoirs, speeches, histories. He had also studied the Dutch struggle for independence and had been influenced by the ideas of Alexis de Tocqueville concerning American institutions. In Boston he had

[6] See below, p. 174.

grown up in reverence of his forebears, who had been among the earliest settlers in Massachusetts and had been prominent in support of liberty. From his heritage of reading, study, knowledge, and belief, Phillips was thus prepared to discover the lines of argument and the appeals disclosed in his justifiably famous reply to the Attorney General of Massachusetts.

Adaptation

How did the speaker adapt his speech to his immediate audience? Invention and adaptation are twin processes, and they often proceed together, particularly when a speech is designed for one and only one audience. Invention can best be conceived, however, as the speaker faces his subject, adaptation as he faces his audience. The adaptation made by Phillips to his immediate audience in Faneuil Hall is clear enough. His specific references to Faneuil Hall, his pointing to the pictured lips of Otis, Hancock, Quincy, and Adams, as well as his numerous references to the arguments just advanced by his opponent, all demonstrate ready adaptation of his materials to his hearers. Nowhere is the adaptation more clearly evident than in Phillips' transposing the lines of argument advanced by Austin, the Attorney General, in a hypothetical application of Austin's doctrine to the news from Bunker Hill. In this part of his speech, Phillips takes phrases (such as, "died as the fool dieth") directly from Austin:

> Imagine yourself present when the first news of Bunker Hill battle reached a New England town. The tale would have run thus: "The patriots are routed,—the redcoats victorious,—Warren lies dead upon the field." With what scorn would that *Tory* have been received, who should have charged Warren with *imprudence!* Who should have said that, bred a physician, he was "out of place" in that battle, and "died as the *fool dieth*"! How would the intimation have been received, that Warren and his associates should have waited a better time? But if success be indeed the only criterion of prudence, *Respice finem,*—wait till the end.[7]

The process of adaptation can be fully understood, however, only when a speech on the same subject is given to different audiences.

[7] See below, p. 173.

It would be interesting to know how Wendell Phillips would have adapted his speech in defense of Lovejoy to an audience in Alton, Illinois, where Lovejoy died, or across the Mississippi River in Missouri, the slave state where Lovejoy's murderers lived. Phillips' beliefs, his dedication to his cause, and the essential facts in the case would not have changed; but, consummate orator that he was, he would doubtless have found other proofs and illustrations than those he employed in New England—proofs and illustrations more readily suasive to audiences in Illinois or Missouri.

Style

In essence, style in speechmaking is the process of putting ideas into suitable words and phrases; and for speeches, the words and phrases must be suitable for an oral, not a written, style. Fortunately, written and oral composition have salient principles in common: for example, unity, coherence, and emphasis. But the differences between an essay designed to be read and a speech designed to be heard are also marked. A good speech must have some of the qualities of a dialogue. Hence it may appear to lack the coherence, the "finish" that it actually possesses in delivery. "Did it read well?" said Charles James Fox, the great debater. "Then it was a bad speech." Good oral style is marked by directness, by first-person utterance. Observe that Wendell Phillips frequently addresses the chairman as "Sir"; that he employs the perpendicular pronoun, "I"; that he quotes from his opponent directly in context. The style is forthright, vivid, direct, clear, urgent, and, withal, simple. It exemplifies Alexander Hamilton's dictum that "Energy without asperity seems best to comport with the dignity of a national language."

For another example of a similar oral style, one may read George William Curtis' "The Public Duty of Educated Men," from which the following excerpt is taken:

> But let us not be deceived. While good men sit at home, not knowing that there is anything to be done, nor caring to know; cultivating a feeling that politics are tiresome and dirty, and politicians vulgar bullies and bravoes; half persuaded that a republic is the contemptible rule of a mob, and secretly longing for a splendid and vigorous despot-

ism—then remember it is not a government mastered by ignorance, it is a government betrayed by intelligence; it is not the victory of the slums, it is the surrender of the schools; it is not that bad men are brave, but that good men are infidels and cowards.[8]

Preparation

How did the speaker prepare his speech? In former times the only method of speech preparation generally approved was memorization. The mastery of the speech was supposed to be so complete that the precise language chosen in advance could be spoken with the easy familiarity of an actor speaking his lines. Today memorization is a lost art, and teachers generally discourage it, as leading to a stilted and absent-minded delivery. Although if the speaker knows his business, the danger to delivery need not be too much feared, still the advice against memorization is doubtless sound; for most speakers today do not have or will not take the time for the thorough preparation required. Indeed, nowadays the speaker sometimes reads his speech (perhaps ghostwritten for him) from a moving tape inserted between him and his audience or the camera.

The other methods available to the speaker are impromptu, manuscript, and extempore. The impromptu speech is one delivered without notice—although the speaker may have spent years of study and reflection on the topic. The manuscript speech is delivered from a reading copy of the text held by the speaker. On some occasions, protocol or other requirements make the manuscript necessary. Most speeches today are extempore. Presumably they have been prepared: the subject matter has been analyzed and the lines of argument laid out. The language may even have been determined and a copy of the speech written out or dictated. But the speech is not memorized and at the moment of delivery the manuscript, if there is one, is discarded. The extemporaneous speaker masters the sequence of his ideas so that he can communicate them in the order best adapted to his audience, but he chooses or adapts his language as he speaks; he rethinks his ideas with a full realization of the meaning at the very moment of utterance.

[8] See below, p. 189.

25

That speaker is fortunate who, like Wendell Phillips, can memorize easily and thoroughly and is yet not bound to a memorized text. Phillips could insert or remove units from his speeches with so little disruption that his audiences did not know when the memorization ended and the extemporization began.

Delivery

How was the speech delivered? At this point the student of speeches must very nearly part company with the text, for although a good text will convey what was said, it will not reveal much about the actual presentation. Sometimes evidence can be gained from witnesses or critics. It was said of Wendell Phillips, for example, that his speeches were those of "a gentleman conversing." He seemed to talk to everyone in the audience, individually. The Richmond *Inquirer* described Phillips as "an infernal machine, set to music." The secret of his delivery was doubtless the one open to all speakers: he spoke with a full realization of the content of his words as he uttered them and with an urgent desire to communicate his message to his hearers. That delivery—called "conversational quality" by the late James A. Winans—is now almost universally advocated but, alas, not universally practiced.

THE ATTITUDE OF THE STUDENT AND CRITIC

Once equipped with an understanding of speechmaking and the characteristics that distinguish it from other forms of human endeavor, those engaged in the study of speeches are well advised to assume that any speech is a response to a problem: perhaps the problem of the speaker, or of the audience, or of both speaker and audience. The following questions might well permeate a study of speeches:

1. What was the problem?
2. How did the speaker (and audience) endeavor to solve it?
3. How well did he (and they) succeed in the solution?

§ Introduction: The Study of Speechmaking

If the student critic looks upon the speech as a human event and endeavors to understand it as a problem in a world of problems, he will have gained a vantage point that may free him from the parochialisms of his own country and the limitations of his own era. Inasmuch as the knowledge of the theory of speechmaking would seem to have some relevancy to its practice, the student critic may also have gained a great personal advantage in solving his own problems of speechmaking in a world greatly in need of good men skilled in speaking. Peter F. Drucker, the economist, has stated well the values of learning to write and to speak and has set forth unmistakably the responsibility of the school in the instruction of students:

> Expressing one's thoughts is one skill that the school can really teach, especially to people born without natural writing or speaking talent. Many other skills can be learned later—in this country there are literally thousands of places that offer training to adult people at work. But the foundations for skill in expression have to be laid early: an interest in and an ear for language; experience in organizing ideas and data, in brushing aside the irrelevant, in wedding outward form and inner content into one structure; and above all, the habit of verbal expression. If you do not lay these foundations during your school years, you may never have an opportunity again.[9]

[9] Peter F. Drucker, "How to Be an Employee," *Fortune* (May 1952), p. 127. Reprinted by permission.

Edmund Burke

꩜ | ꩜

> "I think I know America. If I do not, my ignorance is incurable, for I have spared no pains to understand it." [1] —EDMUND BURKE

BIOGRAPHICAL SKETCH

Edmund Burke, British statesman, orator, and political philosopher, was born in Dublin, probably on January 12, 1729, to Richard Burke, a lawyer, and his wife, Mary Nagle. In 1741 the young Edmund Burke was sent to a school kept by Abraham Shackleton, a member of the Society of Friends, in Ballitore. He entered Trinity College, Dublin, in 1743, obtained a scholarship in 1746, and was awarded the B.A. degree in 1748. In 1750 he went to London, where he was entered at the Middle Temple to study law. Finding literature and politics more to his liking, he abandoned his studies. His *Vindication of Natural Society*, a satire in refutation of the political philosophy of Bolingbroke, and his *Philosophical Enquiry into the Origins of Our Ideas of the Sublime and Beautiful* were both published in 1756. During the winter of 1756–1757, Burke married Jane Nugent, the daughter of a physician at Bath. To the marriage, which was unusually felicitous, were born two sons—Christopher, who died in infancy, and Richard, who died in 1794. In 1759 Burke started the *Annual Register*, an enterprise he continued until 1789.

Following an unfortunate experience as adviser to William Gerard Hamilton, Burke began his sustained career in politics in 1765, when he became secretary to the Marquess of Rockingham,

NOTE: The sources for this essay may be found in the section Suggestions for Further Reading, pp. 101–103. The editors have also consulted newspapers in the British Museum and newspapers and certain ephemeral material in archives in Bristol.

---

[1] "A Letter to John Farr and John Harris, Esqrs., Sheriffs of the City of Bristol, on the Affairs of America," *The Works of Edmund Burke* (London: George Bell and Sons, 1894), Vol. II, p. 16.

and continued it until his retirement two years before he died. In January 1766, Burke delivered his maiden speech in the House of Commons, where—often in opposition to George III and the ministry—he consistently supported measures designed to conciliate the American colonies. He was also consistent in his efforts in behalf of Ireland and for Catholic emancipation, and he was active in the prosecution of Warren Hastings for the injustices charged against Hastings' administration of affairs in India. Toward the close of his career, Burke's forthright stand against the French Revolution gained him some favor with the king and the Tories but led to a break with his friend Charles James Fox and the Whigs.

As a friend of Samuel Johnson and a member of the Literary Club, Burke knew and was respected by the literati of his day including Oliver Goldsmith, James Boswell, Sir Joshua Reynolds, David Garrick, Hannah More, and George Crabbe, whom he befriended. In his own time Burke was greatly respected for his probity as well as for his abilities. He is regarded today as one of the most influential expositors of the conservative point of view derived from the political philosophy of the "Natural Law."

THE SPEAKER

No one has better understood the rights of Englishmen—and of mankind—than the Irishman, Edmund Burke. From reflection and perhaps from intuition he came to believe that freedom, as known in his time, is not found in aboriginal virtue but in civilization, particularly in a civilization where men do not naively assume that they were born free. Every man, Burke thought, is born in debt to his father, from whom he has inherited the code of civilization, and to his son, for whom he is trustee. Inasmuch as man's sentience sets him apart from all other creatures, he has knowledge of ancestry and posterity. Hence no man is a whole unto himself but is bound, spiritually as well as biologically, to the human race. Man, Burke believed, is governed less by laws and statutes than by customs, habits, loyalties, and folkways that may defy rigorous analysis. Burke could hardly have understood and surely would not have sympathized with the statement attributed to Joseph Cannon, once dictatorial Speaker of the House of Representatives, who on being asked to do something "for posterity" replied, "Why should I do anything for posterity? Posterity has never done anything for me."

Burke's ideas applied to the governance of men taught him that the body politic is a delicate organism. One who proposes to keep it in health or to treat its ills should employ the prudence of a good physician. Indeed, the analogy is apt. The physician to the state, like the physician to the human being, may discover that a given remedy is more to be feared than the disease; that unanticipated side effects may develop from the medication; that some anomalies are malignant, others benign; that some diseases may even tend to counteract the effects of certain others; that the body in health sometimes tends to restore itself without benefit of physician.

Edmund Burke knew what Henry David Thoreau was one day to assert, namely that "The mass of men lead lives of quiet desperation." [2] Beneath the skin of some men in civilization there may lurk the savage or the paranoid: such a creature as, for example, could bind eight nurses and cut their throats; such a creature as might take an arsenal of weapons to a steeple and shoot down fifteen unoffending strangers. Translated into national behavior, impulses of this sort become a French Revolution, which Burke observed, or a society that could produce an infamous concentration camp such as Dachau, which he could doubtless have predicted. The great deterrent to wicked folly in humankind, Burke believed, was to be found in a stable social organization relying on prejudices favorable to healthy conduct.

Although, as he said, innovation is not reform, the allegation that Burke was opposed to change is not true; on the contrary he thought opposition to *all* change to be the friend of violent revolution. But change in customs, mores, government, or religion should not be made for the sake of change, nor without a demonstrated need and an accounting for the probabilities. In reckoning the probabilities, the statesman, he thought, must know that there exist in the human race not only impulses of high survival quality—honor and duty, for example—but also unplumbed depths of unreason, alienation, and

[2] *Walden, or Life in the Woods* (New York: Book League of America, 1929), p. 7.

despair. The release of psychic forces destroying reverence for the dead, respect for the living, and hope for oncoming generations, as witnessed in our own time, serves at least to make Burke's views credible.

As an orator and advocate, Burke remains today, as he was in his own time, the subject of controversy. Men of conservative temper regard him as the savior of England and perhaps of America from violent upheavals like the French Revolution. Others less disposed in his favor suggest that even after his death his advocacy was instrumental in delaying for forty years reforms urgently needed in England. Perhaps both of these views grant Burke more power than he owned. Yet through the spoken and the written word he exerted influence on the course of events and exerted it consistently in favor of conservative policies. What were the sources of his persuasive power?

Counted first (because so rare) among Burke's assets as an orator must be intellectual competence of a high order. He was remarkable among men of brilliance in being able to think rhetorically: great thinkers have not always been both able and willing to deal in expedients and probabilities. Allied with his intellectual qualities, his character and reputation as an honest man of simple integrity served him well. Doubtless Burke's religious faith was a source of his ethical proof, as well as of his strength in time of trouble. For Burke was not only a Christian, an Anglo-Catholic, but an ecumenical religionist. It is not right to say that he was a "political Christian"; but it is right to observe that he was never so naive as to suppose that government and religion, church and state, have no concern with each other. In his own life, Burke was reverent without being pious, good without being holy—or at least holier-than-thou—and righteous without being self-righteous. Professing to scorn metaphysics, Burke never escaped religion, for in religion he paid his obeisance to the perplexities of human life on a strange planet in a mysterious universe. He thus observed, ". . . what shadows we are, and what shadows we pursue." [3]

[3] Chauncey A. Goodrich, ed., *Select British Eloquence* (Indianapolis: Bobbs-Merrill, 1963), p. 311.

To be counted among his assets also was his passion in restraint, his commitment to life and to the fortunes of men. His belief in freedom and the rights of men to govern themselves under law was surely as deep and as genuine as that of any person of his time. This passion served as the motive power for his most eloquent efforts in behalf of America, of Ireland, and of India.

Since Burke was always the conservative, counseling caution and urging deliberation in socio-economic affairs, he has been subject to the suspicion, even to the charge, of a lack of sympathy with the downtrodden and the poor. Suspicion, to be sure, never requires evidence; evidence to support this charge is lacking. Burke's willingness to leave a fence standing until he had discovered why it was put up may be plausibly attributed to his perception that in violent upheavals often the first to suffer, and to suffer the most, are those for whom the advocate of the quick change professes devotion. In one of his most felicitous but less well-known speeches he—uncommon man—acknowledges his allegiance to the common people:

> I am accused, I am told abroad, of being a man of aristocratic principles. If by aristocracy they mean the Peers, I have no vulgar admiration, nor any vulgar antipathy, towards them; I hold their order in cold and decent respect. I hold them to be of an absolute necessity in the constitution; but I think they are only good when kept within their proper bounds. I trust, whenever there has been a dispute between these Houses, the part I have taken has not been equivocal. If by the aristocracy, which indeed comes nearer to the point, they mean an adherence to the rich and powerful against the poor and weak, this would indeed be a very extraordinary part. I have incurred the odium of gentlemen in this House for not paying sufficient regard to men of ample property. When, indeed, the smallest rights of the poorest people in the kingdom are in question, I would set my face against any act of pride and power countenanced by the highest that are in it; and if it should come to the last extremity, and to a contest of blood, God forbid! God forbid!—my part is taken; I would take my fate with the poor, and low, and feeble. But if these people came to turn their liberty into a cloak for maliciousness, and to seek a privilege of exemption, not from power, but from the rules of morality and virtuous discipline, then I would join my hand to make them feel the

force which a few, united in a good cause, have over a multitude of the profligate and ferocious.[4]

THE SPEECH

No speech in the English language more clearly exposes the ground of argument in controversy, more explicitly states evidence and presumption, more reasonably sets forth the evidence in a question of policy than does the speech delivered to the House of Commons by Edmund Burke on March 22, 1775. Spoken when Burke was at the fullness of his powers—he was then forty-six years old—and drawing both on his knowledge and his prescience, the speech throughout demonstrates a command of the subject and the probabilities that led Sir James Mackintosh to pronounce it "the most faultless of Mr. Burke's productions" [5] and permitted Professor Houston Peterson, the philosopher-anthologist, to declare that in "the entire history of eloquence, the mind of Edmund Burke stands out supreme." [6]

[4] "Speech on the Second Reading of a Bill for the Repeal of the Marriage Act," *The Works of Edmund Burke*, Vol. VI, pp. 170–171.

[5] Goodrich, *op. cit.*, p. 266.

[6] Houston Peterson, ed., *A Treasury of the World's Great Speeches* (New York: Simon and Schuster, 1954), p. 131.

On Conciliation with the Colonies

‸

I hope, Sir, that notwithstanding the austerity of the chair,[1] your good nature will incline you to some degree of indulgence towards human frailty.[2] You will not think it unnatural, that those who have an object depending, which strongly engages their hopes and fears, should be somewhat inclined to superstition. As I came into the House full of anxiety about the event of my motion,[3] I found to my infinite surprise, that the grand penal bill by which we had passed sentence on the trade and sustenance of America, is to be returned to us from the other House. I do confess, I could not help looking on this event as a fortunate omen. I look upon it as a sort of providential favour; by which we are put once more in possession of our deliberative capacity, upon a business so very questionable in its nature, so very uncertain in its issue. By the return of this bill,[4] which

From "Mr. Burke's Resolutions for Conciliation with the Colonies," as published in *The Speeches of the Right Honourable Edmund Burke in the House of Commons and in Westminster-Hall; in Four Volumes* (London: Printed for Longman, Hurst, Rees, Orme, and Brown, Paternoster Row; and J. Ridgway, Piccadilly, 1816), Vol. I, pp. 272–340. The text is presented as in the original, except for the amendment of minor anomalies in spelling and punctuation. Footnotes incorporated from the original text are indicated by an asterisk.

---

[1] Burke's speech was delivered in the old House of Commons, once St. Stephen's chapel, which was destroyed by fire in 1834.

[2] As he began to speak, Burke addressed the Speaker, Sir Fletcher Norton, who held the office from 1770 to 1780. In Burke's day, as in the present, members of the House of Commons are in order when they speak to the Chair. Members speak *of* each other in certain formal phrases but technically they do not speak *to* each other in debate.

[3] Burke here refers to the motion he is to present at the close of his speech. See p. 97.

[4] The bill by Lord North (Prime Minister 1770 to 1782) to restrict the trade of the New England colonies, passed by the House of Commons on March 8, 1775, was returned by the House of Lords so that its provisions might be extended to other colonies.

35

seemed to have taken its flight for ever, we are at this very instant nearly as free to choose a plan for our American government, as we were on the first day of the session.[5] If, Sir, we incline to the side of conciliation, we are not at all embarrassed (unless we please to make ourselves so) by any incongruous mixture of coercion and restraint. We are therefore called upon, as it were, by a superior warning voice, again to attend to America; to attend to the whole of it together; and to review the subject with an unusual degree of care and calmness.

Surely it is an awful subject; or there is none so on this side of the grave. When I first had the honour of a seat in this House,[6] the affairs of that continent pressed themselves upon us, as the most important and most delicate object of parliamentary attention. My little share in this great deliberation oppressed me. I found myself a partaker in a very high trust; and having no sort of reason to rely on the strength of my natural abilities for the proper execution of that trust, I was obliged to take more than common pains, to instruct myself in every thing which relates to our colonies. I was not less under the necessity of forming some fixed ideas, concerning the general policy of the British empire. Something of this sort seemed to be indispensable; in order, amidst so vast a fluctuation of passions and opinions, to concenter my thoughts; to ballast my conduct; to preserve me from being blown about by every wind of fashionable doctrine. I really did not think it safe, or manly, to have fresh principles to seek upon every fresh mail which should arrive from America.[7]

At that period, I had the fortune to find myself in perfect con-

[5] Burke delivered his speech on March 22, 1775. The session had begun on November 29, 1774.

[6] Burke gave his maiden speech in 1766, and held his seat until 1774, as member for the borough of Wendover. At the time of this speech, he was a representative of the city of Bristol.

[7] Burke had set forth his principles in a speech on American taxation delivered to the House of Commons on April 19, 1774. See Chauncey A. Goodrich, ed., *Select British Eloquence* (Indianapolis: Bobbs-Merrill, 1963), p. 244. Burke's evaluation is also that of Alexander Hamilton, as stated in "A Full Vindication of the Measures of the Congress." Harold C. Syrett and Jacob Cooke, eds., *The Papers of Alexander Hamilton* (New York: Columbia University Press, 1961), Vol. I, p. 48: "How ridiculous then is it to affirm, that we are quarrelling for the trifling sum of three pence a pound on tea; when it is evidently the principle against whi'h we contend."

currence with a large majority in this House.[8] Bowing under that high authority, and penetrated with the sharpness and strength of that early impression, I have continued ever since, without the least deviation in my original sentiments. Whether this be owing to an obstinate perseverance in error, or to a religious adherence to what appears to me truth and reason, it is in your equity to judge.

Sir, parliament having an enlarged view of objects, made, during this interval, more frequent changes in their sentiments and their conduct than could be justified in a particular person upon the contracted scale of private information. But though I do not hazard any thing approaching to a censure on the motives of former parliaments to all those alterations, one fact is undoubted; that under them the state of America has been kept in continual agitation. Every thing administered as a remedy to the public complaint, if it did not produce, was at least followed by, an heightening of the distemper; until, by a variety of experiments, that important country has been brought into her present situation;—a situation which I will not miscall, which I dare not name; which I scarcely know how to comprehend in the terms of any description.

In this posture, Sir, things stood at the beginning of the session. About that time, a worthy member (Mr. Rose Fuller)[9] of great parliamentary experience, who, in the year 1766, filled the chair of the American committee with much ability, took me aside; and, lamenting the present aspect of our politics, told me, things were come to such a pass, that our former methods of proceeding in the House would be no longer tolerated. That the public tribunal (never too indulgent to a long and unsuccessful opposition) would now scrutinize our conduct with unusual severity. That the very vicissitudes and shiftings of ministerial measures, instead of convicting their authors of inconstancy and want of system, would be taken as an occasion of charging us with a predetermined discontent, which nothing could satisfy; whilst we accused every measure of vigour as

---

[8] Burke here refers to his first speech in the House of Commons, in 1766, when, under Rockingham's coalition government, the Stamp Act was repealed by a vote of 275 to 161.

[9] Mr. Fuller, member for Rye, offered the motion (April 18, 1774) to which Burke spoke in his speech on American taxation.

cruel, and every proposal of lenity as weak and irresolute. The public, he said, would not have patience to see us play the game out with our adversaries: we must produce our hand. It would be expected, that those who for many years had been active in such affairs should shew that they had formed some clear and decided idea of the principles of colony government; and were capable of drawing out something like a platform of the ground, which might be laid for future and permanent tranquillity.

I felt the truth of what my honourable friend represented; but I felt my situation too. His application might have been made with far greater propriety to many other gentlemen. No man was indeed ever better disposed, or worse qualified, for such an undertaking than myself. Though I gave so far into his opinion, that I immediately threw my thoughts into a sort of parliamentary form, I was by no means equally ready to produce them. It generally argues some degree of natural impotence of mind, or some want of knowledge of the world, to hazard plans of government, except from a seat of authority. Propositions are made, not only ineffectually, but somewhat disreputably, when the minds of men are not properly disposed for their reception; and for my part, I am not ambitious of ridicule; not absolutely a candidate for disgrace.

Besides, Sir, to speak the plain truth, I have in general no very exalted opinion of the virtue of paper government; nor of any politics in which the plan is to be wholly separated from the execution.[10] But when I saw that anger and violence prevailed every day more and more; and that things were hastening towards an incurable alienation of our colonies; I confess my caution gave way. I felt this, as one of those few moments in which decorum yields to an higher duty. Public calamity is a mighty leveller; and there are occasions when any, even the slightest chance of doing good, must be laid hold on, even by the most inconsiderable person.

To restore order and repose to an empire so great and so distracted as ours, is, merely in the attempt, an undertaking that would ennoble

---

[10] At this point Burke states a distrust of theorizing that he held consistently and expressed more fully in other instances, notably (in 1790) in certain passages of his *Reflections on the Revolution in France*. See, for example, *The Works of Edmund Burke* (London: George Bell and Sons, 1894), Vol. II, pp. 333–334.

the flights of the highest genius, and obtain pardon for the efforts of the meanest understanding. Struggling a good while with these thoughts, by degrees I felt myself more firm. I derived, at length, some confidence from what, in other circumstances, usually produces timidity. I grew less anxious, even from the idea of my own insignificance. For, judging of what you are, by what you ought to be, I persuaded myself that you would not reject a reasonable proposition, because it had nothing but its reason to recommend it. On the other hand, being totally destitute of all shadow of influence, natural or adventitious, I was very sure, that, if my proposition were futile or dangerous; if it were weakly conceived, or improperly timed, there was nothing exterior to it, of power to awe, dazzle, or delude you. You will see it just as it is; and you will treat it just as it deserves.

The proposition is peace. Not peace through the medium of war; not peace to be hunted through the labyrinth of intricate and endless negociations; not peace to arise out of universal discord, fomented from principle, in all parts of the empire; not peace to depend on the juridical determination of perplexing questions, or the precise marking the shadowy boundaries of a complex government. It is simple peace, sought in its natural course, and in its ordinary haunts —it is peace sought in the spirit of peace, and laid in principles purely pacific. I propose, by removing the ground of the difference, and by restoring the *former unsuspecting confidence of the colonies in the mother country*, to give permanent satisfaction to your people; and (far from a scheme of ruling by discord) to reconcile them to each other in the same act, and by the bond of the very same interest, which reconciles them to British government. [11]

My idea is nothing more. Refined policy ever has been the parent of confusion, and ever will be so, as long as the world endures. Plain good intention, which is as easily discovered at the first view, as fraud is surely detected at last, is, let me say, of no mean force in the government of mankind. Genuine simplicity of heart is an healing and cementing principle. My plan, therefore, being formed upon the most simple grounds imaginable, may disappoint some people when they hear it. It has nothing to recommend it to the pruriency

[11] The section of Burke's speech beginning "The proposition is peace" has been much quoted as an example of fluent and forceful statement.

of curious ears. There is nothing at all new and captivating in it. It has nothing of the splendour of the project, which has been lately laid upon your table[12] by the noble lord in the blue ribbon.* It does not propose to fill your lobby with squabbling colony agents, who will require the interposition of your mace,[13] at every instant, to keep the peace amongst them. It does not institute a magnificent auction of finances where captivated provinces come to general ransom by bidding against each other, until you knock down the hammer, and determine a proportion of payments, beyond all the powers of algebra to equalize and settle.[14]

The plan, which I shall presume to suggest, derives, however, one great advantage from the proposition and registry of that noble lord's project. The idea of conciliation is admissible. First, the House in accepting the resolution moved by the noble lord, has admitted, notwithstanding the menacing front of our address, notwithstanding our heavy bill of pains and penalties—that we do not think ourselves precluded from all ideas of free grace and bounty.

The House has gone farther; it has declared conciliation admissible, *previous* to any submission on the part of America. It has even shot a good deal beyond that mark, and has admitted, that the complaints of our former mode of exerting the right of taxation were not wholly unfounded. That right thus exerted is allowed to have had something reprehensible in it; something unwise, or something grievous; since, in the midst of our heat and resentment, we, of ourselves, have proposed a capital alteration; and, in order to get rid of what seemed so very exceptionable, have instituted a mode that is altogether new; one that is, indeed, wholly alien from all the ancient methods and forms of parliament.

The *principle* of this proceeding is large enough for my purpose.

* *Resolution moved by Lord North in the committee; and agreed to by the House, Feb. 27.*

[12] The table referred to was maintained for the parliamentary clerks, who kept pending documents upon it.

[13] When the House of Commons is in session, the mace, a heavily ornamented staff about five feet long, lies on the table as a symbol of authority.

[14] Burke's "magnificent auction of finance" refers to Lord North's proposal that any colony voting funds to the extent approved by King and Parliament should be exempt from taxation by Parliament. The proposal was unacceptable in America.

The means proposed by the noble lord for carrying his ideas into execution, I think, indeed, are very indifferently suited to the end; and this I shall endeavour to shew you before I sit down. But, for the present, I take my ground on the admitted principle. I mean to give peace. Peace implies reconciliation; and where there has been a material dispute, reconciliation does in a manner always imply concession on the one part or on the other. In this state of things I make no difficulty in affirming, that the proposal ought to originate from us. Great and acknowledged force is not impaired, either in effect or in opinion, by an unwillingness to exert itself. The superior power may offer peace with honour and with safety. Such an offer from such a power will be attributed to magnanimity. But the concessions of the weak are the concessions of fear. When such a one is disarmed, he is wholly at the mercy of his superior; and he loses for ever that time and those chances, which, as they happen to all men, are the strength and resources of all inferior power.

The capital leading questions on which you must this day decide, are these two. First, whether you ought to concede; and, secondly, what your concession ought to be. On the first of these questions we have gained (as I have just taken the liberty of observing to you) some ground. But I am sensible that a good deal more is still to be done. Indeed, Sir, to enable us to determine both on the one and the other of these great questions with a firm and precise judgment, I think it may be necessary to consider distinctly the true nature and the peculiar circumstances of the object which we have before us. Because after all our struggle, whether we will or not, we must govern America, according to that nature, and to those circumstances; and not according to our own imaginations; not according to abstract ideas of right; by no means according to mere general theories of government, the resort to which appears to me, in our present situation, no better than arrant trifling. I shall therefore endeavour, with your leave, to lay before you some of the most material of these circumstances in as full and as clear a manner as I am able to state them.

The first thing that we have to consider with regard to the nature of the object is—the number of people in the colonies. I have taken for some years a good deal of pains on that point. I can by no calculation justify myself in placing the number below two millions of inhabitants of our own European blood and colour; besides at least 500,000 others, who form no inconsiderable part of the strength and opulence of the whole. This, Sir, is, I believe, about the true number. There is no occasion to exaggerate, where plain truth is of so much weight and importance. But whether I put the present numbers too high or too low, is a matter of little moment. Such is the strength with which population shoots in that part of the world, that state the numbers as high as we will, whilst the dispute continues, the exaggeration ends. Whilst we are discussing any given magnitude, they are grown to it. Whilst we spend our time in deliberating on the mode of governing two millions, we shall find we have millions more to manage. Your children do not grow faster from infancy to manhood, than they spread from families to communities, and from villages to nations.

I put this consideration of the present and the growing numbers in the front of our deliberation; because, Sir, this consideration will make it evident to a blunter discernment than yours, that no partial, narrow, contracted, pinched, occasional system will be at all suitable to such an object. It will shew you, that it is not to be considered as one of those *minima* which are out of the eye and consideration of the law; not a paltry excrescence of the state; not a mean dependant, who may be neglected with little damage, and provoked with little danger. It will prove, that some degree of care and caution is required in the handling such an object; it will shew that you ought not, in reason, to trifle with so large a mass of the interests and feelings of the human race. You could at no time do so without guilt; and be assured you will not be able to do it long with impunity.

But the population of this country, the great and growing population, though a very important consideration, will lose much of its weight, if not combined with other circumstances. The commerce of your colonies is out of all proportion beyond the numbers of the people. This ground of their commerce indeed has been trod some days ago, and with great ability, by a distinguished person, at your bar.* This gentleman,[15] after thirty-five years—it is so long

* Mr. *Glover.*

[15] Richard Glover (1712–1785), author of *Leonidas,* appeared in January 1742, in

since he first appeared at the same place to plead for the commerce of Great Britain—has come again before you to plead the same cause, without any other effect of time, than, that to the fire of imagination and extent of erudition, which even then marked him as one of the first literary characters of his age, he has added a consummate knowledge in the commercial interest of his country, formed by a long course of enlightened and discriminating experience.

Sir, I should be inexcusable in coming after such a person with any detail, if a great part of the members who now fill the House had not the misfortune to be absent when he appeared at your bar.[16] Besides, Sir, I propose to take the matter at periods of time somewhat different from his. There is, if I mistake not, a point of view, from whence if you will look at this subject it is impossible that it should not make an impression upon you.

I have in my hand two accounts; one a comparative state of the export trade of England to its colonies, as it stood in the year 1704, and as it stood in the year 1772. The other a state of the export trade of this country to its colonies alone, as it stood in 1772, compared with the whole trade of England to all parts of the world (the colonies included) in the year 1704. They are from good vouchers; the latter period from the accounts on your table, the earlier from an original manuscript of Davenant, who first established the inspector general's office, which has been ever since his time so abundant a source of parliamentary information.[17]

The export trade to the colonies consists of three great branches. The African, which, terminating almost wholly in the colonies, must be put to the account of their commerce; the West Indian; and the North American. All these are so interwoven, that the attempt to separate them would tear to pieces the contexture of the whole; and if not entirely destroy, would very much depreciate the value of all

---

behalf of the merchants of London to petition for the protection of their ships from Spanish privateers.

[16] At the entrance to the chamber of the House of Commons is placed a barrier—a bar—beyond which no one except members and officers may go when the House is in session.

[17] Charles Davenant (1656–1714) was appointed Inspector General of imports and exports in 1705.

the parts. I therefore consider these three denominations to be, what in effect they are, one trade.

The trade to the colonies, taken on the export side, at the beginning of this century, that is, in the year 1704, stood thus:

Exports to North America, and the West Indies	£483,265
To Africa	86,665
	£569,930

In the year 1772, which I take as a middle year between the highest and lowest of those lately laid on your table, the account was as follows:

To North America, and the West Indies	£4,791,734
To Africa	866,398
To which if you add the export trade from Scotland, which had in 1704 no existence	364,000
	£6,022,132

From five hundred and odd thousand, it has grown to six millions. It has increased no less than twelve-fold. This is the state of the colony trade as compared with itself at these two periods, within this century;—and this is matter for meditation. But this is not all. Examine my second account. See how the export trade to the colonies alone in 1772 stood in the other point of view, that is, as compared to the whole trade of England in 1704.

The whole export trade of England, including that to the colonies in 1704	£6,509,000
Export to the colonies alone in 1772	6,024,000
Difference	£ 485,000

The trade with America alone is now within less than 500,000*l.* of being equal to what this great commercial nation, England, carried on at the beginning of this century with the whole world! If I had taken the largest year of those on your table, it would rather have exceeded. But it will be said, is not this American trade an unnatural protuberance, that has drawn the juices from the rest of the body? The reverse. It is the very food that has nourished every other part into its present magnitude. Our general trade has been greatly augmented; and augmented more or less in almost every part to which it ever extended; but with this material difference, that of the six millions which in the beginning of the century constituted the whole mass of our export commerce, the colony trade was but one twelfth part; it is now (as a part of sixteen millions) considerably more than a third of the whole. This is the relative proportion of the importance of the colonies at these two periods: and all reasoning concerning our mode of treating them must have this proportion as its basis; or it is a reasoning weak, rotten, and sophistical.

Mr. Speaker, I cannot prevail on myself to hurry over this great consideration. It is good for us to be here. We stand where we have an immense view of what is, and what is past. Clouds indeed, and darkness, rest upon the future. Let us, however, before we descend from this noble eminence, reflect that this growth of our national prosperity has happened within the short period of the life of man. It has happened within 68 years. There are those alive whose memory might touch the two extremities. For instance, my Lord Bathurst[18] might remember all the stages of the progress. He was in 1704 of an age at least to be made to comprehend such things. He was then old enough *acta parentum jam legere, et quæ sit poterit cognoscere virtus.*[19]—Suppose, Sir, that the angel of this auspicious youth, fore-seeing the many virtues, which made him one of the most amiable, as he is one of the most fortunate men of his age, had opened to him in vision, that, when, in the fourth generation, the third prince of the house of Brunswick had sat twelve years on the throne of that nation, which (by the happy issue of moderate and healing councils) was to be made Great Britain, he should see his son, lord chancellor of England, turn back the current of hereditary dignity to its foun-tain, and raise him to an higher rank of peerage, whilst he enriched the family with a new one;—if amidst these bright and happy scenes of domestic honour and prosperity, that angel should have drawn up the curtain, and unfolded the rising glories of his country, and whilst he was gazing with admiration on the then commercial gran-deur of England, the genius should point out to him a little speck,

[18] Allen Bathurst, Earl Bathurst (1684–1775).
[19] Apparently the allusion is to Virgil's *Eclogues*, IV, 26: "He could examine the deeds of his forefathers and learn to recognize virtue."

scarce visible in the mass of the national interest, a small seminal principle, rather than a formed body, and should tell him—"Young man, there is America—which at this day serves for little more than to amuse you with stories of savage men, and uncouth manners; yet shall, before you taste of death, shew itself equal to the whole of that commerce which now attracts the envy of the world. Whatever England has been growing to by a progressive increase of improvement, brought in by varieties of people, by succession of civilising conquests and civilising settlements in a series of 1,700 years, you shall see as much added to her by America in the course of a single life!" If this state of his country had been foretold to him, would it not require all the sanguine credulity of youth, and all the fervid glow of enthusiasm, to make him believe it? Fortunate man, he has lived to see it! Fortunate indeed, if he lives to see nothing that shall vary the prospect, and cloud the setting of his day!

Excuse me, Sir, if turning from such thoughts, I resume this comparative view once more. You have seen it on a large scale; look at it on a small one. I will point out to your attention a particular instance of it in the single province of Pennsylvania. In the year 1704, that province called for 11,459*l.* in value of your commodities, native and foreign. This was the whole. What did it demand in 1772? Why nearly fifty times as much; for in that year the export to Pennsylvania was 507,909*l.* nearly equal to the export of all the colonies together in the first period.

I choose, Sir, to enter into these minute and particular details; because generalities, which in all other cases are apt to heighten and raise the subject, have here a tendency to sink it. When we speak of the commerce with our colonies, fiction lags after truth; invention is unfruitful, and imagination cold and barren.

So far, Sir, as to the importance of the object in the view of its commerce, as concerned in the exports from England. If I were to detail the imports, I could shew how many enjoyments they procure, which deceive the burthen of life; how many materials which invigorate the springs of national industry, and extend and animate every part of our foreign and domestic commerce. This would be a curious subject indeed—but I must prescribe bounds to myself in a matter so vast and various.

I pass therefore to the colonies in another point of view, their agriculture. This they have prosecuted with such a spirit, that, besides feeding plentifully their own growing multitude, their annual export of grain, comprehending rice, has some years ago exceeded a million in value. Of their last harvest, I am persuaded, they will export much more. At the beginning of the century, some of these colonies imported corn from the mother country. For some time past, the old world has been fed from the new. The scarcity which you have felt would have been a desolating famine, if this child of your old age, with a true filial piety, with a Roman charity, had not put the full breast of its youthful exuberance to the mouth of its exhausted parent.[20]

As to the wealth which the colonies have drawn from the sea by their fisheries, you had all that matter fully opened at your bar. You surely thought those acquisitions of value, for they seemed even to excite your envy; and yet the spirit, by which that enterprising employment has been exercised, ought rather, in my opinion, to have raised your esteem and admiration. And pray, Sir, what in the world is equal to it? Pass by the other parts, and look at the manner in which the people of New England have of late carried on the whale fishery. Whilst we follow them among the tumbling mountains of ice, and behold them penetrating into the deepest frozen recesses of Hudson's Bay, and Davis's Streights, whilst we are looking for them beneath the arctic circle, we hear that they have pierced into the opposite region of polar cold, that they are at the antipodes, and engaged under the frozen serpent of the south. Falkland Island, which seemed too remote and romantic an object for the grasp of national ambition, is but a stage and resting-place in the progress of their victorious industry. Nor is the equinoctial heat more discouraging to them than the accumulated winter of both the poles. We know that whilst some of them draw the line, and strike the harpoon on the coast of Africa, others run the longitude, and pursue their gigantic game along the coast of Brazil. No sea but what is vexed by their fisheries. No climate that is not witness to their toils. Neither

[20] In a number of versions, a Roman legend recounts the story of a father, condemned to death by starvation, who was visited in his cell by a daughter who kept him alive with the milk from her own breasts.

47

the perseverance of Holland, nor the activity of France, nor the dexterous and firm sagacity of English enterprise, ever carried this most perilous mode of hard industry to the extent to which it has been pushed by this recent people; a people who are still, as it were, but in the gristle, and not yet hardened into the bone of manhood. When I contemplate these things; when I know that the colonies in general owe little or nothing to any care of ours, and that they are not squeezed into this happy form by the constraints of watchful and suspicious government, but that through a wise and salutary neglect, a generous nature has been suffered to take her own way to perfection; when I reflect upon these effects, when I see how profitable they have been to us, I feel all the pride of power sink, and all presumption in the wisdom of human contrivances melt, and die away within me. My rigour relents. I pardon something to the spirit of liberty.

I am sensible, Sir, that all which I have asserted, in my detail, is admitted in the gross; but that quite a different conclusion is drawn from it. America, gentlemen say, is a noble object. It is an object well worth fighting for. Certainly it is, if fighting a people be the best way of gaining them. Gentlemen in this respect will be led to their choice of means by their complexions and their habits. Those who understand the military art will of course have some predilection for it. Those who wield the thunder of the state, may have more confidence in the efficacy of arms. But I confess, possibly for want of this knowledge, my opinion is much more in favour of prudent management, than of force; considering force not as an odious but a feeble instrument, for preserving a people so numerous, so active, so growing, so spirited as this, in a profitable and subordinate connection with us.

First, Sir, permit me to observe, that the use of force alone is but *temporary*. It may subdue for a moment; but it does not remove the necessity of subduing again: and a nation is not governed, which is perpetually to be conquered.

My next objection is *uncertainty*. Terror is not always the effect of force; and an armament is not a victory. If you do not succeed, you are without resourse; for, conciliation failing, force remains; but, force failing, no further hope of reconciliation is left. Power and authority are sometimes bought by kindness; but they can never be begged as alms, by an impoverished and defeated violence.

A further objection to force is, that you *impair the object* by your very endeavours to preserve it. The thing you fought for is not the thing which you recover; but depreciated, sunk, wasted, and consumed in the contest. Nothing less will content me, than *whole America*. I do not choose to consume its strength along with our own; because in all parts it is the British strength that I consume. I do not choose to be caught by a foreign enemy at the end of this exhausting conflict, and still less in the midst of it. I may escape; but I can make no insurance against such an event. Let me add, that I do not choose wholly to break the American spirit, because it is the spirit that has made the country.

Lastly, we have no sort of *experience* in favour of force as an instrument in the rule of our colonies. Their growth and their utility has been owing to methods altogether different. Our ancient indulgence has been said to be pursued to a fault. It may be so. But we know, if feeling is evidence, that our fault was more tolerable than our attempt to mend it; and our sin far more salutary than our penitence. These, Sir, are my reasons for not entertaining that high opinion of untried force, by which many gentlemen, for whose sentiments in other particulars I have great respect, seem to be so greatly captivated. But there is still behind a third consideration concerning this object, which serves to determine my opinion on the sort of policy which ought to be pursued in the management of America, even more than its population and its commerce,—I mean its *temper and character*.

In this character of the Americans, a love of freedom is the predominating feature which marks and distinguishes the whole; and as an ardent is always a jealous affection, your colonies become suspicious, restive, and untractable, whenever they see the least attempt to wrest from them by force, or shuffle from them by chicane, what they think the only advantage worth living for. This fierce spirit of liberty is stronger in the English colonies probably than in any other people of the earth; and this from a great variety of powerful causes; which, to understand the true temper of their minds, and the direction which this spirit takes, it will not be amiss to lay open somewhat more largely.

First, the people of the colonies are descendants of Englishmen. England, Sir, is a nation, which still I hope respects, and formerly adored, her freedom. The colonists emigrated from you, when this part of your character was most predominant; and they took this bias and direction the moment they parted from your hands. They are therefore not only devoted to liberty, but to liberty according to English ideas, and on English principles. Abstract liberty, like other mere abstractions, is not to be found. Liberty inheres in some sensible object; and every nation has formed to itself some favourite point, which by way of eminence becomes the criterion of their happiness. It happened, you know, Sir, that the great contests for freedom in this country were from the earliest times chiefly upon the question of taxing. Most of the contests in the ancient commonwealths turned primarily on the right of election of magistrates; or on the balance among the several orders of the state. The question of money was not with them so immediate. But in England it was otherwise. On this point of taxes the ablest pens, and most eloquent tongues, have been exercised; the greatest spirits have acted and suffered. In order to give the fullest satisfaction concerning the importance of this point, it was not only necessary for those who in argument defended the excellence of the English constitution, to insist on this privilege of granting money as a dry point of fact, and to prove, that the right had been acknowledged in ancient parchments, and blind usages, to reside in a certain body called a House of Commons. They went much further; they attempted to prove, and they succeeded, that in theory it ought to be so, from the particular nature of a House of Commons, as an immediate representative of the people; whether the old records had delivered this oracle or not. They took infinite pains to inculcate, as a fundamental principle, that, in all monarchies, the people must in effect themselves mediately or immediately possess the power of granting their own money, or no shadow of liberty could subsist. The colonies draw from you, as with their lifeblood, these ideas and principles. Their love of liberty, as with you, fixed and attached on this specific point of taxing. Liberty might be safe, or might be endangered in twenty other particulars, without their being much pleased or alarmed. Here they felt its pulse; and as they found that beat, they thought themselves sick or sound. I do not say whether they were right or wrong in applying your general arguments to their own case. It is not easy indeed to make a monopoly of theorems and corollaries. The fact is, that they did thus apply those general arguments; and your mode of governing them, whether through lenity or indolence, through wisdom or mistake, confirmed them in the imagination, that they, as well as you, had an interest in these common principles.

They were further confirmed in this pleasing error, by the form of their provincial legislative assemblies. Their governments are popular in a high degree; some are merely popular; in all, the popular representative is the most weighty; and this share of the people in their ordinary government never fails to inspire them with lofty sentiments, and with a strong aversion from whatever tends to deprive them of their chief importance.

If any thing were wanting to this necessary operation of the form of government, religion would have given it a complete effect. Religion, always a principle of energy, in this new people, is no way worn out or impaired; and their mode of professing it is also one main cause of this free spirit. The people are Protestants; and of that kind which is the most adverse to all implicit submission of mind and opinion. This is a persuasion not only favourable to liberty, but built upon it. I do not think, Sir, that the reason of this averseness in the dissenting churches from all that looks like absolute government is so much to be sought in their religious tenets as in their history. Every one knows that the Roman Catholic religion is at least coeval with most of the governments where it prevails; that it has generally gone hand in hand with them; and received great favour and every kind of support from authority. The church of England too was formed from her cradle under the nursing care of regular government. But the dissenting interests have sprung up in direct opposition to all the ordinary powers of the world; and could justify that opposition only on a strong claim to natural liberty. Their very existence depended on the powerful and unremitted assertion of that claim. All Protestantism, even the most cold and passive, is a sort of dissent. But the religion most prevalent in our northern colonies is a refinement on the principle of resistance; it is the diffidence of dissent; and the Protestantism of the Protestant religion. This religion, under a variety of denominations, agreeing in nothing but in the communion of the spirit of liberty, is predominant in most of the northern provinces; where the church of England, notwithstanding its legal rights, is in reality no more than a sort of private sect, not composing most probably the tenth of the people. The colonists left England when this spirit was high; and in the emigrants was the highest of all; and even that stream of foreigners, which has been constantly flowing into these colonies, has, for the greatest part, been composed of dissenters from the establishments of their several countries, and have brought with them a temper and character far from alien to that of the people with whom they mixed.

Sir, I can perceive by their manner, that some gentlemen object to the latitude of this description; because in the southern colonies the church of England forms a large body, and has a regular establishment. It is certainly true. There is, however, a circumstance attending these colonies, which, in my opinion, fully counterbalances this difference, and makes the spirit of liberty still more high and haughty than in those to the northward. It is that in Virginia and the Carolinas, they have a vast multitude of slaves. Where this is the case in any part of the world, those who are free, are by far the most proud and jealous of their freedom. Freedom is to them not only an enjoyment, but a kind of rank and privilege. Not seeing there, that freedom, as in countries where it is a common blessing, and as broad and general as the air, may be united with much abject toil, with great misery, with all the exterior of servitude, liberty looks, amongst them, like something that is more noble and liberal. I do not mean, Sir, to commend the superior morality of this sentiment, which has at least as much pride as virtue in it; but I cannot alter the nature of man. The fact is so; and these people of the southern colonies are much more strongly, and with a higher and more stubborn spirit, attached to liberty, than those to the northward. Such were all the ancient commonwealths; such were our Gothic ancestors; such in our days were the Poles; and such will be all masters of slaves, who are not slaves themselves. In such a people the haughtiness of domination combines with the spirit of freedom, fortifies it, and renders it invincible.

Permit me, Sir, to add another circumstance in our colonies, which contributes no mean part towards the growth and effect of this untractable spirit. I mean their education. In no country perhaps in the world is the law so general a study. The profession itself is numerous and powerful; and in most provinces it takes the lead. The greater number of the deputies sent to the congress were lawyers. But all who read, and most do read, endeavour to obtain some smattering in that science. I have been told by an eminent bookseller, that in no branch of his business, after tracts of popular devotion, were so many books as those on the law exported to the plantations. The colonists have now fallen into the way of printing them for their own use. I hear that they have sold nearly as many of Blackstone's Commentaries in America[21] as in England. General Gage marks out this disposition very particularly in a letter on your table.[22] He states, that all the people in his government are lawyers, or smatterers in law; and that in Boston they have been enabled, by successful chicane, wholly to evade many parts of one of your capital penal constitutions. The smartness of debate will say, that this knowledge ought to teach them more clearly the rights of legislature, their obligations to obedience, and the penalties of rebellion. All this is mighty well. But my honourable and learned friend on the floor (the Attorney General) who condescends to mark what I say for animadversion, will disdain that ground.[23] He has heard, as well as I, that when great honours and great emoluments do not win over this knowledge to the service of the state, it is a formidable adversary to government. If the spirit be not tamed and broken by these happy methods, it is stubborn and litigious. *Abeunt studia in mores.*[24]

[21] Sir William Blackstone (1723–1780), the first Vinerian Professor of Law at Oxford University, published his lectures as *Commentaries on the Law of England* in 1765–1769.

[22] General Thomas Gage (1721–1787) came to America with General Braddock, under whom he served in the French and Indian War. In 1774 he became Governor of Massachusetts, where he attempted to put down the colonial opposition to British rule.

[23] Edward Thurlow (1731–1806), Lord Thurlow, the Attorney General, was thought to be preparing a reply to Burke.

[24] "One's studies influence one's character."

This study renders men acute, inquisitive, dexterous, prompt in attack, ready in defence, full of resources. In other countries, the people, more simple, and of a less mercurial cast, judge of an ill principle in government only by an actual grievance; here they anticipate the evil, and judge of the pressure of the grievance by the badness of the principle. They augur misgovernment at a distance; and snuff the approach of tyranny in every tainted breeze.

The last cause of this disobedient spirit in the colonies is hardly less powerful than the rest, as it is not merely moral, but laid deep in the natural constitution of things. Three thousand miles of ocean lie between you and them. No contrivance can prevent the effect of this distance, in weakening government. Seas roll, and months pass, between the order and the execution: and the want of a speedy explanation of a single point, is enough to defeat a whole system. You have, indeed, winged ministers of vengeance, who carry your bolts in their pounces to the remotest verge of the sea. But there a power steps in, that limits the arrogance of raging passions and furious elements, and says, "So far shalt thou go, and no farther." Who are you, that should fret and rage, and bite the chains of nature? Nothing worse happens to you, than does to all nations, who have extensive empire; and it happens in all the forms into which empire can be thrown. In large bodies, the circulation of power must be less vigorous at the extremities. Nature has said it. The Turk cannot govern Egypt, and Arabia, and Curdistan, as he governs Thrace; nor has he the same dominion in Crimea and Algiers, which he has at Brusa and Smyrna. Despotism itself is obliged to truck and huckster. The sultan gets such obedience as he can. He governs with a loose rein, that he may govern at all; and the whole of the force and vigour of his authority in his centre, is derived from a prudent relaxation in all his borders. Spain, in her provinces, is, perhaps, not so well obeyed, as you are in yours. She complies too; she submits; she watches times. This is the immutable condition, the eternal law, of extensive and detached empire.[25]

Then, Sir, from these six capital sources; of descent; of form of government; of religion in the northern provinces; of manners in the

[25] This passage has often been cited as an example of Burke's concrete, particularizing style.

southern; of education; of the remoteness of situation from the first mover of government; from all these causes a fierce spirit of liberty has grown up. It has grown with the growth of the people in your colonies, and increased with the increase of their wealth; a spirit, that unhappily meeting with an exercise of power in England, which, however lawful, is not reconcileable to any ideas of liberty, much less with theirs, has kindled this flame, that is ready to consume us.

I do not mean to commend either the spirit in this excess, or the moral causes which produce it. Perhaps a more smooth and accommodating spirit of freedom in them would be more acceptable to us. Perhaps ideas of liberty might be desired more reconcileable with an arbitrary and boundless authority. Perhaps we might wish the colonists to be persuaded, that their liberty is more secure when held in trust for them by us (as their guardians during a perpetual minority) than with any part of it in their own hands. But the question is, not whether their spirit deserves praise or blame;—what, in the name of God, shall we do with it? You have before you the object; such as it is, with all its glories, with all its imperfections on its head. You see the magnitude; the importance; the temper; the habits; the disorders. By all these considerations, we are strongly urged to determine something concerning it. We are called upon to fix some rule and line for our future conduct, which may give a little stability to our politics, and prevent the return of such unhappy deliberations as the present. Every such return will bring the matter before us in a still more untractable form. For, what astonishing and incredible things have we not seen already? What monsters have not been generated from this unnatural contention? Whilst every principle of authority and resistance has been pushed, upon both sides, as far as it would go, there is nothing so solid and certain, either in reasoning or in practice, that has not been shaken. Until very lately, all authority in America seemed to be nothing but an emanation from yours. Even the popular part of the colony constitution derived all its activity, and its first vital movement from the pleasure of the crown. We thought, Sir, that the utmost which the discontented colonists could do, was to disturb authority; we never dreamt they could of themselves supply it; knowing in general what an operose business it is, to establish a government absolutely new. But having, for our purposes in this contention, resolved, that none but an obedient assembly should sit, the humours of the people there, finding all passage through the legal channel stopped, with great violence broke out another way. Some provinces have tried their experiment, as we have tried ours; and theirs has succeeded. They have formed a government sufficient for its purposes, without the bustle of a revolution, or the troublesome formality of an election. Evident necessity, and tacit consent, have done the business in an instant. So well they have done it, that Lord Dunmore[26] (the account is among the fragments on your table) tells you, that the new institution is infinitely better obeyed than the ancient government ever was in its most fortunate periods. Obedience is what makes government, and not the names by which it is called; not the name of governor, as formerly, or committee, as at present. This new government has originated directly from the people; and was not transmitted through any of the ordinary artificial media of a positive constitution. It was not a manufacture ready formed, and transmitted to them in that condition from England. The evil arising from hence is this; that the colonists having once found the possibility of enjoying the advantages of order, in the midst of a struggle for liberty, such struggles will not henceforward seem so terrible to the settled and sober part of mankind, as they had appeared before the trial.

Pursuing the same plan of punishing by the denial of the exercise of government to still greater lengths, we wholly abrogated the ancient government of Massachusetts.[27] We were confident that the first feeling, if not the very prospect of anarchy, would instantly enforce a complete submission. The experiment was tried. A new, strange, unexpected face of things appeared. Anarchy is found tolerable. A vast province has now subsisted, and subsisted in a considerable degree of health and vigour, for near a twelvemonth, without governor, without public council, without judges, without executive magistrates. How long it will continue in this state, or what may arise out of this unheard-of situation, how can the wisest of us conjecture?

[26] John Murray Dunmore (1732–1809), first Earl of Dunmore, Governor of Virginia, was forced to flee under threats against his life in 1775. He burned Norfolk in January 1776, and in July of that year was forced to return to England.

[27] The Massachusetts charter was abrogated on May 11, 1774.

Our late experience has taught us, that many of those fundamental principles, formerly believed infallible, are either not of the importance they were imagined to be; or that we have not at all adverted to some other far more important and far more powerful principles, which entirely over-rule those we had considered as omnipotent. I am much against further experiments, which tend to put to the proof any more of these allowed opinions, which contribute so much to the public tranquillity. In effect, we suffer as much at home, by this loosening of all ties, and this concussion of all established opinions, as we do abroad. For, in order to prove, that the Americans have no right to their liberties, we are every day endeavouring to subvert the maxims which preserve the whole spirit of our own.[28] To prove that the Americans ought not to be free, we are obliged to depreciate the value of freedom itself; and we never seem to gain a paltry advantage over them in debate, without attacking some of those principles, or deriding some of those feelings, for which our ancestors have shed their blood.

But, Sir, in wishing to put an end to pernicious experiments, I do not mean to preclude the fullest enquiry. Far from it. Far from deciding on a sudden or partial view, I would patiently go round and round the subject, and survey it minutely in every possible aspect. Sir, if I were capable of engaging you to an equal attention, I would state, that, as far as I am capable of discerning, there are but three ways of proceeding relative to this stubborn spirit which prevails in your colonies and disturbs your government. These are —to change that spirit, as inconvenient, by removing the causes; to prosecute it as criminal; or, to comply with it as necessary. I would not be guilty of an imperfect enumeration; I can think of but these three. Another has indeed been started, that of giving up the colonies; but it met so slight a reception, that I do not think myself obliged to dwell a great while upon it. It is nothing but a little sally of anger, like the frowardness of peevish children, who, when they cannot get all they would have, are resolved to take nothing.

The first of these plans, to change the spirit as inconvenient, by removing the causes, I think is the most like a systematic proceeding.

[28] Observe that Burke consistently hews to the line of *principle*. He repeats here the reasoning in his speech "On American Taxation." See Goodrich, *op. cit.*, p. 245.

It is radical in its principle; but it is attended with great difficulties, some of them little short, as I conceive, of impossibilities. This will appear, by examining into the plans which have been proposed.

As the growing population of the colonies is evidently one cause of their resistance, it was last session mentioned in both Houses, by men of weight, and received not without applause, that, in order to check this evil, it would be proper for the crown to make no further grants of land. But to this scheme there are two objections. The first, that there is already so much unsettled land in private hands, as to afford room for an immense future population, although the crown not only withheld its grants, but annihilated its soil. If this be the case, then the only effect of this avarice of desolation, this hoarding of a royal wilderness, would be to raise the value of the possessions in the hands of the great private monopolists, without any adequate check to the growing and alarming mischief of population.

But if you stopped your grants, what would be the consequence? The people would occupy without grants. They have already so occupied in many places. You cannot station garrisons in every part of these deserts. If you drive the people from one place, they will carry on their annual tillage, and remove with their flocks and herds to another. Many of the people in the back settlements are already little attached to particular situations. Already they have topped the Appalachian mountains. From thence they behold before them an immense plain, one vast, rich, level meadow; a square of five hundred miles. Over this they would wander, without a possibility of restraint; they would change their manners with the habits of their life; would soon forget a government, by which they were disowned; would become hordes of English Tartars; and, pouring down upon your unfortified frontiers a fierce and irresistible cavalry, become masters of your governors and your counsellors, your collectors and comptrollers, and of all the slaves that adhered to them. Such would, and, in no long time, must be, the effect of attempting to forbid as a crime, and to suppress as an evil, the command and blessing of Providence, "Increase and multiply." Such would be the happy result of an endeavour to keep as a lair of wild beasts, that earth, which God, by an express charter, has given to the children of men. Far different, and surely much wiser, has been our policy hitherto. Hitherto we have invited our people, by every kind of bounty, to fixed establishments. We have invited the husbandman to look to authority for his title. We have taught him piously to believe in the mysterious virtue of wax and parchment. We have thrown each tract of land, as it was peopled, into districts; that the ruling power should never be wholly out of sight. We have settled all we could; and we have carefully attended every settlement with government.

Adhering, Sir, as I do, to this policy, as well as for the reasons I have just given, I think this new project of hedging in population to be neither prudent nor practicable.

To impoverish the colonies in general, and in particular to arrest the noble course of their marine enterprises, would be a more easy task. I freely confess it. We have shewn a disposition to a system of this kind; a disposition even to continue the restraint after the offence; looking on ourselves as rivals to our colonies, and persuaded that of course we must gain all that they shall lose. Much mischief we may certainly do. The power inadequate to all other things is often more than sufficient for this. I do not look on the direct and immediate power of the colonies to resist our violence, as very formidable. In this, however, I may be mistaken. But when I consider, that we have colonies for no purpose but to be serviceable to us, it seems to my poor understanding a little preposterous, to make them unserviceable, in order to keep them obedient. It is, in truth, nothing more than the old, and, as I thought, exploded problem of tyranny, which proposes to beggar its subjects into submission. But remember, when you have completed your system of impoverishment, that nature still proceeds in her ordinary course; that discontent will increase with misery; and that there are critical moments in the fortune of all states, when they who are too weak to contribute to your prosperity may be strong enough to complete your ruin. *Spoliatis arma supersunt.*[29]

The temper and character, which prevail in our colonies, are, I am afraid, unalterable by any human art. We cannot, I fear, falsify the pedigree of this fierce people, and persuade them that they are not sprung from a nation, in whose veins the blood of freedom cir-

[29] Juvenal, *Satires*, VIII, 124: "Those who are robbed still have recourse to arms."

culates. The language in which they would hear you tell them this tale, would detect the imposition; your speech would betray you. An Englishman is the unfittest person on earth to argue another Englishman into slavery.

I think it is nearly as little in our power to change their republican religion, as their free descent; or to substitute the Roman Catholic, as a penalty; or the church of England, as an improvement. The mode of inquisition and dragooning is going out of fashion in the old world; and I should not confide much to their efficacy in the new. The education of the Americans is also on the same unalterable bottom with their religion. You cannot persuade them to burn their books of curious science; to banish their lawyers from the courts of law; or to quench the lights of their assemblies, by refusing to choose those persons who are best read in their privileges. It would be no less impracticable to think of wholly annihilating the popular assemblies, in which these lawyers sit. The army, by which we must govern in their place, would be far more chargeable to us; not quite so effectual; and perhaps, in the end, full as difficult to be kept in obedience.

With regard to the high aristocratic spirit of Virginia and the southern colonies, it has been proposed, I know, to reduce it, by declaring a general enfranchisement of their slaves. This project has had its advocates and panegyrists; yet I never could argue myself into any opinion of it. Slaves are often much attached to their masters. A general wild offer of liberty would not always be accepted. History furnishes few instances of it. It is sometimes as hard to persuade slaves to be free, as it is to compel freemen to be slaves; and in this auspicious scheme, we should have both these pleasing tasks on our hands at once. But when we talk of enfranchisement, do we not perceive that the American master may enfranchise too; and arm servile hands in defence of freedom? A measure to which other people have had recourse more than once, and not without success, in a desperate situation of their affairs.

Slaves as these unfortunate black people are, and dull as all men are from slavery, must they not a little suspect the offer of freedom from that very nation which has sold them to their present masters? From that nation, one of whose causes of quarrel with those masters, is their refusal to deal any more in that inhuman traffic? An offer of freedom from England, would come rather oddly, shipped to them in an African vessel, which is refused an entry into the ports of Virginia or Carolina, with a cargo of three hundred Angola negroes. It would be curious to see the Guinea captain attempting at the same instant to publish his proclamation of liberty, and to advertise his sale of slaves.[30]

But let us suppose all these moral difficulties got over. The ocean remains. You cannot pump this dry; and as long as it continues in its present bed, so long all the causes which weaken authority by distance will continue. "Ye gods, annihilate but space and time, and make two lovers happy!" [31]—was a pious and passionate prayer;—but just as reasonable as many of the serious wishes of very grave and solemn politicians.

If then, Sir, it seems almost desperate to think of any alterative course, for changing the moral causes (and not quite easy to remove the natural) which produce prejudices irreconcileable to the late exercise of our authority; but that the spirit infallibly will continue; and, continuing, will produce such effects, as now embarrass us; the second mode under consideration is, to prosecute that spirit in its overt acts as *criminal*.

At this proposition, I must pause a moment. The thing seems a great deal too big for my ideas of jurisprudence. It should seem, to my way of conceiving such matters, that there is a very wide difference in reason and policy, between the mode of proceeding on the irregular conduct of scattered individuals, or even of bands of men, who disturb order within the state, and the civil dissentions which may, from time to time, on great questions, agitate the several communities which compose a great empire. It looks to me to be

[30] Although the British may not have imposed slavery on the colonists, as has been alleged, they certainly condoned and fostered it. Slavery was not outlawed in Britain until 1807, and not in the West Indies (under British dominion) until the legislation of 1833. Thereafter slavery as an accepted practice was gradually exterminated throughout all lands under the control of the British.

[31] From *Peri Bathous: or Of the Art of Sinking in Poetry* by Martinus Scriblerus, a pseudonym employed jointly by Alexander Pope (1688–1744), Jonathan Swift (1667–1745), and John Arbuthnot (1667–1735). The lines were probably written principally by Arbuthnot, a scientist, physician, and pamphleteer.

narrow and pedantic, to apply the ordinary ideas of criminal justice to this great public contest. I do not know the method of drawing up an indictment against a whole people. I cannot insult and ridicule the feelings of millions of my fellow creatures, as Sir Edward Coke insulted one excellent individual (Sir Walter Raleigh)[32] at the bar.* I am not ripe to pass sentence on the gravest public bodies, entrusted with magistracies of great authority and dignity, and charged with the safety of their fellow-citizens, upon the very same title that I am. I really think, that for wise men this is not judicious; for sober men, not decent; for minds tinctured with humanity, not mild and merciful.

Perhaps, Sir, I am mistaken in my idea of an empire, as distinguished from a single state or kingdom. But my idea of it is this; that an empire is the aggregate of many states under one common head: whether this head be a monarch, or a presiding republic. It does, in such constitutions, frequently happen (and nothing but the dismal, cold, dead uniformity of servitude can prevent its happening) that the subordinate parts have many local privileges and immunities. Between these privileges, and the supreme common authority, the line may be extremely nice. Of course disputes, often too very bitter disputes, and much ill blood, will arise. But though every privilege is an exemption (in the case) from the ordinary exercise of the supreme authority, it is no denial of it. The claim of a privilege seems rather *ex vi termini*,[33] to imply a superior power. For to talk of the privileges of a state or of a person, who has no superior, is hardly any better than speaking nonsense. Now, in such unfortunate quarrels, among the component parts of a great political union of communities, I can scarcely conceive any thing more completely imprudent, than for the head of the empire to insist, that, if any privilege is pleaded against his will, or his acts, that his whole authority is denied; instantly to proclaim rebellion, to beat to arms, and to put the offending provinces under the ban. Will not this,

* *See Howell's State Trials, vol. ii, p. 7. et seq.*

[32] Sir Edward Coke (1552–1634), the great lawyer, jurist, and commentator on English law, was appointed Attorney General in 1593. In 1603 he conducted the trial of Sir Walter Raleigh (1552–1618), who, after a lapse of some years, was condemned and executed.

[33] "From the meaning of the term."

Sir, very soon teach the provinces to make no distinctions on their part? Will it not teach them that the government, against which a claim of liberty is tantamount to high treason, is a government to which submission is equivalent to slavery? It may not always be quite convenient to impress dependent communities with such an idea.

We are, indeed, in all disputes with the colonies, by the necessity of things, the judge. It is true, Sir. But I confess, that the character of judge in my own cause, is a thing that frightens me. Instead of filling me with pride, I am exceedingly humbled by it. I cannot proceed with a stern, assured, judicial confidence, until I find myself in something more like a judicial character. I must have these hesitations as long as I am compelled to recollect, that, in my little reading upon such contests as these, the sense of mankind has, at least, as often decided against the superior as the subordinate power. Sir, let me add too, that the opinion of my having some abstract right in my favour would not put me much at my ease in passing sentence; unless I could be sure that there were no rights which, in their exercise under certain circumstances, were not the most odious of all wrongs, and the most vexatious of all injustice. Sir, these considerations have great weight with me, when I find things so circumstanced, that I see the same party, at once a civil litigant against me in point of right, and a culprit before me; while I sit as criminal judge, on acts of his, whose moral quality is to be decided upon the merits of that very litigation. Men are every now and then put, by the complexity of human affairs, into strange situations; but justice is the same, let the judge be in what situation he will.

There is, Sir, also a circumstance which convinces me, that this mode of criminal proceeding is not (at least in the present stage of our contest) altogether expedient; which is nothing less than the conduct of those very persons who have seemed to adopt that mode, by lately declaring a rebellion in Massachusetts Bay, as they had formerly addressed to have traitors brought hither under an act of Henry VIII. for trial.[34] For though rebellion is declared, it is not

[34] In 1769, Parliament requested that traitors be brought to England for trial. In 1775, Parliament, in an address to the king, declared the Massachusetts Bay Colony to be in a state of rebellion.

6 3

proceeded against as such; nor have any steps been taken towards the apprehension or conviction of any individual offender, either on our late or our former address; but modes of public coercion have been adopted, and such as have much more resemblance to a sort of qualified hostility towards an independent power than the punishment of rebellious subjects. All this seems rather inconsistent; but it shews how difficult it is to apply these juridical ideas to our present case.[35]

In this situation, let us seriously and coolly ponder. What is it we have got by all our menaces, which have been many and ferocious? What advantage have we derived from the penal laws we have passed, and which, for the time, have been severe and numerous? What advances have we made towards our object, by the sending of a force, which by land and sea is no contemptible strength? Has the disorder abated? Nothing less.—When I see things in this situation, after such confident hopes, bold promises, and active exertions, I cannot, for my life, avoid a suspicion, that the plan itself is not correctly right.

If then the removal of the causes of this spirit of American liberty be, for the greater part, or rather entirely, impracticable; if the ideas of criminal process be inapplicable, or, if applicable, are in the highest degree inexpedient, what way yet remains? No way is open, but the third and last—to comply with the American spirit as necessary; or if you please to submit to it, as a necessary evil.

If we adopt this mode; if we mean to conciliate and concede; let us see of what nature the concession ought to be: to ascertain the nature of our concession, we must look at their complaint. The colonies complain, that they have not the characteristic mark and seal of British freedom. They complain, that they are taxed in a parliament, in which they are not represented. If you mean to satisfy them at all, you must satisfy them with regard to this complaint. If you mean to please any people, you must give them the boon which they ask; not what you may think better for them, but of a kind totally different.

[35] In his *Letter to the Sheriffs of Bristol* (1777), Burke stated explicitly his objections to the application of the Act of Henry VIII to the American colonies. See *The Works of Edmund Burke*, Vol. II, pp. 3–4.

Such an act may be a wise regulation, but it is no concession; whereas our present theme is the mode of giving satisfaction.

Sir, I think you must perceive, that I am resolved this day to have nothing at all to do with the question of the right of taxation. Some gentlemen startle—but it is true: I put it totally out of the question. It is less than nothing in my consideration. I do not indeed wonder, nor will you, Sir, that gentlemen of profound learning are fond of displaying it on this profound subject. But my consideration is narrow, confined, and wholly limited to the policy of the question. I do not examine, whether the giving away a man's money be a power excepted and reserved out of the general trust of government; and how far all mankind, in all forms of polity, are entitled to an exercise of that right by the charter of nature. Or whether, on the contrary, a right of taxation is necessarily involved in the general principle of legislation, and inseparable from the ordinary supreme power. These are deep questions, where great names militate against each other; where reason is perplexed; and an appeal to authorities only thickens the confusion. For high and reverend authorities lift up their heads on both sides; and there is no sure footing in the middle. This point is the "great Serbonian bog, betwixt Damiata and Mount Casius old, where armies whole have sunk." [36] I do not intend to be overwhelmed in that bog, though in such respectable company. The question with me is, not whether you have a right to render your people miserable; but whether it is not your interest to make them happy. It is not, what a lawyer tells me, I may do; but what humanity, reason, and justice tell me, I ought to do. Is a politic act the worse for being a generous one? Is no concession proper, but that which is made from your want of right to keep what you grant? Or does it lessen the grace or dignity of relaxing in the exercise of an odious claim, because you have your evidence-room full of titles, and your magazines stuffed with arms to enforce them? What signify all those titles, and all those arms? Of what avail are they, when the reason of the thing tells me, that the assertion of my title is the loss of my suit; and that I could do nothing but wound myself by the use of my own weapons? [37]

[36] John Milton, *Paradise Lost*, II, 592–594.

[37] Burke's line of reasoning was not unknown on the other side of the Atlantic. Com-

§ *Edmund Burke*

Such is stedfastly my opinion of the absolute necessity of keeping up the concord of this empire by a unity of spirit, though in a diversity of operations, that, if I were sure the colonists had, at their leaving this country, sealed a regular compact of servitude; that they had solemnly abjured all the rights of citizens; that they had made a vow to renounce all ideas of liberty for them and their posterity, to all generations, yet I should hold myself obliged to conform to the temper I found universally prevalent in my own day, and to govern two million of men, impatient of servitude, on the principles of freedom. I am not determining a point of law; I am restoring tranquillity; and the general character and situation of a people must determine what sort of government is fitted for them. That point nothing else can or ought to determine.

My idea, therefore, without considering whether we yield as matter of right, or grant as matter of favour, is *to admit the people of our colonies into an interest in the constitution,* and, by recording that admission in the journals of parliament, to give them as strong an assurance as the nature of the thing will admit, that we mean for ever to adhere to that solemn declaration of systematic indulgence.

Some years ago, the repeal of a revenue act, upon its understood principle, might have served to shew, that we intended an unconditional abatement of the exercise of a taxing power. Such a measure was then sufficient to remove all suspicion, and to give perfect content. But unfortunate events, since that time, may make something further necessary; and not more necessary for the satisfaction of the colonies, than for the dignity and consistency of our own future proceedings.

I have taken a very incorrect measure of the disposition of the

---

pare Alexander Hamilton's views as set forth in his pamphlet "The Farmer Refuted . . ." (1775). Harold C. Syrett and Jacob E. Cooke, eds., *The Papers of Alexander Hamilton,* Vol. I, pp. 121–122: "It is true, that New-York has no Charter. But, if it could support it's claim to liberty in no other way, it might, with justice, plead the common principles of colonization: for, it would be unreasonable, to seclude one colony, from the enjoyment of the most important privileges of the rest. There is no need, however, of this plea: The sacred rights of mankind are not to be rummaged for, among old parchments, or musty records. They are written, as with a sun beam, in the whole *volume* of human nature, by the hand of the divinity itself; and can never be erased or obscured by mortal power."

House, if this proposal in itself would be received with dislike. I think, Sir, we have few American financiers. But our misfortune is, we are too acute; we are too exquisite in our conjectures of the future, for men oppressed with such great and present evils. The more moderate among the opposers of parliamentary concession freely confess, that they hope no good from taxation; but they apprehend the colonists have further views; and if this point were conceded, they would instantly attack the trade laws. These gentlemen are convinced, that this was the intention from the beginning; and the quarrel of the Americans with taxation was no more than a cloak and cover to this design. Such has been the language even of a gentleman (Mr. Rice)[38] of real moderation, and of a natural temper so well adjusted to fair and equal government. I am, however, Sir, not a little surprised at this kind of discourse, whenever I hear it: and I am the more surprised, on account of the arguments which I constantly find in company with it, and which are often urged from the same mouths, and on the same day.

For instance, when we allege, that it is against reason to tax a people under so many restraints in trade as the Americans, the noble lord (North) in the blue ribband shall tell you, that the restraints on trade are futile and useless; of no advantage to us, and of no burthen to those on whom they are imposed; that the trade to America is not secured by the acts of navigation, but by the natural and irresistible advantage of a commercial preference.[39]

Such is the merit of the trade laws in this posture of the debate. But when strong internal circumstances are urged against the taxes: when the scheme is dissected; when experience and the nature of things are brought to prove, and do prove, the utter impossibility of obtaining an effective revenue from the colonies; when these things are pressed, or rather press themselves, so as to drive the advocates of colony taxes to a clear admission of the futility of the scheme; then, Sir, the sleeping trade laws revive from their trance; and this useless taxation is to be kept sacred, not for its own sake, but as a counter-guard and security of the laws of trade.

Then, Sir, you keep up revenue laws which are mischievous, in

[38] George Rice (1724–1779), Member of Parliament from Wales.
[39] At this point Burke recounts admissions made by Lord North.

order to preserve trade laws that are useless. Such is the wisdom of our plan in both its members. They are separately given up as of no value, and yet one is always to be defended for the sake of the other. But I cannot agree with the noble lord, nor with the pamphlet from whence he seems to have borrowed these ideas, concerning the inutility of the trade laws. For without idolizing them, I am sure they are still, in many ways, of great use to us; and in former times, they have been of the greatest. They do confine, and they do greatly narrow, the market for the Americans. But my perfect conviction of this does not help me in the least to discern how the revenue laws form any security whatsoever to the commercial regulations; or that these commercial regulations are the true ground of the quarrel; or, that the giving way in any one instance of authority, is to lose all that may remain unconceded.

One fact is clear and indisputable. The public and avowed origin of this quarrel was on taxation. This quarrel has indeed brought on new disputes on new questions; but certainly the least bitter and the fewest of all on trade laws. To judge which of the two be the real radical cause of quarrel, we have to see whether the commercial dispute did, in order of time, precede the dispute on taxation. There is not a shadow of evidence for it. Next, to enable us to judge whether at this moment a dislike to the trade laws be the real cause of quarrel, it is absolutely necessary to put the taxes out of the question by a repeal. See how the Americans act in this position, and then you will be able to discern correctly what is the true object of the controversy, or whether any controversy at all will remain. Unless you consent to remove this cause of difference, it is impossible, with decency, to assert that the dispute is not upon what it is avowed to be. And I would, Sir, recommend to your serious consideration, whether it be prudent to form a rule for punishing people, not on their own acts, but on your conjectures. Surely it is preposterous at the very best. It is not justifying your anger, by their misconduct; but it is converting your ill-will into their delinquency.

But the colonies will go further.—Alas! alas! when will this speculating against fact and reason end? What will quiet these panic fears which we entertain of the hostile effect of the conciliatory conduct? Is it true, that no case can exist, in which it is proper for the sovereign to accede to the desires of his discontented subjects? Is there any thing peculiar in this case, to make a rule for itself? Is all authority of course lost, when it is not pushed to the extreme? Is it a certain maxim, that, the fewer causes of dissatisfaction are left by government, the more the subject will be inclined to resist and rebel?

All these objections being in fact no more than suspicions, conjectures, divinations, formed in defiance of fact and experience; they did not, Sir, discourage me from entertaining the idea of a conciliatory concession, founded on the principles which I have just stated.

In forming a plan for this purpose, I endeavoured to put myself in that frame of mind, which was the most natural, and the most reasonable; and which was certainly the most probable means of securing me from all error. I set out with a perfect distrust of my own abilities; a total renunciation of every speculation of my own; and with a profound reverence for the wisdom of our ancestors, who have left us the inheritance of so happy a constitution, and so flourishing an empire, and what is a thousand times more valuable, the treasury of the maxims and principles which formed the one, and obtained the other.

During the reigns of the kings of Spain of the Austrian family, whenever they were at a loss in the Spanish councils, it was common for their statesmen to say, that they ought to consult the genius of Philip the Second.[40] The genius of Philip the Second might mislead them; and the issue of their affairs shewed, that they had not chosen the most perfect standard. But, Sir, I am sure that I shall not be misled, when, in a case of constitutional difficulty, I consult the genius of the English constitution. Consulting at that oracle (it was with all due humility and piety) I found four capital examples in a similar case before me: those of Ireland, Wales, Chester, and Durham.

Ireland, before the English conquest, though never governed by a despotic power, had no parliament.[41] How far the English parliament itself was at that time modelled according to the present form,

[40] Philip II of Spain sent the Armada against England in 1588.
[41] In 1171–1172, Henry II, in an expedition into Ireland, consolidated temporarily the conquests made theretofore.

is disputed among antiquaries. But we have all the reason in the world to be assured, that a form of parliament, such as England then enjoyed, she instantly communicated to Ireland; and we are equally sure, that almost every successive improvement in constitutional liberty, as fast as it was made here, was transmitted thither. The feudal baronage, and the feudal knighthood, the roots of our primitive constitution, were early transplanted into that soil; and grew and flourished there. Magna Charta, if it did not give us originally the House of Commons, gave us at least a House of Commons of weight and consequence.[42] But your ancestors did not churlishly sit down alone to the feast of Magna Charta. Ireland was made immediately a partaker. This benefit of English laws and liberties, I confess, was not at first extended to *all* Ireland. Mark the consequence. English authority and English liberty had exactly the same boundaries. Your standard could never be advanced an inch before your privileges. Sir John Davis[43] shews beyond a doubt, that the refusal of a general communication of these rights, was the true cause why Ireland was 500 years in subduing; and after the vain projects of a military government, attempted in the reign of Queen Elizabeth, it was soon discovered, that nothing could make that country English, in civility and allegiance, but your laws and your forms of legislature. It was not English arms, but the English constitution, that conquered Ireland. From that time, Ireland has ever had a general parliament, as she had before a partial parliament. You changed the people; you altered the religion; but you never touched the form or the vital substance of free government in that kingdom. You deposed kings; you restored them; you altered the succession to theirs, as well as to your own crown; but you never altered their constitution; the principle of which was respected by usurpation; restored with the restoration of monarchy, and established, I trust, for ever, by the glorious Revolution.[44] This has made Ireland the great and flourishing kingdom that it is; and from a disgrace and a burthen intolerable to this nation, has rendered her a principal part of our strength and ornament. This

[42] Magna Charta was signed by King John at Runnymede in 1215.
[43] Sir John Davies (1569–1626) was appointed Solicitor General of Ireland in 1603.
[44] Following the Glorious (or Bloodless) Revolution of 1688, James II was deposed and William and Mary enthroned.

country cannot be said to have ever formally taxed her. The irregular things done in the confusion of mighty troubles, and on the hinge of great revolutions, even if all were done that is said to have been done, form no example. If they have any effect in argument, they make an exception to prove the rule. None of your own liberties could stand a moment if the casual deviations from them, at such times, were suffered to be used as proofs of their nullity. By the lucrative amount of such casual breaches in the constitution, judge what the stated and fixed rule of supply has been in that kingdom. Your Irish pensioners would starve, if they had no other fund to live on than taxes granted by English authority. Turn your eyes to those popular grants from whence all your great supplies are come; and learn to respect that only source of public wealth in the British empire.

My next example is Wales. This country was said to be reduced by Henry the Third.[45] It was said more truly to be so by Edward the First.[46] But though then conquered, it was not looked upon as any part of the realm of England. Its old constitution, whatever that might have been, was destroyed; and no good one was substituted in its place. The care of that tract was put into the hands of lords marchers—a form of government of a very singular kind; a strange heterogeneous monster, something between hostility and government; perhaps it has a sort of resemblance, according to the modes of those times, to that of commander in chief at present, to whom all civil power is granted, as secondary.[47] The manners of the Welsh nation followed the genius of the government; the people were ferocious, restiff, savage, and uncultivated; sometimes composed, never pacified. Wales, within itself, was in perpetual disorder; and it kept the frontier of England in perpetual alarm. Benefits from it to the state there were none. Wales was only known to England by incursion and invasion.

Sir, during that state of things, parliament was not idle. They attempted to subdue the fierce spirit of the Welsh by all sorts of

[45] Henry III reigned from 1216 to 1272.
[46] Edward I reigned from 1272 to 1307.
[47] The Lords Marchers were vested with special powers and responsibilities for the marches, or borders, between England and Wales and between England and Scotland.

rigorous laws. They prohibited by statute the sending all sorts of arms into Wales, as you prohibit by proclamation (with something more of doubt on the legality) the sending arms to America. They disarmed the Welsh by statute, as you attempted (but with still more question on the legality) to disarm New England by an instruction. They made an act to drag offenders from Wales into England for trial, as you have done (but with more hardship) with regard to America. By another act, where one of the parties was an Englishman, they ordained that his trial should be always by English. They made acts to restrain trade, as you do; and they prevented the Welsh from the use of fairs and markets, as you do the Americans from fisheries and foreign ports. In short, when the statute-book was not quite so much swelled as it is now, you find no less than fifteen acts of penal regulation on the subject of Wales.

Here we rub our hands—a fine body of precedents for the authority of parliament and the use of it!—I admit it fully; and pray add likewise to those precedents, that all the while, Wales rid this kingdom like an *incubus*; that it was an unprofitable and oppressive burthen; and that an Englishman travelling in that country could not go six yards from the high road without being murdered.

The march of the human mind is slow. Sir, it was not, until after 200 years, discovered, that by an eternal law, Providence had decreed vexation to violence; and poverty to rapine. Your ancestors did however at length open their eyes to the ill husbandry of injustice. They found that the tyranny of a free people could of all tyrannies the least be endured; and that laws made against a whole nation were not the most effectual methods for securing its obedience. Accordingly, in the 27th year of Henry the Eighth, the course was entirely altered. With a preamble stating the entire and perfect rights of the crown of England, it gave to the Welsh all the rights and privileges of English subjects. A political order was established; the military power gave way to the civil; the marches were turned into counties. But that a nation should have a right to English liberties, and yet no share at all in the fundamental security of these liberties, the grant of their own property, seemed a thing so incongruous; that eight years after, that is, in the 35th year of that reign, a complete and not ill-proportioned representation by counties and boroughs was be-

stowed upon Wales, by act of parliament. From that moment, as by
a charm, the tumult subsided; obedience was restored; peace, order,
and civilization followed in the train of liberty.—When the day-star
of the English constitution had arisen in their hearts, all was harmony within and without—

> "Simul alba nautis
> "Stella refulsit,
> "Defluit saxis agitatus humor:
> "Concidunt venti, fugiuntque nubes:
> "Et minax (quòd sic voluere) ponto
> "Unda recumbit." [48]

The very same year the county palatine[49] of Chester received the
same relief from its oppressions, and the same remedy to its disorders. Before this time Chester was little less distempered than
Wales. The inhabitants, without rights themselves, were the fittest
to destroy the rights of others, and from thence Richard the Second [50]
drew the standing army of archers, with which for a time he oppressed England. The people of Chester applied to parliament in a
petition penned as I shall read to you.

"To the king our sovereign lord, in most humble wise shewn unto
your excellent majesty, the inhabitants of your grace's county palatine of Chester; that where the said county palatine of Chester is
and hath been always hitherto exempt, excluded, and separated out
and from your high court of parliament, to have any knights and
burgesses within the said court; by reason whereof the said inhabitants have hitherto sustained manifold disherisons, losses, and dam-
ages, as well in their lands, goods, and bodies, as in the good, civil,
and politic governance and maintenance of the commonwealth of
their said country: (2.) And for as much as the said inhabitants have
always hitherto been bound by the acts and statutes made and or-

---

[48] Horace, *Odes*, I, 12, 27–32: "As soon as the bright star amid the tempest shines
upon the mariner, the spray subsides, the winds are quieted, the clouds disperse, and
(such is their power) the tremendous waves sink down into the sea."

[49] A County Palatine was ruled by a Count who in theory exercised absolute power
within his jurisdiction. By Burke's time the system had long since been superseded in
England.

[50] Richard II reigned from 1377 to 1399.

dained by your said highness, and your most noble progenitors, by authority of the said court, as far forth as other counties, cities, and boroughs have been, that have had their knights and burgesses within your said court of parliament, and yet have had neither knight nor burgess there for the said county palatine; the said inhabitants, for lack thereof, have been oftentimes touched and grieved with acts and statutes made within the said court, as well derogatory unto the most ancient jurisdictions, liberties, and privileges of your said county palatine, as prejudicial unto the commonwealth, quietness, rest, and peace of your grace's most bounden subjects inhabiting within the same."

What did parliament with this audacious address?—Reject it as a libel? Treat it as an affront to government? Spurn it as a derogation from the rights of legislature? Did they toss it over the table? Did they burn it by the hands of the common hangman?—They took the petition of grievance, all rugged as it was, without softening or temperament, unpurged of the original bitterness and indignation of complaint; they made it the very preamble to their act of redress; and consecrated its principle to all ages in the sanctuary of legislation.

Here is my third example. It was attended with the success of the two former. Chester, civilized as well as Wales, has demonstrated, that freedom and not servitude is the cure of anarchy; as religion, and not atheism, is the true remedy for superstition. Sir, this pattern of Chester was followed in the reign of Charles the Second,[51] with regard to the county palatine of Durham, which is my fourth example. This county had long lain out of the pale of free legislation. So scrupulously was the example of Chester followed, that the style of the preamble is nearly the same with that of the Chester act; and without affecting the abstract extent of the authority of parliament, it recognizes the equity of not suffering any considerable district, in which the British subjects may act as a body, to be taxed without their own voice in the grant.

Now, if the doctrines of policy contained in these preambles, and the force of these examples in the acts of parliaments, avail any thing, what can be said against applying them with regard to Amer-

[51] Charles II reigned from 1660 until his death in 1685.

ica? Are not the people of America as much Englishmen as the Welsh? The preamble of the act of Henry VIII. says, the Welsh speak a language no way resembling that of his majesty's English subjects. Are the Americans not as numerous? If we may trust the learned and accurate Judge Barrington's[52] account of North Wales, and take that as a standard to measure the rest, there is no comparison. The people cannot amount to above 200,000: not a tenth part of the number in the colonies. Is America in rebellion? Wales was hardly ever free from it. Have you attempted to govern America by penal statutes? You made fifteen for Wales. But your legislative authority is perfect with regard to America; was it less perfect in Wales, Chester, and Durham? But America is virtually represented. What! does the electric force of virtual representation[53] more easily pass over the Atlantic, than pervade Wales, which lies in your neighbourhood: or than Chester and Durham, surrounded by abundance of representation that is actual and palpable? But, Sir, your ancestors thought this sort of virtual representation, however ample, to be totally insufficient for the freedom of the inhabitants of territories that are so near, and comparatively so inconsiderable. How then can I think it sufficient for those which are infinitely greater, and infinitely more remote?

You will now, Sir, perhaps imagine, that I am on the point of proposing to you a scheme for a representation of the colonies in parliament. Perhaps I might be inclined to entertain some such thought; but a great flood stops me in my course. *Opposuit natura*[54] —I cannot remove the eternal barriers of the creation. The thing in that mode, I do not know to be possible. As I meddle with no theory, I do not absolutely assert the impracticability of such a representation. But I do not see my way to it; and those who have been more confident, have not been more successful. However, the arm

---

[52] In 1757 Daines Barrington (1727–1800) was appointed justice of the Welsh counties of Merioneth, Carnarvon, and Anglesey.

[53] The doctrine of virtual representation was advanced by the "King's Friends" to justify withholding the franchise from the American colonists. It was argued that once a member was elected to the House of Commons he represented all the king's subjects, including the colonists, so that they were "virtually" represented in the Parliament.

[54] Juvenal, *Satires*, X, 152: "Nature opposes."

of public benevolence is not shortened; and there are often several means to the same end. What nature has disjoined in one way, wisdom may unite in another. When we cannot give the benefit as we would wish, let us not refuse it altogether. If we cannot give the principal, let us find a substitute. But how? Where? What substitute?

Fortunately I am not obliged for the ways and means of this substitute to tax my own unproductive invention. I am not even obliged to go to the rich treasury of the fertile framers of imaginary commonwealths: not to the Republic of Plato; not to the Utopia of More; not to the Oceana of Harrington. It is before me—it is at my feet, "*and the rude swain treads daily on it with his clouted shoon.*" [55] I only wish you to recognize, for the theory, the ancient constitutional policy of this kingdom with regard to representation, as that policy has been declared in acts of parliament; and, as to the practice, to return to that mode which an uniform experience has marked out to you as best; and in which you walked with security, advantage, and honour, until the year 1763.

My resolutions, therefore, mean to establish the equity and justice of a taxation of America, by *grant* and not by *imposition*. To mark the *legal competency* of the colony assemblies for the support of their government in peace, and for public aids in time of war. To acknowledge that this legal competency has had *a dutiful and beneficial exercise;* and that experience has shewn the *benefit of their grants,* and the *futility of parliamentary taxation as a method of supply.*

These solid truths compose six fundamental propositions. There are three more resolutions corollary to these. If you admit the first set, you can hardly reject the others. But if you admit the first, I shall be far from solicitous whether you accept or refuse the last. I think these six massive pillars will be of strength sufficient to support the temple of British concord. I have no more doubt than I entertain of my existence, that, if you admitted these, you would command an immediate peace; and with but tolerable future management, a lasting obedience in America. I am not arrogant in this

[55] See John Milton, *Comus,* 631–635.

confident assurance. The propositions are all mere matters of fact; and if they are such facts as draw irresistible conclusions even in the stating, this is the power of truth, and not any management of mine.

Sir, I shall open the whole plan to you together, with such observations on the motions as may tend to illustrate them where they may want explanation. The first is a resolution—"That the colonies and plantations of Great Britain in North America, consisting of fourteen separate governments, and containing two millions and upwards of free inhabitants, have not had the liberty and privilege of electing and sending any knights and burgesses, or others to represent them in the high court of parliament."—This is a plain matter of fact, necessary to be laid down, and (excepting the description) it is laid down in the language of the constitution; it is taken nearly *verbatim* from acts of parliament.

The second is like unto the first—"That the said colonies and plantations have been liable to, and bounden by, several subsidies, payments, rates, and taxes, given and granted by parliament, though the said colonies and plantations have not their knights and burgesses, in the said high court of parliament, of their own election, to represent the condition of their country; by lack whereof they have been oftentimes touched and grieved by subsidies, given, granted, and assented to, in the said court, in a manner prejudicial to the commonwealth, quietness, rest, and peace of the subjects inhabiting within the same."

Is this description too hot, or too cold, too strong, or too weak? Does it arrogate too much to the supreme legislature? Does it lean too much to the claims of the people? If it runs into any of these errors, the fault is not mine. It is the language of your own ancient acts of parliament. "Non meus hic sermo, sed quæ præcepit Ofellus, rusticus, abnormis sapiens." [56] It is the genuine produce of the ancient, rustic, manly, home-bred sense of this country.—I did not dare to rub off a particle of the venerable rust that rather adorns and preserves, than destroys the metal. It would be a profanation to touch with a tool the stones which construct the sacred altar of peace.[57]

[56] Horace, *Satires*, II, 2–3: "It is not an essay original with me but comprises the teaching of the peasant Ofellus, an uneducated natural philosopher."
[57] See Exodus, XX, 25.

77

I would not violate with modern polish the ingenuous and noble roughness of these truly constitutional materials. Above all things, I was resolved not to be guilty of tampering, the odious vice of restless and unstable minds. I put my foot in the tracks of our forefathers; where I can neither wander nor stumble. Determining to fix articles of peace, I was resolved not to be wise beyond what was written; I was resolved to use nothing else than the form of sound words; to let others abound in their own sense; and carefully to abstain from all expressions of my own. What the law has said, I say. In all things else I am silent. I have no organ but for her words. This, if it be not ingenious, I am sure is safe.

There are indeed words expressive of grievance in this second resolution, which those who are resolved always to be in the right, will deny to contain matter of fact, as applied to the present case; although parliament thought them true, with regard to the counties of Chester and Durham. They will deny that the Americans were ever "touched and grieved" with the taxes. If they consider nothing in taxes but their weight as pecuniary impositions, there might be some pretence for this denial. But men may be sorely touched and deeply grieved in their privileges, as well as in their purses. Men may lose little in property by the act which takes away all their freedom. When a man is robbed of a trifle on the highway, it is not the twopence lost that constitutes the capital outrage. This is not confined to privileges. Even ancient indulgences withdrawn, without offence on the part of those who enjoyed such favours, operate as grievances. But were the Americans then not touched and grieved by the taxes, in some measure, merely as taxes? If so, why were they almost all, either wholly repealed or exceedingly reduced? Were they not touched and grieved, even by the regulating duties of the sixth of George the Second?[58] Else why were the duties first reduced to one third in 1764, and afterwards to a third of that third in the year 1766? Were they not touched and grieved by the stamp-act? I shall say they were, until that tax is revived. Were they not touched and grieved by the duties of 1767, which were likewise repealed, and

[58] In his speech "On American Taxation" (1774), Burke refers to the regulating duties (the "Molasses Act").

which, Lord Hillsborough[59] tells you (for the ministry) were laid contrary to the true principle of commerce? Is not the assurance given by that noble person to the colonies of a resolution to lay no more taxes on them, an admission that taxes would touch and grieve them? Is not the resolution of the noble lord in the blue ribband, now standing on your Journals, the strongest of all proofs that parliamentary subsidies really touched and grieved them? Else why all these changes, modifications, repeals, assurances, and resolutions?

The next proposition is—"That, from the distance of the said colonies, and from other circumstances, no method hath hitherto been devised for procuring a representation in parliament for the said colonies." This is an assertion of a fact. I go no further on the paper; though in my private judgment an useful representation is impossible; I am sure it is not desired by them; nor ought it perhaps by us; but I abstain from opinions.

The fourth resolution is—"That each of the said colonies hath within itself a body, chosen in part, or in the whole, by the freemen, freeholders, or other free inhabitants thereof, commonly called the General Assembly, or general court, with powers legally to raise, levy, and assess, according to the several usage of such colonies, duties and taxes towards defraying all sorts of public services."

This competence in the colony assemblies is certain. It is proved by the whole tenor of their acts of supply in all the assemblies, in which the constant style of granting is, "an aid to his majesty"; and acts granting to the crown have regularly for near a century passed the public offices without dispute. Those who have been pleased paradoxically to deny this right, holding that none but the British parliament can grant to the crown, are wished to look to what is done, not only in the colonies, but in Ireland, in one uniform unbroken tenor every session. Sir, I am surprised, that this doctrine should come from some of the law servants of the crown. I say, that if the crown could be responsible, his majesty—but certainly the ministers, and even these law officers themselves, through whose hands the acts pass biennially in Ireland, or annually in the colonies, are in habitual course of committing impeachable offences. What

[59] Lord Hillsborough (1718–1793) was Secretary of State for the colonies from 1768 to 1772.

habitual offenders have been all presidents of the council, all secretaries of state, all first lords of trade, all attornies and all solicitors general! However, they are safe; as no one impeaches them; and there is no ground of charge against them, except in their own unfounded theories.

The fifth resolution is also a resolution of fact—"That the said general assemblies, general courts, or other bodies legally qualified as aforesaid, have at sundry times freely granted several large subsidies and public aids for his majesty's service, according to their abilities, when required thereto by letter from one of his majesty's principal secretaries of state; and that their right to grant the same, and their cheerfulness and sufficiency in the said grants, have been at sundry times acknowledged by parliament." To say nothing of their great expences in the Indian wars; and not to take their exertion in foreign ones, so high as the supplies in the year 1695; not to go back to their public contributions in the year 1710; I shall begin to travel only where the Journals give me light; resolving to deal in nothing but fact, authenticated by parliamentary record; and to build myself wholly on that solid basis.

On the 4th of April, 1748, a committee of this House came to the following resolution:

"Resolved, That it is the opinion of this committee, *that it is just and reasonable* that the several provinces and colonies of Massachusetts Bay, New Hampshire, Connecticut, and Rhode Island, be reimbursed the expences they have been at in taking and securing to the crown of Great Britain the island of Cape Breton and its dependencies."

These expences were immense for such colonies. They were above 200,000*l.* sterling; money first raised and advanced on their public credit.

On the 28th of January, 1756, a message from the king came to us, to this effect—"His majesty, being sensible of the zeal and vigour with which his faithful subjects of certain colonies in North America have exerted themselves in defence of his majesty's just rights and possessions, recommends it to this House to take the same into their consideration, and to enable his majesty to give them such assistance as may be a *proper reward and encouragement.*"

On the 3d of February 1756, the House came to a suitable resolution, expressed in words nearly the same as those of the message: but with the further addition, that the money then voted was as an *encouragement* to the colonies to exert themselves with vigour. It will not be necessary to go through all the testimonies which your own records have given to the truth of my resolutions. I will only refer you to the places in the Journals: Vol. xxvii.—16th and 19th May, 1757. Vol. xxviii.—June 1st, 1758; April 26th and 30th, 1759; March 26th and 31st, and April 28th, 1760; Jan. 9th and 20th, 1761. Vol. xxix.—Jan. 22d and 26th, 1762; March 14th and 17th, 1763.

Sir, here is the repeated acknowledgement of parliament, that the colonies not only gave, but gave to satiety. This nation has formerly acknowledged two things; first, that the colonies had gone beyond their abilities, parliament having thought it necessary to reimburse them; secondly, that they had acted legally and laudably in their grants of money, and their maintenance of troops, since the compensation is expressly given as reward and encouragement. Reward is not bestowed for acts that are unlawful; and encouragement is not held out to things that deserve reprehension. My resolution therefore does nothing more than collect into one proposition what is scattered through your Journals. I give you nothing but your own; and you cannot refuse in the gross what you have so often acknowledged in detail. The admission of this, which will be so honourable to them and to you, will, indeed, be mortal to all the miserable stories by which the passions of the misguided people have been engaged in an unhappy system. The people heard, indeed, from the beginning of these disputes, one thing continually dinned in their ears, that reason and justice demanded, that the Americans, who paid no taxes, should be compelled to contribute. How did that fact of their paying nothing stand, when the taxing system began? When Mr. Grenville[60] began to form his system of American revenue, he stated in this House, that the colonies were then in debt 2,600,000*l.* sterling money; and was of opinion they would discharge that debt in four years. On this state, those untaxed people were actually subject to the payment of taxes to the amount of 650,000*l.* a year. In

[60] George Grenville (1712–1770), Prime Minister from 1763 to 1765, initiated the Stamp Act of 1765.

fact, however, Mr. Grenville was mistaken. The funds given for sinking the debt did not prove quite so ample as both the colonies and he expected. The calculation was too sanguine: the reduction was not completed till some years after, and at different times in different colonies. However, the taxes after the war continued too great to bear any addition, with prudence or propriety; and when the burthens imposed in consequence of former requisitions were discharged, our tone became too high to resort again to requisition. No colony, since that time, ever has had any requisition whatsoever made to it.

We see the sense of the crown, and the sense of parliament, on the productive nature of a *revenue by grant*. Now search the same Journals for the produce of the *revenue by imposition*—Where is it? —Let us know the volume and the page—what is the gross, what is the net produce?—To what service is it applied?—How have you appropriated its surplus?—What, can none of the many skilful index-makers, that we are now employing, find any trace of it?—Well, let them, and that, rest together.—But are the Journals, which say nothing of the revenue, as silent on the discontent? Oh no! a child may find it. It is the melancholy burthen and blot of every page.

I think then I am, from those Journals, justified in the sixth and last resolution, which is—"That it hath been found by experience, that the manner of granting the said supplies and aids, by the said general assemblies, hath been more agreeable to the said colonies, and more beneficial and conducive to the public service, than the mode of giving and granting aids in parliament, to be raised and paid in the said colonies." This makes the whole of the fundamental part of the plan. The conclusion is irresistible. You cannot say, that you were driven by any necessity to an exercise of the utmost rights of legislature. You cannot assert, that you took on yourselves the task of imposing colony taxes, from the want of another legal body, that is competent to the purpose of supplying the exigencies of the state without wounding the prejudices of the people. Neither is it true that the body so qualified, and having that competence, had neglected the duty.

The question now, on all this accumulated matter, is;—whether you will choose to abide by a profitable experience, or a mischievous theory; whether you choose to build on imagination or fact; whether you prefer enjoyment or hope; satisfaction in your subjects, or discontent?

If these propositions are accepted, every thing which has been made to enforce a contrary system, must, I take it for granted, fall along with it. On that ground, I have drawn the following resolution, which, when it comes to be moved, will naturally be divided in a proper manner: "That it may be proper to repeal an act, made in the seventh year of the reign of his present majesty, intituled, An act for granting certain duties in the British colonies and plantations in America; for allowing a drawback of the duties of customs upon the exportation from this kingdom, of coffee and cocoa-nuts of the produce of the said colonies or plantations; for discontinuing the drawbacks payable on China earthenware exported to America; and for more effectually preventing the clandestine running of goods in the said colonies and plantations. And that it may be proper to repeal an act, made in the 14th year of the reign of his present majesty, intituled, An act to discontinue in such manner, and for such time, as are therein mentioned, the landing and discharging, lading or shipping, of goods, wares, and merchandize, at the town and within the harbour of Boston, in the province of Massachusetts Bay, in North America. And that it may be proper to repeal an act, made in the 14th year of the reign of his present majesty, intituled, An act for the impartial administration of justice, in the cases of persons questioned for any acts done by them, in the execution of the law, or for the suppression of riots and tumults, in the province of Massachusetts Bay, in New England. And that it may be proper to repeal an act, made in the 14th year of the reign of his present majesty, intituled, An act for the better regulating the government of the province of Massachusetts Bay in New England. And also, that it may be proper to explain and amend an act made in the 35th year of the reign of King Henry VIII., intituled, An act for the trial of treasons committed out of the king's dominions."

I wish, Sir, to repeal the Boston port bill, because (independently of the dangerous precedent of suspending the rights of the subject during the king's pleasure) it was passed, as I apprehend, with less regularity, and on more partial principles, than it ought. The corporation of Boston was not heard before it was condemned. Other towns, full as guilty as she was, have not had their ports blocked up. Even the restraining bill of the present session does not go to the length of the Boston port act. The same ideas of prudence, which induced you not to extend equal punishment to equal guilt, even when you were punishing, induce me, who mean not to chastise, but to reconcile, to be satisfied with the punishment already partially inflicted.[61]

Ideas of prudence, and accommodation to circumstances, prevent you from taking away the charters of Connecticut and Rhode Island, as you have taken away that of Massachusetts colony, though the crown has far less power in the two former provinces than it enjoyed in the latter; and though the abuses have been full as great, and as flagrant, in the exempted as in the punished. The same reasons of prudence and accommodation have weight with me in restoring the charter of Massachusetts Bay. Besides, Sir, the act which changes the charter of Massachusetts is in many particulars so exceptionable, that if I did not wish absolutely to repeal, I would by all means desire to alter it; as several of its provisions tend to the subversion of all public and private justice. Such, among others, is the power in the governor to change the sheriff at his pleasure; and to make a new returning officer for every special cause. It is shameful to behold such a regulation standing among English laws.

The act for bringing persons accused of committing murder under the orders of government to England for trial, is but temporary. That act has calculated the probable duration of our quarrel with the colonies; and is accommodated to that supposed duration. I would hasten the happy moment of reconciliation; and therefore must, on my principle, get rid of that most justly obnoxious act.

The act of Henry VIII.[62] for the trial of treasons, I do not mean to take away, but to confine it to its proper bounds and original intention; to make it expressly for trial of treasons (and the greatest treasons may be committed) in places where the jurisdiction of the crown does not extend.

[61] Lord North had chosen to make an example of the town of Boston.
[62] Henry VIII (1491–1547) was king of England from 1509 to 1547. The act referred to permitted the trial of a subject charged with treason to be held outside his normal jurisdiction.

Having guarded the privileges of local legislature, I would next secure to the colonies a fair and unbiassed judicature: for which purpose, Sir, I propose the following resolution: "That, from the time when the general assembly or general court of any colony or planta-tion in North America shall have appointed by act of assembly, duly confirmed, a settled salary to the offices of the chief justice and other judges of the superior court, it may be proper, that the said chief justice and other judges of the superior courts of such colony, shall hold his and their office and offices during their good behaviour; and shall not be removed therefrom, but when the said removal shall be adjudged by his majesty in council, upon a hearing on complaint from the general assembly, or on a complaint from the governor, or council, or the house of representatives severally, of the colony in which the said chief justice and other judges have exercised the said offices."

The next resolution relates to the courts of admiralty. It is this: —"That it may be proper to regulate the courts of admiralty or vice-admiralty, authorized by the 15th chap. of the 4th of George III. in such a manner as to make the same more commodious to those who sue or are sued, in the said courts, and to provide for the more decent maintenance of the judges in the same."

These courts I do not wish to take away: they are in themselves proper establishments. This court is one of the capital securities of the Act of Navigation. The extent of its jurisdiction, indeed, has been increased; but this is altogether as proper, and is, indeed, on many accounts, more eligible, where new powers were wanted, than a court absolutely new. But courts incommodiously situated, in effect, deny justice; and a court, partaking in the fruits of its own con-demnation, is a robber. The congress complain, and complain justly of this grievance.*

These are the three consequential propositions. I have thought of two or three more; but they came rather too near detail, and to the province of executive government, which I wish parliament al-ways to superintend, never to assume. If the first six are granted,

* *The Solicitor-General informed Mr. Burke when the resolutions were separately moved, that the grievance of the judges partaking of the profits of the seizure had been redressed by office; accordingly the resolution was amended.*

congruity will carry the latter three. If not, the things that remain unrepealed will be, I hope, rather unseemly incumbrances on the building, than very materially detrimental to its strength and stability.

Here, Sir, I should close; but that I plainly perceive some objections remain which I ought, if possible, to remove. The first will be, that, in resorting to the doctrine of our ancestors, as contained in the preamble to the Chester Act, I prove too much; that the grievance from a want of representation stated in that preamble, goes to the whole of legislation as well as to taxation. And that the colonies grounding themselves upon that doctrine, will apply it to all parts of legislative authority.

To this objection, with all possible deference and humility, and wishing as little as any man living to impair the smallest particle of our supreme authority, I answer, that *the words are the words of parliament, and not mine*; and, that all false and inconclusive inferences, drawn from them, are not mine; for I heartily disclaim any such inference. I have chosen the words of an act of parliament, which Mr. Grenville, surely a tolerably zealous and very judicious advocate for the sovereignty of parliament, formerly moved to have read at your table, in confirmation of his tenets.[63] It is true, that Lord Chatham[64] considered these preambles as declaring strongly in favour of his opinions. He was a no less powerful advocate for the privileges of the Americans. Ought I not from hence to presume, that these preambles are as favourable as possible to both, when properly understood; favourable both to the rights of parliament, and to the privilege of the dependencies of this crown? But, Sir, the object of grievance in my resolution, I have not taken from the Chester, but from the Durham Act, which confines the hardship of want of representation to the case of subsidies; and which therefore falls in exactly with the case of the colonies. But whether the unrepresented

[63] Inasmuch as the members of Parliament were well acquainted with Grenville's zeal to uphold the prerogatives of the kingdom in the governance of the colonies, the language of Burke is clearly an understatement.

[64] William Pitt (1708–1778), the Earl of Chatham, consistently supported the claims of the colonies to the rights of Englishmen but not to independence. See below, pp. 111–123.

counties were *de jure*, or *de facto*,[65] bound, the preambles do not accurately distinguish; nor indeed was it necessary; for whether *de jure*, or *de facto*, the legislature thought the exercise of the power of taxing, as of right, or as of fact without right, equally a grievance, and equally oppressive.

I do not know that the colonies have, in any general way, or in any cool hour, gone much beyond the demand of immunity in relation to taxes. It is not fair to judge of the temper or dispositions of any man, or any set of men, when they are composed and at rest, from their conduct, or their expressions, in a state of disturbance and irritation. It is besides a very great mistake to imagine, that mankind follow up practically any speculative principle, either of government or of freedom, as far as it will go in argument and logical illation. We Englishmen stop very short of the principles upon which we support any given part of our constitution; or even the whole of it together. I could easily, if I had not already tired you, give you very striking and convincing instances of it. This is nothing but what is natural and proper. All government, indeed every human benefit and enjoyment, every virtue, and every prudent act, is founded on compromise and barter. We balance inconveniences; we give and take; we remit some rights, that we may enjoy others; and, we chuse rather to be happy citizens, than subtle disputants. As we must give away some natural liberty, to enjoy civil advantages; so we must sacrifice some civil liberties, for the advantages to be derived from the communion and fellowship of a great empire. But in all fair dealings the thing bought must bear some proportion to the purchase paid. None will barter away the immediate jewel of his soul. Though a great house is apt to make slaves haughty,[66] yet it is purchasing a part of the artificial importance of a great empire too dear, to pay for it all the essential rights, and all the intrinsic dignity of human nature. None of us who would not risk his life, rather than fall under a government purely arbitrary. But, although there are some amongst us who think our constitution wants many improvements, to make it a complete system of liberty, perhaps none

---

[65] *De jure*: "in law"; *de facto*: "in fact."

[66] See Juvenal, *Satires*, V, 66.

who are of that opinion would think it right to aim at such improvement, by disturbing his country, and risking every thing that is dear to him. In every arduous enterprise, we consider what we are to lose, as well as what we are to gain; and the more and better stake of liberty every people possess, the less they will hazard in a vain attempt to make it more. These are *the cords of man*. Man acts from adequate motives relative to his interest; and not on metaphysical speculations. Aristotle, the great master of reasoning, cautions us, and with great weight and propriety, against this species of delusive geometrical accuracy in moral arguments, as the most fallacious of all sophistry.[67]

The Americans will have no interest contrary to the grandeur and glory of England, when they are not oppressed by the weight of it; and they will rather be inclined to respect the acts of a superintending legislature; when they see them the acts of that power, which is itself the security, not the rival, of their secondary importance. In this assurance, my mind most perfectly acquiesces; and I confess, I feel not the least alarm, from the discontents which are to arise, from putting people at their ease; nor do I apprehend the destruction of this empire, from giving, by an act of free grace and indulgence, to two millions of my fellow-citizens, some share of those rights, upon which I have always been taught to value myself.

It is said, indeed, that this power of granting, vested in American assemblies, would dissolve the unity of the empire; which was preserved entire, although Wales, and Chester, and Durham, were added to it. Truly, Mr. Speaker, I do not know what this unity means; nor has it ever been heard of, that I know, in the constitutional policy of this country. The very idea of subordination of parts, excludes this notion of simple and undivided unity. England is the head; but she is not the head and the members too. Ireland has ever had from the beginning a separate, but not an independent, legislature; which, far from distracting, promoted the union of the whole. Every thing was sweetly and harmoniously disposed through

[67] *The Nichomachean Ethics*, I, 3 (trans. J. A. K. Thomson): "It is a mark of an educated man and a proof of his culture that in every subject he looks only for so much precision as its nature permits. For example, it is absurd to demand logical demonstrations from a professional speaker; we might as well expect mere probabilities from a mathematician."

both islands for the conservation of English dominion, and the communication of English liberties. I do not see that the same principles might not be carried into twenty islands, and with the same good effect. This is my model with regard to America, as far as the internal circumstances of the two countries are the same. I know no other unity of this empire, than I can draw from its example during these periods, when it seemed to my poor understanding more united than it is now, or than it is likely to be by the present methods.

But since I speak of these methods, I recollect, Mr. Speaker, almost too late, that I promised, before I finished, to say something of the proposition of the noble lord (North) on the floor, which has been so lately received, and stands on your Journals. I must be deeply concerned, whenever it is my misfortune to continue a difference with the majority of this House. But as the reasons for that difference are my apology for thus troubling you, suffer me to state them in a very few words. I shall compress them into as small a body as I possibly can, having already debated that matter at large, when the question was before the committee.

First, then, I cannot admit that proposition of a ransom by auction;—because it is a mere project. It is a thing new; unheard of; supported by no experience; justified by no analogy; without example of our ancestors, or root in the constitution.

It is neither regular parliamentary taxation, nor colony grant. *Experimentum in corpore vili*,[68] is a good rule, which will ever make me adverse to any trial of experiments on what is certainly the most valuable of all subjects; the peace of this empire.

Secondly, it is an experiment which must be fatal in the end to our constitution. For what is it but a scheme for taxing the colonies in the anti-chamber of the noble lord and his successors? To settle the quotas and proportions in this House, is clearly impossible. You, Sir, may flatter yourself, you shall sit a state auctioneer, with your hammer in your hand, and knock down to each colony as it bids. But to settle (on the plan laid down by the noble lord) the true proportional payment for four or five and twenty governments, according to the absolute and the relative wealth of each, and according to the British proportion of wealth and burthen, is a wild and

---

[68] "The experiment should be tried on something worthless."

chimerical notion. This new taxation must therefore come in by the back-door of the constitution. Each quota must be brought to this House ready formed; you can neither add nor alter. You must register it. You can do nothing further. For on what grounds can you deliberate either before or after the proposition? You cannot hear the counsel for all these provinces quarrelling each on its own quantity of payment, and its proportion to others. If you should attempt it, the committee of provincial ways and means, or by whatever other name it will delight to be called, must swallow up all the time of parliament.

Thirdly, it does not give satisfaction to the complaint of the colonies. They complain, that they are taxed without their consent; you answer, that you will fix the sum at which they shall be taxed. That is, you give them the very grievance for the remedy. You tell them indeed, that you will leave the mode to themselves. I really beg pardon: it gives me pain to mention it; but you must be sensible that you will not perform this part of the compact. For, suppose the colonies were to lay the duties which furnished their contingent, upon the importation of your manufactures; you know you would never suffer such a tax to be laid. You know too, that you would not suffer many other modes of taxation. So that, when you come to explain yourself it will be found, that you will neither leave to themselves the quantum nor the mode; nor indeed any thing. The whole is delusion from one end to the other.

Fourthly, this method of ransom by auction, unless it be *universally* accepted, will plunge you into great and inextricable difficulties. In what year of our Lord are the proportions of payments to be settled? To say nothing of the impossibility that colony agents should have general powers of taxing the colonies at their discretion; consider, I implore you, that the communication by special messages, and orders between these agents and their constituents, on each variation of the case, when the parties come to contend together, and to dispute on their relative proportions, will be a matter of delay, perplexity, and confusion, that never can have an end.

If all the colonies do not appear at the outcry, what is the condition of those assemblies, who offer, by themselves or their agents, to tax themselves up to your ideas of their proportion? The refractory colonies, who refuse all composition, will remain taxed only to your old impositions, which, however grievous in principle, are trifling as to production. The obedient colonies in this scheme are heavily taxed; the refractory remain unburthened. What will you do? Will you lay new and heavier taxes by parliament on the disobedient? Pray consider in what way you can do it. You are perfectly convinced that in the way of taxing, you can do nothing but at the ports. Now suppose it is Virginia that refuses to appear at your auction, while Maryland and North Carolina bid handsomely for their ransom, and are taxed to your quota: how will you put these colonies on a par? Will you tax the tobacco of Virginia? If you do, you give its death wound to your English revenue at home, and to one of the very greatest articles of your own foreign trade. If you tax the import of that rebellious colony, what do you tax but your own manufactures, or the goods of some other obedient, and already well taxed colony? Who has said one word on this labyrinth of detail, which bewilders you more and more as you enter into it? Who has presented, who can present you, with a clue, to lead you out of it? I think, Sir, it is impossible, that you should not recollect that the colony bounds are so implicated in one another (you know it by your other experiments in the bill for prohibiting the New England fishery) that you can lay no possible restraints on almost any of them which may not be presently eluded, if you do not confound the innocent with the guilty, and burthen those whom upon every principle you ought to exonerate. He must be grossly ignorant of America, who thinks, that, without falling into this confusion of all rules of equity and policy, you can restrain any single colony, especially Virginia and Maryland, the central, and most important of them all.

Let it also be considered, that, either in the present confusion you settle a permanent contingent, which will and must be trifling; and then you have no effectual revenue; or you change the quota at every exigency; and then on every new repartition you will have a new quarrel.

Reflect, besides, that when you have fixed a quota for every colony, you have not provided for prompt and punctual payment. Suppose one, two, five, ten years arrears. You cannot issue a treasury extent against the failing colony. You must make new Boston port bills, new restraining laws, new acts for dragging men to England for trial. You must send out new fleets, new armies. All is to begin again. From this day forward the empire is never to know an hour's tranquillity. An intestine fire will be kept alive in the bowels of the colonies, which one time or other must consume this whole empire. I allow indeed that the empire of Germany[69] raises her revenue and her troops by quotas and contingents; but the revenue of the empire, and the army of the empire, is the worst revenue, and the worst army, in the world.

Instead of a standing revenue, you will therefore have a perpetual quarrel. Indeed the noble lord, who proposed this project of a ransom by auction, seemed himself to be of that opinion. His project was rather designed for breaking the union of the colonies, than for establishing a revenue. He confessed, he apprehended that his proposal would not be to *their taste*. I say, this scheme of disunion seems to be at the bottom of the project; for I will not suspect that the noble lord meant nothing but merely to delude the nation by an airy phantom which he never intended to realize. But whatever his views may be, as I propose the peace and union of the colonies as the very foundation of my plan, it cannot accord with one whose foundation is perpetual discord.

Compare the two. This I offer to give you is plain and simple. The other full of perplexed and intricate mazes. This is mild; that harsh. This is found by experience effectual for its purposes; the other is a new project. This is universal; the other calculated for certain colonies only. This is immediate in its conciliatory operation; the other remote, contingent, full of hazard. Mine is what becomes the dignity of a ruling people; gratuitous, unconditional, and not held out as matter of bargain and sale. I have done my duty in proposing it to you. I have indeed tired you by a long discourse; but this is the misfortune of those to whose influence nothing will be conceded, and who must win every inch of their ground by argument. You have heard me with goodness. May you decide with wisdom! For my part, I feel my mind greatly disburthened by what I have done to-day. I have been the less fearful of trying your patience, because on this subject I mean to spare it altogether in future. I have this

[69] The Holy Roman Empire.

comfort, that in every stage of the American affairs, I have steadily opposed the measures that have produced the confusion, and may bring on the destruction of this empire. I now go so far as to risk a proposal of my own. If I cannot give peace to my country, I give it to my conscience.

But what (says the financier) is peace to us without money? Your plan gives us no revenue. No! But it does—For it secures to the subject the power of refusal; the first of all revenues. Experience is a cheat, and fact a liar, if this power in the subject of proportioning his grant, or of not granting at all, has not been found the richest mine of revenue ever discovered by the skill or by the fortune of man. It does not indeed vote you 152,752*l*. 11*s*. 2¾*d*., nor any other paltry limited sum. But it gives the strong box itself, the fund, the bank, from whence only revenues can arise amongst a people sensible of freedom: *Posita luditur arca.*[70] Cannot you in England; cannot you at this time of day; cannot you, a House of Commons, trust to the principle which has raised so mighty a revenue, and accumulated a debt of near 140 millions in this country? Is this principle to be true in England, and false every where else? Is it not true in Ireland? Has it not hitherto been true in the colonies? Why should you presume, that, in any country, a body duly constituted for any function, will neglect to perform its duty, and abdicate its trust? Such a presumption would go against all governments in all modes. But, in truth, this dread of penury of supply, from a free assembly, has no foundation in nature. For first observe, that besides the desire which all men have naturally of supporting the honour of their own government; that sense of dignity, and that security to property, which ever attends freedom, has a tendency to increase the stock of the free community. Most may be taken where most is accumulated. And what is the soil or climate where experience has not uniformly proved, that the voluntary flow of heaped-up plenty, bursting from the weight of its own rich luxuriance, has ever run with a more copious stream of revenue, than could be squeezed from the dry husks of oppressed indigence, by the straining of all the politic machinery in the world.

Next we know, that parties must ever exist in a free country.

[70] Juvenal, *Satires*, I, 90: "The treasure chest is bet upon the game."

We know too, that the emulations of such parties, their contradictions, their reciprocal necessities, their hopes, and their fears, must send them all in their turns to him that holds the balance of the state. The parties are the gamesters; but government keeps the table, and is sure to be the winner in the end. When this game is played, I really think it is more to be feared, that the people will be exhausted, than that government will not be supplied. Whereas, whatever is got by acts of absolute power ill obeyed, because odious, or by contracts ill kept, because constrained; will be narrow, feeble, uncertain, and precarious. "Ease would retract vows made in pain, as violent and void." [71]

I, for one, protest against compounding our demands: I declare against compounding, for a poor limited sum, the immense, overgrowing, eternal debt, which is due to generous government from protected freedom. And so may I speed in the great object I propose to you, as I think it would not only be an act of injustice, but would be the worst economy in the world, to compel the colonies to a sum certain, either in the way of ransom, or in the way of compulsory compact.

But to clear up my ideas on this subject—a revenue from America transmitted hither—do not delude yourselves—you never can receive it—No, not a shilling. We have experience that from remote countries it is not to be expected. If, when you attempted to extract revenue from Bengal,[72] you were obliged to return in loan what you had taken in imposition; what can you expect from North America? for certainly, if ever there was a country qualified to produce wealth, it is India; or an institution fit for the transmission, it is the East-India Company. America has none of these aptitudes. If America gives you taxable objects, on which you lay your duties here, and gives you, at the same time, a surplus by a foreign sale of her commodities to pay the duties on these objects which you tax at home, she has performed her part to the British revenue. But with regard to her own internal establishments, she may, I doubt not she will, contribute in moderation. I say in moderation; for she ought not to be permitted to exhaust herself. She ought to be reserved to a war;

[71] John Milton, *Paradise Lost*, IV, 96–97.

[72] This reference reflects another of Burke's deep concerns, that for India.

the weight of which, with the enemies that we are most likely to have, must be considerable in her quarter of the globe. There she may serve you, and serve you essentially.

For that service, for all service, whether of revenue, trade, or empire, my trust is in her interest in the British constitution. My hold of the colonies is in the close affection which grows from common names, from kindred blood, from similar privileges, and equal protection. These are ties, which, though light as air, are as strong as links of iron. Let the colonies always keep the idea of their civil rights associated with your government;—they will cling and grapple to you; and no force under heaven will be of power to tear them from their allegiance. But let it be once understood, that your government may be one thing, and their privileges another; that these two things may exist without any mutual relation; the cement is gone; the cohesion is loosened; and every thing hastens to decay and dissolution. As long as you have the wisdom to keep the sovereign authority of this country as the sanctuary of liberty, the sacred temple consecrated to our common faith, wherever the chosen race and sons of England worship freedom, they will turn their faces towards you. The more they multiply, the more friends you will have; the more ardently they love liberty, the more perfect will be their obedience. Slavery they can have any where. It is a weed that grows in every soil. They may have it from Spain, they may have it from Prussia. But until you become lost to all feeling of your true interest and your natural dignity, freedom they can have from none but you. This is the commodity of price, of which you have the monopoly. This is the true act of navigation, which binds to you the commerce of the colonies, and through them secures to you the wealth of the world. Deny them this participation of freedom, and you break that sole bond, which originally made, and must still preserve, the unity of the empire. Do not entertain so weak an imagination, as that your registers and your bonds, your affidavits and your sufferances, your cockets and your clearances, are what form the great securities of your commerce. Do not dream that your letters of office, and your instructions, and your suspending clauses, are the things that hold together the great contexture of this mysterious whole. These things do not make your government. Dead instruments, passive tools as they are, it is the spirit of the English communion, that gives all their life and efficacy to them. It is the spirit of the English constitution, which, infused through the mighty mass, pervades, feeds, unites, invigorates, vivifies, every part of the empire, even down to the minutest member.

Is it not the same virtue which does every thing for us here in England? Do you imagine then, that it is the Land Tax Act which raises your revenue; that it is the annual vote in the committee of supply, which gives you your army? or that it is the Mutiny Bill which inspires it with bravery and discipline? No! surely no! It is the love of the people; it is their attachment to their government from the sense of the deep stake they have in such a glorious institution, which gives you your army and your navy, and infuses into both that liberal obedience, without which your army would be a base rabble, and your navy nothing but rotten timber.

All this, I know well enough, will sound wild and chimerical to the profane herd of those vulgar and mechanical politicians, who have no place among us; a sort of people who think that nothing exists but what is gross and material; and who therefore, far from being qualified to be directors of the great movement of empire, are not fit to turn a wheel in the machine. But to men truly initiated and rightly taught, these ruling and master principles, which, in the opinion of such men as I have mentioned, have no substantial existence, are in truth every thing, and all in all. Magnanimity in politics is not seldom the truest wisdom; and a great empire and little minds go ill together. If we are conscious of our situation, and glow with zeal to fill our places as becomes our station and ourselves, we ought to auspicate all our public proceedings on America with the old warning of the church, *Sursum corda!*[73] We ought to elevate our minds to the greatness of that trust to which the order of Providence has called us. By adverting to the dignity of this high calling, our ancestors have turned a savage wilderness into a glorious empire; and have made the most extensive, and the only honourable conquests; not by destroying, but by promoting, the wealth, the number, the happiness of the human race. Let us get an American

[73] *Sursum corda* ("Lift up your hearts") is a phrase employed in the Roman Catholic Mass and in the Communion Service of certain other churches.

revenue as we have got an American empire. English privileges have made it all that it is; English privileges alone will make it all it can be.

In full confidence of this unalterable truth, I now (quod felix faustumque sit)[74]—lay the first stone of the temple of peace; and I move you, &c.

[Mr. Burke concluded with moving the first of the following Resolutions:]

1. That the colonies and plantations of Great Britain in North America, consisting of fourteen separate governments, and containing two millions and upwards of free inhabitants, have not had the liberty and privilege of electing and sending any knights and burgesses, or others, to represent them in the high court of parliament.

2. That the said colonies and plantations have been made liable to, and bounden by, several subsidies, payments, rates, and taxes, given and granted by parliament; though the said colonies and plantations have not their knights and burgesses, in the said high court of parliament, of their own election, to represent the condition of their country, *by lack whereof, they have been oftentimes touched and grieved by subsidies given, granted, and assented to, in the said court, in a manner prejudicial to the commonwealth, quietness, rest, and peace, of the subjects inhabiting within the same.**

3. That, from the distance of the said colonies, and from other circumstances, no method hath hitherto been devised for procuring a representation in parliament for the said colonies.

4. That each of the said colonies hath within itself a body, chosen, in part or in the whole, by the freemen, freeholders, or other free inhabitants thereof, commonly called the general assembly, or general court; with powers legally to raise, levy, and assess, according to the several usage of such colonies, duties and taxes towards defraying all sorts of public services.

5. That the said general assemblies, general courts, or other bodies, legally qualified as aforesaid, have at sundry times freely granted several large subsidies and public aids for his majesty's serv-

---

* *The words in italics were, by an amendment that was carried, left out of the motion.*
[74] "May all be happy and prosperous." The Romans offered this invocation at the outset of important ventures.

ice, according to their abilities, when required thereto by letter from one of his majesty's principal secretaries of state; and that their right to grant the same, and their cheerfulness and sufficiency in the said grants, have been at sundry times acknowledged by parliament.

6. That it hath been found by experience, that the manner of granting the said supplies and aids, by the said general assemblies, hath been more agreeable to the inhabitants of the said colonies, and more beneficial and conducive to the public service, than the mode of giving and granting aids and subsidies in parliament to be raised and paid in the said colonies.

7. That it may be proper to repeal an act, made in the 7th year of the reign of his present majesty, intituled, An act for granting certain duties in the British colonies and plantations in America; for allowing a drawback of the duties of customs, upon the exportation from this kingdom, of coffee and cocoa-nuts, of the produce of the said colonies or plantations; for discontinuing the drawbacks payable on China earthenware exported to America; and for more effectually preventing the clandestine running of goods in the said colonies and plantations.

8. That it may be proper to repeal an act, made in the 14th year of the reign of his present majesty, intituled, An act to discontinue, in such manner, and for such time, as are therein mentioned, the landing and discharging, lading or shipping of goods, wares, and merchandize, at the town, and within the harbour, of Boston, in the province of Massachusetts Bay, in North America.

9. That it may be proper to repeal an act, made in the 14th year of the reign of his present majesty, intituled, An act for the impartial administration of justice, in cases of persons questioned for any acts done by them in the execution of the law, or for the suppression of riots and tumults, in the province of Massachusetts Bay, in New England.

10. That it is proper to repeal an act, made in the 14th year of the reign of his present majesty, intituled, An act for the better regulating the government of the province of Massachusetts Bay, in New England.

11. That it is proper to explain and amend an act, made in the

35th year of the reign of King Henry VIII., intituled, An act for the trial of treasons committed out of the king's dominions.

12. That, from the time when the general assembly, or general court, of any colony or plantation, in North America, shall have appointed, by act of assembly duly confirmed, a settled salary to the offices of the chief justice and judges of the superior courts, it may be proper that the said chief justice and other judges of the superior courts of such colony shall hold his and their office and offices during their good behaviour; and shall not be removed therefrom, but when the said removal shall be adjudged by his majesty in council, upon a hearing on complaint from the general assembly, or on a complaint from the governor, or council, or the house of representatives, severally, of the colony in which the said chief justice and other judges have exercised the said office.

13. That it may be proper to regulate the courts of admiralty, or vice-admiralty, authorised by the 15th chapter of the 4th of George III., in such a manner as to make the same more commodious to those who sue, or are sued, in the said courts; *and to provide for the more decent maintenance of the judges of the same.*

§ Critical Analysis

It has been said that the measure of a man more truly lies in the assumptions he makes than in the propositions he argues. What do Burke's assumptions about the proper relationship of strong and weak powers, the appropriate motives for setting government policy, the effective methods of dealing with peoples, and the workings of human nature suggest about his character and statesmanship? How well do his assumptions bear out his avowed purpose set forth early in the speech of making "plain good intention" the basis of policy?

§

What kinds of reasoning does Burke use in developing and supporting his proposal? enthymeme? emotional appeal? example? What kind of enthymemes does he marshal for his contentions? How does he make use of the *a fortiori* argument? the alternatives enthymeme? How does he meet possible objections (when he sees gentlemen startle, for instance)? He devotes an extensive discussion to the examples of Ireland, Wales, Chester, and Durham, which he goes to the trouble of introducing with a full paragraph of preparation—a paragraph well worth careful scrutiny. Can you see its purpose? What kind of evidence do the examples of Wales, *et al.*, constitute? What other kinds of evidence does Burke offer in the speech? What efforts does he make so that the speech itself enhances his ultimate proof?

§

Aristotle's rationale of rhetoric takes its departure from the premise that the audience is the end and object of the speaker's efforts. What evidence in the speech suggests that Burke held the same opinion?

§

Burke's style has been generally praised by critics as eloquent for its dignity, its fervor, and its originality. John Morley, himself a statesman and writer of note, says in his biography of Burke,

> In the midst of the torrent of his most strenuous and passionate deliverances, he suddenly rises aloof from his immediate subject, and in

100

all tranquillity reminds us of some permanent relation of things, some enduring truth of human life or society.[1]

How does this speech bear out Morley's statement? Can you identify some of the gem-like epigrams for which Burke is famous? Another feature of his style is the use of ordinary words in fresh and unusual ways, as in the phrase, "Some gentlemen startle," in which Burke has shifted "startle" to an intransitive use. Can you find other examples?

§ SUGGESTIONS FOR FURTHER READING

As a historical event, Burke's speech "On Conciliation with the Colonies" may serve as a point of departure in the study not only of history but also of politics, rhetoric, and literature. The published works relevant to the speech are thus formidable in quantity if somewhat uneven in value. Taken as a whole, they are not as satisfying as they might be, particularly if one accepts the dictum that Sir Leslie Stephen expressed in his *History of English Thought in the Eighteenth Century* (New York: G. P. Putnam's, 1902), Vol. II, p. 219, that as a master of English prose "Burke has not, in my judgment, been surpassed in any period of our literature." The inadequacy of the Burke material is noteworthy in the texts of his speeches, for which there is no really satisfactory edition offering both textual and rhetorical criticism. Chauncey A. Goodrich's *Select British Eloquence* (Indianapolis: Bobbs-Merrill, 1963) may be consulted for certain of the texts as well as for Goodrich's insightful commentaries. Texts of some of Burke's speeches, as well as of his letters and pamphlets, are available in *Bohn's Standard Library*, 6 vols. (London: George Bell and Sons, 1894).

For the history of the period during which Burke participated in the debates on the American question, one may read the three volumes of Sir George Otto Trevelyan's *The American Revolution* (London: Longmans, Green, 1909). Trevelyan's leisurely narrative is enriched by many quotations from contemporary sources. W. E. H. Lecky's *A History of England in the Eighteenth Century* (New York: D. Appleton, 1891) is a standard work. More recent and perhaps more serviceable is L. B.

[1] *Burke* (London: Macmillan, 1902), p. 311.

Namier's *England in the Age of the American Revolution* (London: Macmillan, 1930). Chapter III ("The Parliament of 1761") and Chapter IV ("The House of Commons and America") cast illumination on the immediate audience that Burke could anticipate in speaking to the Commons. For a well-nigh exhaustive treatment of the House of Commons during the years of Burke's active life, see *The House of Commons: 1754–1790* (London: H. M. Stationery Office, 1964), by Sir Lewis Namier and John Brooke. *The Coming of the Revolution: 1763–1775* (New York: Harper & Brothers, 1954) by Lawrence Henry Gipson contributes a succinct and authoritative account of the colonies during the period of Burke's chief interest in America. In addition, Gipson's work supplies an excellent bibliography. In *Fundamental Law and the American Revolution: 1760–1776* (New York: Columbia University Press, 1933), Charles F. Mullett considers, from twentieth-century perspective, the propositions that Burke and his colleagues argued in the eighteenth century. In his admirable study *The War for America: 1775–1783* (Cambridge: Harvard University Press, 1964), Piers Mackesy writes charitably of the British ministers without approving British policy.

Edmund Burke awaits a definitive biography. Meanwhile, the most recent accounts of him are serviceable: *Edmund Burke: A Biography* (New York: Oxford University Press, 1931) by Robert H. Murray, and *Edmund Burke: A Life* (London: John Murray, 1939) by Sir Philip Magnus. Although John Morley's *Burke* (London: Macmillan, 1902) is designed as a critical review rather than as a narrative, it remains indispensable both for biography and for criticism.

The several aspects of Burke's career have been the subject of books, chapters, monographs, and scholarly articles. The following may be mentioned: Louis I. Bredvold, *The Brave New World of the Enlightenment* (Ann Arbor: University of Michigan Press, 1961); Donald Cross Bryant, *Edmund Burke and His Literary Friends* (St. Louis: Washington University Studies, 1939); Alfred Cobban, *Edmund Burke and the Revolt Against the Eighteenth Century*, 2nd ed. (London: George Allen and Unwin, 1960); Thomas W. Copeland, *Our Eminent Friend Edmund Burke: Six Essays* (New Haven: Yale University Press, 1949); Ross J. S. Hoffman, *Edmund Burke, New York Agent: With His Letters to the New York Assembly and Intimate Correspondence with Charles O'Hara 1751–1776* (Philadelphia: American Philosophical Society, 1956); Charles Parkin, *The Moral Basis of Burke's Political Thought: An Essay* (New York: Cambridge University Press, 1956); and Leo Straus, *Natural Right and History* (Chicago: University of Chicago Press, 1963).

Special mention should be made of some recent contributions: *Burke and the Nature of Politics: The Age of the American Revolution* (Lexington: University of Kentucky Press, 1957) and *Burke and the Nature of Politics: The Age of the French Revolution* (Lexington: University of Kentucky Press, 1964), both by Carl B. Cone; *The Conservative Mind from Burke to Santayana* (Chicago: Regnery, 1953) by Russell Kirk; *Edmund Burke and Ireland* (Cambridge: Harvard University Press, 1960) by Thomas H. D. Mahony; and *Edmund Burke and the Natural Law* (Ann Arbor: University of Michigan Press, 1958) by Peter J. Stanlis.

Cone's substantial contribution to the biography of Edmund Burke is the first to reflect the advantages gained from access to the Burke papers deposited in the Sheffield Central Library and to the smaller collection in the Northamptonshire Record Office. Kirk's volume is noteworthy for its perceptive and sympathetic account (pp. 11–61) of Burke's contribution to conservative thought. Mahony's book is unique in the extent and quality of its treatment of Burke's concern for Ireland and for Catholic emancipation. It includes helpful notes on sources and a selected bibliography. Stanlis' work (particularly his chapters "Burke and the Natural Law" and "Burke and the Sovereignty of Natural Law") provides a counterweight to the criticism offered by logical positivists of Burke's conception of the natural law.

Of the three divisions of *Burke, Disraeli, and Churchill: The Politics of Perseverance* (Cambridge: Harvard University Press, 1961), by Stephen R. Graubard, the essay entitled "Edmund Burke: The Old Whig" is, as the author says, an attempt to rescue Burke from his disciples. In *Edmund Burke: The Practical Imagination* (Cambridge: Harvard University Press, 1967), Gerald W. Chapman treats Burke as "a practical and imaginative thinker unpredictable in the range and depth of his insights." Chapman's work, particularly the chapter on "Burke and America" is immediately relevant to the speech "On Conciliation with the Colonies"; and the first chapter entitled "The Organic Premise" should be meaningful to all rhetoricians as well as to historians and students of Edmund Burke.

William B. Todd's A *Bibliography of Edmund Burke* (London: Rupert Hart-Davis, 1964) is a scholarly endeavor invaluable for locating early editions of Burke.

William Pitt, Lord Chatham

"If I were an American, as I am an Englishman, while a foreign troop was landed in my country, I never would lay down my arms —never—never—never." [1] —LORD CHATHAM

BIOGRAPHICAL SKETCH

William Pitt, first Earl of Chatham, was born in London on November 15, 1708. He was the son of Robert and Harriet Pitt and the grandson of Thomas Pitt, known as "Governor" Pitt, who was the founder of the family fortunes. As a boy of ten or eleven, Pitt was placed at Eton, where he seems to have been diligent and proficient in the study of the classics. In January 1727, he entered Trinity College, Oxford, as a gentleman-commoner. Beset by the gout, a disease that continued to afflict him, he left Oxford without a degree. Later, it appears, he studied at Utrecht, prior to accepting a commission (1730–1731) as Cornet of Horse. In 1733, he took the "grand tour" thought desirable to the standing of the English gentry and visited France and Switzerland.

On his return to England, Pitt was chosen (February 18, 1735) as Member of Parliament for Old Sarum and, in April 1736, delivered in the House of Commons a maiden speech as notable for its irony as for its impertinence. In consequence of the speech Pitt was dismissed from his post as Cornet of Horse and thus immediately attracted the attention of all those opposed to Walpole and

NOTE: The sources for this essay will be found in the section Suggestions for Further Reading, pp. 125–126. Special indebtedness is acknowledged to Chauncey A. Goodrich's critiques of Chatham's speechmaking. Taken together they constitute perhaps the most perspicuous and the most stimulating examples of Goodrich's rhetorical criticism.

[1] William Pitt, "Speech of Lord Chatham on a Motion for an Address to the Throne, at the Opening of Parliament, Delivered in the House of Lords, November 18, 1777," in Chauncey A. Goodrich, ed., *Select British Eloquence* (Indianapolis: Bobbs-Merrill, 1963), p. 135.

George II, as well as the partisans of the Prince of Wales. Afterward, except during spells of illness, Pitt was never to be out of the turmoil of politics. To Pitt may be attributed in part the downfall of Walpole as Prime Minister (1742), an event that doubtless still further alienated George II. Even so, in 1756 the disasters that befell British policy required the king to call Pitt to the government as Secretary of State. In the following year, Pitt headed a coalition ministry that conducted the Seven Years' (French and Indian) War with such force and brilliance that France was defeated in India, Africa, America, and Europe. No small measure of Pitt's success was owing to his ability to appeal to all classes of men, a quality that gained him the name of "the Great Commoner."

On November 16, 1754, Pitt was married to Lady Hester Grenville, to whom were born five children. One of these was William Pitt, the younger, who, like his father, became famous as parliamentarian, orator, and war minister. In 1760, George III forced Pitt out of office and he joined the opposition to the king and the "King's friends." Pitt's opposition, notably in his support of the American colonists, was continued in the House of Lords after he was made Earl of Chatham (1766), and even after he was forced, probably by a mental disability, to leave public life except for occasional visits to the House of Lords. Following Chatham's last speech (April 17, 1778) in the House of Lords, he collapsed and was carried home to die. William Pitt, the Earl of Chatham, is generally reckoned to hold a high place among British politicians, statesmen, war ministers, and orators. Proud, imperious, eccentric, he was indubitably an English patriot and a major contributor to the building of the British Empire.

THE SPEAKER

Lord Chatham's career as a speechmaker exemplifies the principle that every speech moving a hearer to thought and action does so by a combination of three forces: the reason inhering in the language, the appeals to the feelings and attitudes existing within the hearer, and the character of the speaker as revealed by the speech. In persuasion no one of these forces exists alone. And neither the speaker nor the hearer is likely to analyze a discourse at the moment of utterance in order to discover which element of the combination is uppermost. Yet in retrospect one may examine a speaker's practice to find his characteristic modes of persuasion and to assess their effect.

The Persuasion of Reason

In a quiet, orderly, and reasonable society persuasion would presumably be quiet, orderly, and reasonable. A speaker would offer cogent demonstrations of the validity of his premises without recourse to other means of persuasion. Inasmuch, however, as neither men in particular nor societies in general are consistently quiet, orderly, and reasonable, the orator who would give effect to his counsels must be prepared to employ the accessories of proof. The accessories must be employed particularly in questions of policy for which solutions must be sought symbolically—since otherwise they cannot be demonstrated—under such legal or ethical limitations as the orator imposes on himself or society imposes on him.

Of William Pitt, Earl of Chatham, it has been said that in eloquence he was not a reasoner but depended on the vigor of his personality to achieve the results he sought. Admittedly, Chatham was imperious, but examination of the surviving texts of his speeches fails to confirm the notion that he was "not a reasoner." Another explanation is more probable. Unlike Burke, Chatham did not endeavor to expose every element of his enthymemes to the attention of his hearers. Rather than to tease out the proofs that might have been required of another speaker, or to cite authority for his premises, he depended in his major speeches either on his own authority or on the members of the House of Commons or the House of Lords to complete his reasoning, and thus to participate in the process for which he stated only the results. Hence one does not find in Chatham, as in Burke, full inventories of argument against the policies of the king's ministers. One is likely to find a conclusion that is not unreasonable, one that in fact is—or has been—reasoned, with the expectation presumably that the hearer will supply the minor premises or recall evidence and assumptions perhaps unavailable to a current reader of the text.

For example, when Chatham said to the peers, "France, my Lords, has insulted you; she has encouraged and sustained America; and, whether America be wrong or right, the dignity of this country ought to spurn at the officious insult of French interference," [2] he did not cite chapter and verse. He did not spell out the proofs. He did not bring out the law books "doubled down in dog's ears." He relied—as he had done twenty years before—on a mighty premise, the pride of the English in their race and land, and on the cogency of reasoning developed therefrom. No expert witness was called. Chatham was his own sufficient authority:

> My Lords, this ruinous and ignominious situation, where we can not act with success, nor suffer with honor, calls upon us to remonstrate in the strongest and loudest language of truth, to rescue the ear of majesty from the delusions which surround it. The desperate state of our arms abroad is in part known. No man thinks more highly of them than I do. I love and honor the English troops. I know their virtues and their valor. I know they can achieve any thing except impossibilities; and I know that the conquest of English America *is an impossibility*. You can not, I venture to say it, *you can not* conquer America. Your armies last war effected every thing that could be effected; and what was it? It cost a numerous army, under the command of a most able general [Lord Amherst], now a noble Lord in this House, a long and laborious campaign, to expel five thousand Frenchmen from French America. My Lords, *you can not conquer America*.[3]

The Appeals to Feelings and Attitudes

To be sure, nothing in Chatham's obeisance to the rhetoric of cogency required him to employ only the pallid language of ratiocination or to abstain from appeals to mood or sentiment. A man of passion himself, he thought he could observe it, perhaps arouse it, in others. He was thus moved to passionate reply to Lord Suffolk's defense of the employment of Indian warriors against the colonists:

[2] See below, pp. 112–113.

[3] See below, p. 114.

These abominable principles, and this more abominable avowal of them, demand the most decisive indignation. I call upon that right reverend bench, those holy ministers of the Gospel, and pious pastors of our Church—I conjure them to join in the holy work, and vindicate the religion of their God. I appeal to the wisdom and the law of this learned bench, to defend and support the justice of their country. I call upon the Bishops, to interpose the unsullied sanctity of their lawn; upon the learned Judges, to interpose the purity of their ermine, to save us from this pollution. I call upon the honor of your Lordships, to reverence the dignity of your ancestors, and to maintain your own. I call upon the spirit and humanity of my country, to vindicate the national character. I invoke the genius of the Constitution. From the tapestry that adorns these walls, the immortal ancestor of this noble Lord frowns with indignation at the disgrace of his country. . . . Spain armed herself with blood-hounds to extirpate the wretched natives of America, and we improve on the inhuman example even of Spanish cruelty; we turn loose these savage hell-hounds against our brethren and countrymen in America, of the same language, laws, liberties, and religion, endeared to us by every tie that should sanctify humanity.[4]

The Character of the Speaker

On November 18, 1777, Chatham, old and ill, had less than a year to live. He was no longer, as he had been a generation before, the imperious minister saying to the Duke of Devonshire, "My Lord, I am sure that I can save this country, and that nobody else can." Yet the will to command, the habit of speaking with authority, remained with him. To the uses of his oratory he brought the three cardinal virtues—courage, integrity, and commitment to England.

[4] See below, pp. 122–123. In the House of Lords on December 5, 1777, Lord Chatham "moved for copies of all instructions relative to the employment of Indians in conjunction with the British troops against the inhabitants of the British colonies in North America." Lord Gower, opposing the motion, asserted that Chatham had himself employed savages in the operations of the last war. Chatham vigorously denied that Indians had been employed, except to gain intelligence. In this statement he was supported by Lord Townshend, who had been in command at Quebec. Townshend testified that Indians "were never under military command, nor arrayed for military purposes." *Correspondence of William Pitt, Earl of Chatham* (London: John Murray, 1840), Vol. IV, pp. 476–477.

As William Pitt, Chatham had earned the approbation of his countrymen for his bold, his audacious, conduct of the Seven Years' War, from whence came the Empire. In a venal age, his financial as well as his political integrity was well known: he could not be bought. His loyalty to his country had been amply demonstrated. Chatham thus brought to bear with the language of reason and the appeals to his hearers an ethical proof of the highest order.

THE SPEECH

Goodrich observes laconically, "The speech had no effect. The amendment was rejected by a vote of 97 to 24." [5] The speech and its reception thus stand in support of the Aristotelian dictum that the function of rhetoric "is not simply to succeed in persuading, but rather to discover the means of coming as near such success as the circumstances of each particular case allow." [6] The orator is gratified when he "wins" a verdict or a decision. The critic of oratory knows that great speeches are sometimes delivered in causes foredoomed to failure.

[5] Goodrich, *op. cit.*, p. 138.
[6] Aristotle, *Rhetoric*, 1355b.

On an Address to the Throne

I rise, my Lords, to declare my sentiments on this most solemn and serious subject. It has imposed a load upon my mind, which, I fear, nothing can remove, but which impels me to endeavor its alleviation, by a free and unreserved communication of my sentiments.

In the first part of the address, I have the honor of heartily concurring with the noble Earl who moved it. No man feels sincerer joy than I do; none can offer more genuine congratulations on every accession of strength to the Protestant succession. I therefore join in every congratulation on the birth of another princess, and the happy recovery of her Majesty.[1]

But I must stop here. My courtly complaisance will carry me no farther. I will not join in congratulation on misfortune and disgrace. I can not concur in a blind and servile address, which approves, and endeavors to sanctify the monstrous measures which have heaped disgrace and misfortune upon us. This, my Lords, is a perilous and tremendous moment! It is not a time for adulation. The smoothness of flattery can not now avail—can not save us in this rugged and awful crisis. It is now necessary to instruct the Throne in the language of truth. We must dispel the illusion and the darkness which envelop it, and display, in its full danger and true colors, the ruin that is brought to our doors.

This, my Lords, is our duty. It is the proper function of this noble assembly, sitting, as we do, upon our honors in this House, the hereditary council of the Crown. *Who* is the minister—*where* is the minister, that has dared to suggest to the Throne the contrary, un-

From *Select British Eloquence*, edited by Chauncey A. Goodrich, D.D., with an Introduction by Bower Aly. Copyright © 1963, by The Bobbs-Merrill Company, Inc., reprinted by permission of the publisher. According to Goodrich, the speech was reported by Hugh Boyd and is said to have been corrected by Lord Chatham himself. Footnotes supplied by Goodrich are indicated by an asterisk.

[1] In 1761 George III married Charlotte Sophia, princess of Mecklenburg-Strelitz. The felicitations extended by the House of Lords concerned the birth of their daughter Sophia (b. 1777).

constitutional language this day delivered from it? The accustomed language from the Throne has been application to Parliament for advice, and a reliance on its constitutional advice and assistance.[2] As it is the right of Parliament to give, so it is the duty of the Crown to ask it. But on this day, and in this extreme momentous exigency, no reliance is reposed on our constitutional counsels! no advice is asked from the sober and enlightened care of Parliament! but the Crown, from itself and by itself, declares an unalterable determination to pursue measures—and what measures, my Lords? The measures that have produced the imminent perils that threaten us;[3] the measures that have brought ruin to our doors.

Can the minister of the day now presume to expect a continuance of support in this ruinous infatuation? Can Parliament be so dead to its dignity and its duty as to be thus deluded into the loss of the one and the violation of the other? To give an unlimited credit and support for the steady perseverance in measures not proposed for our parliamentary advice, but dictated and forced upon us—in measures, I say, my Lords, which have reduced this late flourishing empire to ruin and contempt! "But yesterday, and England might have stood against the world: now none so poor to do her reverence." [4] I use the words of a poet; but, though it be poetry, it is no fiction. It is a shameful truth, that not only the power and strength of this country are wasting away and expiring, but her well-earned glories, her true honor, and substantial dignity are sacrificed.

France, my Lords, has insulted you; she has encouraged and sustained America; and, whether America be wrong or right, the dignity of this country ought to spurn at the officious insult of

[2] Chatham here states the theory of the British constitution: the king reigns but does not rule. George III undertook consciously and consistently to rule as well as to reign under a principle of personal government by the king.

[3] When Chatham delivered his speech he did not know that one of the greatest of the perils he foresaw was already an accomplished fact. On October 17, 1777, General John Burgoyne had surrendered to General Horatio Gates following the battle of Saratoga, considered to be the turning point of the American Revolution. The news of the loss of Burgoyne's forces reached Chatham on December 3, and on December 5 he spoke again in the House of Lords. On December 11, to Chatham's unconcealed disgust, the House of Lords adjourned for six weeks to celebrate the holiday season.

[4] See William Shakespeare, *Julius Caesar*, Act III, sc. II.

French interference. The ministers and embassadors of those who are called rebels and enemies are in Paris; in Paris they transact the reciprocal interests of America and France.[5] Can there be a more mortifying insult? Can even our ministers sustain a more humiliating disgrace? Do they dare to resent it? Do they presume even to hint a vindication of their honor, and the dignity of the state, by requiring the dismission of the plenipotentiaries of America? Such is the degradation to which they have reduced the glories of England! The people whom they affect to call contemptible rebels, but whose growing power has at last obtained the name of enemies; the people with whom they have engaged this country in war, and against whom they now command our implicit support in every measure of desperate hostility—this people, despised as rebels, or acknowledged as enemies, are abetted against you, supplied with every military store, their interests consulted, and their embassadors entertained, by your inveterate enemy! and our ministers dare not interpose with dignity or effect. Is this the honor of a great kingdom? Is this the indignant spirit of England, who "but yesterday" gave law to the house of Bourbon?[6] My Lords, the dignity of nations demands a decisive conduct in a situation like this. Even when the greatest prince that perhaps this country ever saw, filled our throne, the requisition of a Spanish general, on a similar subject, was attended to, and complied with; for, on the spirited remonstrance of the Duke of Alva,[7] Elizabeth found herself obliged to deny the Flemish exiles all countenance, support, or even entrance into her dominions; and the

[5] In November 1777, the American ministers and "embassadors" to whom Chatham refers included Benjamin Franklin, Arthur Lee, and Silas Deane, who had already succeeded in enlisting the covert assistance of the French; in 1778, Franklin and Vergennes negotiated an alliance between France and the American commonwealths. The French alliance, largely the outcome of Franklin's talents in diplomacy, was crucially important to the colonies. Doubtless it was particularly galling to Chatham, who remembered the years 1756–1763 when under his administration the French had been beaten in India, Africa, Europe, and—with the assistance of the colonial troops —North America.

[6] In 1589, the house of Bourbon, French ducal and royal family, first gave a king to France in the person of Henry IV (1553–1610). In 1777 the ruling monarch was Louis XVI (1754–1793), who had succeeded his grandfather, Louis XV, in 1774.

[7] Fernando Alvarez de Toledo, Duke of Alva (1508–1582), appointed in 1567 to rule the Netherlands on behalf of Philip II, advocated and carried out a policy of stern repression of religious and political liberty.

Count Le Marque, with his few desperate followers, were expelled the kingdom. Happening to arrive at the Brille, and finding it weak in defense, they made themselves masters of the place; and this was the foundation of the United Provinces.[8]

My Lords, this ruinous and ignominious situation, where we can not act with success, nor suffer with honor, calls upon us to remonstrate in the strongest and loudest language of truth, to rescue the ear of majesty from the delusions which surround it. The desperate state of our arms abroad is in part known. No man thinks more highly of them than I do. I love and honor the English troops. I know their virtues and their valor. I know they can achieve any thing except impossibilities; and I know that the conquest of English America *is an impossibility*. You can not, I venture to say it, *you can not* conquer America. Your armies last war effected every thing that could be effected; and what was it? It cost a numerous army, under the command of a most able general [Lord Amherst],[9] now a noble Lord in this House, a long and laborious campaign, to expel five thousand Frenchmen from French America. My Lords, *you can not conquer America*. What is your present situation there? We do not know the worst; but we know that in three campaigns we have done nothing and suffered much. Besides the sufferings, perhaps *total loss* of the Northern force,[10] the best appointed army that ever took the field, commanded by Sir William Howe, has retired from the Ameri-

[8] The seeming digression concerning "Count Le Marque" served to remind the Lords of the impotence of English policy. Under Queen Elizabeth, the so-called "sea beggars" under De la Marck, Treslong, Brand, and other Dutch seamen, upon the remonstrance of the Duke of Alva, had been denied asylum in England, whereupon they sailed (March–April 1572) to the Netherlands and in desperation demanded and obtained the surrender of The Brill, a port city. As John Lothrop Motley observes in *The Rise of the Dutch Republic* (London: J. M. Dent, 1920), Vol. II, pp. 286–290, the sea beggars laid the foundations of the Dutch Republic. Obviously George III was in no position to require the French to dismiss from Paris the Americans rebelling against the English king.

[9] Lord Jeffery Amherst, appointed by Chatham during the Seven Years' War (1756–1763), first as major general and later as supreme commander in North America, achieved a brilliant reputation as a commanding officer, strategist, and military administrator.

[10] In 1777, the British forces in North America were divided between General John Burgoyne's northern force, based in Canada, and General William Howe's southern force, based in New York.

can lines.[11] *He was obliged* to relinquish his attempt, and with great delay and danger to adopt a new and distant plan of operations. We shall soon know, and in any event have reason to lament, what may have happened since. As to conquest, therefore, my Lords, I repeat, it is impossible. You may swell every expense and every effort still more extravagantly; pile and accumulate every assistance you can buy or borrow; traffic and barter with every little pitiful German prince that sells and sends his subjects to the shambles of a foreign prince; your efforts are forever vain and impotent—doubly so from this mercenary aid on which you rely; for it irritates, to an incurable resentment, the minds of your enemies, to overrun them with the mercenary sons of rapine and plunder, devoting them and their possessions to the rapacity of hireling cruelty! [12] If I were an American, as I am an Englishman, while a foreign troop was landed in my country, I never would lay down my arms—never—never— never.

Your own army is infected with the contagion of these illiberal allies. The spirit of plunder and of rapine is gone forth among them. I know it; and, notwithstanding what the noble Earl [Lord Percy] who moved the address has given as his opinion of the American army, I know from authentic information, and the *most experienced officers*, that our discipline is deeply wounded. While this is notoriously our sinking situation, America grows and flourishes; while our strength and discipline are lowered, hers are rising and improving.

But, my Lords, who is the man that, in addition to these disgraces and mischiefs of our army, has dared to authorize and associate to our arms the tomahawk and scalping-knife of the savage? to call into civilized alliance the wild and inhuman savage of the woods;

[11] Sir William Howe (1729–1814) served with the British forces in North America during the Seven Years' War. At the outset of the American Revolution, he was a commanding officer at Bunker Hill. The slaughter of British troops under the fire of the Americans at Bunker Hill is thought so to have impressed him that he became unduly cautious in committing his troops thereafter. In 1777, he captured Philadelphia and defeated the Americans at the battle of Brandywine. However, he was unable to destroy Washington's army or to join forces with Burgoyne.

[12] Many of the troops who fought under the British flag were obtained from German principalities, notably from Hesse, and were known somewhat indiscriminately as "Hessians."

to delegate to the merciless Indian the defense of disputed rights, and to wage the horrors of his barbarous war against our brethren? My Lords, these enormities cry aloud for redress and punishment. Unless thoroughly done away, it will be a stain on the national character. It is a violation of the Constitution. I believe it is against law. It is not the least of our national misfortunes that the strength and character of our army are thus impaired. Infected with the mercenary spirit of robbery and rapine; familiarized to the horrid scenes of savage cruelty, it can no longer boast of the noble and generous principles which dignify a soldier; no longer sympathize with the dignity of the royal banner, nor feel the pride, pomp, and circumstance of glorious war, "that make ambition virtue!" What makes ambition virtue?—the sense of honor. But is the sense of honor consistent with a spirit of plunder, or the practice of murder? Can it flow from mercenary motives, or can it prompt to cruel deeds? Besides these murderers and plunderers, let me ask our ministers, What other allies have they acquired? What *other powers* have they associated to their cause? Have they entered into alliance with the *king of the gipsies?* Nothing, my Lords, is too low or too ludicrous to be consistent with their counsels.

The independent views of America have been stated and asserted as the foundation of this address. My Lords, no man wishes for the due dependence of America on this country more than I do. To preserve it, and not confirm that state of independence into which *your measures* hitherto have *driven them,* is the object which we ought to unite in attaining. The Americans, contending for their rights against arbitrary exactions, I love and admire. It is the struggle of free and virtuous patriots. But, contending for independency and total disconnection from England, as an Englishman, I can not wish them success; for in a due constitutional dependency, including the ancient supremacy of this country in regulating their commerce and navigation, consists the mutual happiness and prosperity both of England and America. She derived assistance and protection from us; and we reaped from her the most important advantages. She was, indeed, the fountain of our wealth, the nerve of our strength, the nursery and basis of our naval power. It is our duty, therefore, my Lords, if we wish to save our country, most seriously to endeavor the recovery of these most beneficial subjects; and in this perilous crisis, perhaps the present moment may be the only one in which we can hope for success. For in their negotiations with France, they have, or think they have, reason to complain; though it be notorious that they have received from that power important supplies and assistance of various kinds, yet it is certain they expected it in a more decisive and immediate degree. America is in ill humor with France; on some points they have not entirely answered her expectations. Let us wisely take advantage of every possible moment of reconciliation. Besides, the natural disposition of America herself still leans toward England; to the old habits of connection and mutual interest that united both countries. This *was* the established sentiment of all the Continent; and still, my Lords, in the great and principal part, the sound part of America, this wise and affectionate disposition prevails. And there is a very considerable part of America yet sound—the middle and the southern provinces. Some parts may be factious and blind to their true interests; but if we express a wise and benevolent disposition to communicate with them those immutable rights of nature and those constitutional liberties to which they are equally entitled with ourselves, by a conduct so just and humane we shall confirm the favorable and conciliate the adverse. I say, my Lords, the rights and liberties to which they are equally entitled with ourselves, *but no more.* I would participate to them every enjoyment and freedom which the colonizing subjects of a free state can possess, or wish to possess; and I do not see why they should not enjoy every fundamental right in their property, and every original substantial liberty, which Devonshire, or Surrey, or the county I live in, or any other county in England, can claim; reserving always, as the sacred right of the mother country, the due constitutional dependency of the colonies. The inherent supremacy of the state in regulating and protecting the navigation and commerce of all her subjects, is necessary for the mutual benefit and preservation of every part, to constitute and preserve the prosperous arrangement of the whole empire.[13]

[13] Chatham steadfastly supported the claims of the colonists to the rights of Englishmen and just as steadfastly denied their claims to independence. He opposed the pretensions of the Parliament to levy internal taxes in North America, but consistently asserted the obligation of the British Parliament to control trade by means of tariffs.

The sound parts of America, of which I have spoken, must be sensible of these great truths and of their real interests. America is not in that state of desperate and contemptible rebellion which this country has been deluded to believe. It is not a wild and lawless banditti, who, having nothing to lose, might hope to snatch something from public convulsions. Many of their leaders and great men have a great stake in this great contest. The gentleman who conducts their armies,[14] I am told, has an estate of four or five thousand pounds a year; and when I consider these things, I can not but lament the inconsiderate violence of our penal acts, our declarations of treason and rebellion, with all the fatal effects of attainder and confiscation.

As to the disposition of foreign powers which is asserted [in the King's speech] to be pacific and friendly, let us judge, my Lords, rather by their actions and the nature of things than by interested assertions. The uniform assistance supplied to America by France, suggests a different conclusion. The most important interests of France in aggrandizing and enriching herself with what she most wants, supplies of every naval store from America, must inspire her with different sentiments. The extraordinary preparations of the house of Bourbon, by land and by sea, from Dunkirk to the Straits, equally ready and willing to overwhelm these defenseless islands, should rouse us to a sense of their real disposition and our own danger. Not five thousand troops in England! hardly three thousand in Ireland! What can we oppose to the combined force of our enemies? Scarcely twenty ships of the line so fully or sufficiently manned, that any admiral's reputation would permit him to take the command of. The river of Lisbon in the possession of our enemies! The seas swept by American privateers! Our Channel trade torn to pieces by them! In this complicated crisis of danger, weakness at home, and calamity abroad, terrified and insulted by the neighboring powers, unable to act in America, or acting only to be destroyed, where is the man with the forehead to promise or hope for success in such a situation, or from perseverance in the measures that have driven us to it? Who has the forehead to do so? Where is that man? I should be glad to see his face.

You can not *conciliate* America by your present measures. You

[14] George Washington.

can not *subdue* her by your present or by any measures. What, then, can you do? You can not conquer; you can not gain; but you can *address*; you can lull the fears and anxieties of the moment into an ignorance of the danger that should produce them. But, my Lords, the time demands the language of truth. We must not now apply the flattering unction of servile compliance or blind complaisance. In a just and necessary war, to maintain the rights or honor of my country, I would strip the shirt from my back to support it. But in such a war as this, unjust in its principle, impracticable in its means, and ruinous in its consequences, I would not contribute a single effort nor a single shilling. I do not call for vengeance on the heads of those who have been guilty; I only recommend to them to make their retreat. Let them walk off; and let them make haste, or they may be assured that speedy and condign punishment will overtake them.

My Lords, I have submitted to you, with the freedom and truth which I think my duty, my sentiments on your present awful situation. I have laid before you the ruin of your power, the disgrace of your reputation, the pollution of your discipline, the contamination of your morals, the complication of calamities, foreign and domestic, that overwhelm your sinking country. Your dearest interests, your own liberties, the Constitution itself, totters to the foundation. All this disgraceful danger, this multitude of misery, is the monstrous offspring of this unnatural war. We have been deceived and deluded too long. Let us now stop short. This is the crisis—the only crisis* of time and situation, to give us a possibility of escape from the fatal effects of our delusions. But if, in an obstinate and infatuated perseverance in folly, we slavishly echo the peremptory words this day presented to us, nothing can save this devoted country from complete and final ruin. We madly rush into multiplied miseries, and "confusion worse confounded."

Is it possible, can it be believed, that ministers are yet blind to this impending destruction? I did hope, that instead of this false and

---

* It can not have escaped observation, says Chapman, with what urgent anxiety the noble speaker has pressed this point throughout his speech; the critical necessity of instantly treating with America. But the warning voice was heard in vain; the address triumphed; Parliament adjourned; ministers enjoyed the festive recess of a long Christmas; and America ratified her alliance with France.

empty vanity, this overweening pride, engendering high conceits and presumptuous imaginations, ministers would have humbled themselves in their errors, would have confessed and retracted them, and by an active, though a late repentance, have endeavored to redeem them. But, my Lords, since they had neither sagacity to foresee, nor justice nor humanity to shun these oppressive calamities—since not even severe experience can make them feel, nor the imminent ruin of their country awaken them from their stupefaction, the guardian care of Parliament must interpose. I shall therefore, my Lords, propose to you an amendment of the address to his Majesty, to be inserted immediately after the two first paragraphs of congratulation on the birth of a princess, to recommend an immediate cessation of hostilities, and the commencement of a treaty to restore peace and liberty to America, strength and happiness to England, security and permanent prosperity to both countries. This, my Lords, is yet in our power; and let not the wisdom and justice of your Lordships neglect the happy, and, perhaps the only opportunity. By the establishment of irrevocable law, founded on mutual rights, and ascertained by treaty, these glorious enjoyments may be firmly perpetuated. And let me repeat to your Lordships, that the strong bias of America, at least of the wise and sounder parts of it, naturally inclines to this happy and constitutional reconnection with you. Notwithstanding the temporary intrigues with France, we may still be assured of their ancient and confirmed partiality to us. America and France can not be congenial. There is something decisive and confirmed in the honest American, that will not assimilate to the futility and levity of Frenchmen.

My Lords, to encourage and confirm that innate inclination to this country, founded on every principle of affection, as well as consideration of interest; to restore that favorable disposition into a permanent and powerful reunion with this country; to revive the mutual strength of the empire; again to awe the house of Bourbon, instead of meanly truckling, as our present calamities compel us, to every insult of French caprice and Spanish punctilio; to re-establish our commerce; to reassert our rights and our honor; to confirm our interests, and renew our glories forever—a consummation most devoutly to be endeavored! and which, I trust, may yet arise from reconciliation with

America—I have the honor of submitting to you the following amendment, which I move to be inserted after the two first paragraphs of the address:

"And that this House does most humbly advise and supplicate his Majesty to be pleased to cause the most speedy and effectual measures to be taken for restoring peace in America; and that no time may be lost in proposing an immediate cessation of hostilities there, in order to the opening of a treaty for the final settlement of the tranquillity of these invaluable provinces, by a removal of the unhappy causes of this ruinous civil war, and by a just and adequate security against the return of the like calamities in times to come. And this House desire to offer the most dutiful assurances to his Majesty, that they will, in due time, cheerfully co-operate with the magnanimity and tender goodness of his Majesty for the preservation of his people, by such explicit and most solemn declarations, and provisions of fundamental and irrevocable laws, as may be judged necessary for the ascertaining and fixing forever the respective rights of Great Britain and her colonies."

[In the course of this debate, Lord Suffolk,[15] secretary for the northern department, undertook to defend the employment of the Indians in the war. His Lordship contended that, besides its *policy* and *necessity*, the measure was also allowable on *principle*; for that "it was perfectly justifiable to use all the means that *God and nature put into our hands!*"]

I am astonished! (exclaimed Lord Chatham, as he rose), shocked! to hear such principles confessed—to hear them avowed in this House, or in this country; principles equally unconstitutional, inhuman, and unchristian!

My Lords, I did not intend to have encroached again upon your attention, but I can not repress my indignation. I feel myself impelled by every duty. My Lords, we are called upon as members of this House, as men, as Christian men, to protest against such notions standing near the Throne, polluting the ear of Majesty. "That God and nature put into our hands!" I know not what ideas that Lord may

---

[15] It took courage to stand up to Chatham in debate. The member who spoke up on this occasion was Henry, 12th Earl of Suffolk and 5th Earl of Berkshire, sometime Lord Privy Seal.

entertain of God and nature, but I know that such abominable principles are equally abhorrent to religion and humanity. What! to
attribute the sacred sanction of God and nature to the massacres of
the Indian scalping-knife—to the cannibal savage torturing, murder-
ing, roasting, and eating—literally, my Lords, *eating* the mangled
victims of his barbarous battles! Such horrible notions shock every
precept of religion, divine or natural, and every generous feeling of
humanity. And, my Lords, they shock every sentiment of honor;
they shock me as a lover of honorable war, and a detester of murder-
ous barbarity.[16]

These abominable principles, and this more abominable avowal
of them, demand the most decisive indignation. I call upon that right
reverend bench, those holy ministers of the Gospel, and pious pastors
of our Church—I conjure them to join in the holy work, and vindicate the religion of their God. I appeal to the wisdom and the law
of this learned bench, to defend and support the justice of their
country. I call upon the Bishops, to interpose the unsullied sanctity
of their lawn; upon the learned Judges, to interpose the purity of their
ermine, to save us from this pollution. I call upon the honor of your
Lordships, to reverence the dignity of your ancestors, and to maintain
your own. I call upon the spirit and humanity of my country, to
vindicate the national character. I invoke the genius of the Constitution. From the tapestry that adorns these walls, the immortal ancestor of this noble Lord frowns with indignation at the disgrace of
his country.* In vain he led your victorious fleets against the boasted
Armada of Spain; in vain he defended and established the honor,
the liberties, the religion—the *Protestant religion*—of this country,
against the arbitrary cruelties of popery and the Inquisition, if these
more than popish cruelties and inquisitorial practices are let loose
among us—to turn forth into our settlements, among our ancient
connections, friends, and relations, the merciless cannibal, thirsting
for the blood of man, woman, and child! to send forth the infidel

---

* *The tapestry of the House of Lords represented the English fleet led by the ship of
the lord admiral, Effingham Howard (ancestor of Suffolk), to engage the Spanish
Armada.*

[16] Chatham was the victim of the propaganda of his day. The Indians of North
America were not cannibals.

savage—against whom? against your Protestant brethren; to lay waste their country, to desolate their dwellings, and extirpate their race and name with these horrible hell-hounds of savage war—*hell-hounds, I say, of savage war!* Spain armed herself with blood-hounds to extirpate the wretched natives of America, and we improve on the inhuman example even of Spanish cruelty; we turn loose these savage hell-hounds against our brethren and countrymen in America, of the same language, laws, liberties, and religion, endeared to us by every tie that should sanctify humanity.

My Lords, this awful subject, so important to our honor, our Constitution, and our religion, demands the most solemn and effectual inquiry. And I again call upon your Lordships, and the united powers of the state, to examine it thoroughly and decisively, and to stamp upon it an indelible stigma of the public abhorrence. And I again implore those holy prelates of our religion to do away these iniquities from among us. Let them perform a lustration; let them purify this House, and this country, from this sin.

My Lords, I am old and weak, and at present unable to say more; but my feelings and indignation were too strong to have said less.[17] I could not have slept this night in my bed, nor reposed my head on my pillow, without giving this vent to my eternal abhorrence of such preposterous and enormous principles.

[17] On April 7, 1778, Chatham appeared for the last time in Parliament, expressly to speak against the Duke of Richmond's motion advising George III to seek peace with America by granting independence. Manifestly ill, Chatham collapsed and was taken by his seventeen-year-old son, William Pitt the younger, to his home at Hayes, where he died on May 11, 1778.

§ Critical Analysis

In his biography of Chatham, Lord Rosebery quotes the words of Pitt's nephew, Lord Camelford, on the eloquence of his famous uncle:

> His wit was elegant, his imagination inexhaustible, his sensibility exquisite, and his diction flowed like a torrent, impure often, but always varied and abundant. There was a style of conscious superiority, a tone, a gesture of manner, which was quite peculiar to him—everything shrunk before it; and even facts, truth and argument were over-awed and vanquished by it.[1]

Where does this speech offer evidence to bear out these statements? How does it reveal the powers of the speaker himself? Does Chatham at any point seek directly to establish ethical proof?

§

How well would you say Chatham has judged his audience in the assumptions that underlie his enthymemes? What assumptions, for example, does he make about the motives of the French? the motives of the Americans? the proper relationship of England and America? the conduct of Indians in battle, and the duty of civilized men? Would his audience be likely to agree with his attitudes? What kind of evidence does Chatham offer in support of his arguments? Does he present new evidence or rely chiefly on knowledge the audience already has? How much use does he make of the argument from authority? To what extent does this speech bear out Bishop Newton's judgment that Pitt "spoke more to your passions than to your reason"?[2] To what passions does he appeal in "On an Address to the Throne"? As motivating forces for action, would they tend to debase or to ennoble men? What appeals to reason does he make?

§

Chatham was particularly famous for the invectives described respectfully by various people who heard him as so powerful they

[1] *Chatham: His Early Life and Connections* (London: Hodder and Stoughton, 1922), p. 521.

[2] *Ibid.*, p. 519.

were like thunder and flashes of lightning. What passages in this address might be considered to merit the description?

§

Various critics have suggested that Pitt's speeches were loosely structured, sometimes to the point of rambling. Is this criticism applicable here, or does the address seem to follow a pattern? How much does the ordering of ideas derive from refutation?

§

Chatham's speeches are almost invariably described by his contemporaries as showing a remarkable command of language, rising at times to sublime bursts of eloquence. Can you identify phrasings in this address that would justify such commendation? Where, for example, does Pitt make effective use of metaphor, climactic statement, emphatic repetition, original combinations of words?

§ SUGGESTIONS FOR FURTHER READING

For the historical background of Britain and America in 1777 (when Chatham delivered the speech said by Goodrich to be "Lord Chatham's greatest effort"), the works cited for Burke's speech "On Conciliation with the Colonies" may be consulted. (See above, pp. 101–103.) Especially useful for students of speechmaking is Chauncey Goodrich's *Select British Eloquence* (Indianapolis: Bobbs-Merrill, 1963) since it includes texts and commentaries for other speeches by Chatham on the American question (pp. 102–153) as well as for Lord Mansfield's address "On the Right of Taxing America" (pp. 143–153) and for the "Letters of Junius" (pp. 163–205).

Although Lord Rosebery, himself one of Chatham's biographers, declared in *Chatham: His Early Life and Connections* (London: Hodder and Stoughton, 1922), p. vii, that the "life of Chatham is extremely difficult to write, and, strictly speaking, never can be written at all," numerous biographers have been courageous enough to attempt the impossible. The difficulties of Chatham's biography chiefly concern his private rather than his public life, the latter being documented in correspondence in official or quasi-official papers and in reports (there are no adequate texts) of his speeches.

Rosebery's account (noted above) of Chatham's early years includes a number of letters. The two volumes of Basil Williams' *The Life of William Pitt: Earl of Chatham* (London: Longmans, Green, 1914) provide a dependable account of Chatham's public life on the principle that "Lord Chatham was a great, illustrious, faulty human being, whose character, like all the noblest works of human composition, should be determined by its excellences, not by its defects." Williams' book offers portraits and maps, as does J. C. Long's *Mr. Pitt and America's Birthright* (New York: Frederick A. Stokes, 1940). Long's book, a lively narrative, is written in the American idiom. Arthur S. McDowall's *Chatham* (New York: Dutton, 1903), a competent, short account (223 pages), offers the portrait by Hoare as a frontispiece as well as portraits of Chatham's contemporaries, including Walpole, Newcastle, Mansfield, Burke, and George III. Frederic Harrison's *Chatham* (London: Macmillan, 1922) develops the thesis that Chatham was the founder of the British Empire.

Doubtless the account of Chatham's life and contributions that is most influential in America will be found in Lord Macaulay's essays, once widely read in American secondary schools. These essays have passed through many editions since they first appeared in the *Edinburgh Review,* for they are thought to be not only notable studies of Chatham but also worthy examples of the style of Thomas Babington Macaulay. The essays may be found in F. C. Montague, ed., *Critical and Historical Essays Contributed to the Edinburgh Review by Lord Macaulay,* 3 vols. (London: Methuen, 1903).

Personal and Party Government (Cambridge: Harvard University Press, 1910) by D. A. Winstanley covers the political history of the early years (1760–1766) of the reign of George III. *The Chatham Administration: 1766–1768* (London: Macmillan, 1956) by John Brooke is a study in the origins of parties in Britain and of the debacle leading to the resignation of Chatham and eventually to the American War.

Chatham's correspondence is a source for the chief biographical accounts and is thus widely disseminated. For those who wish to review it consecutively, the major portion of the correspondence appears in the four volumes of *Correspondence of William Pitt, Earl of Chatham* (London: John Murray, 1838–1840), as edited by the executors of his son, John, Earl of Chatham, and published from the original manuscripts in their possession.

Alexander Hamilton

> "If these states are not united under a federal government, they will infalliably have wars with each other; and their divisions will subject them to all the mischiefs of foreign influence and intrigue."[1]
> —ALEXANDER HAMILTON

BIOGRAPHICAL SKETCH

Alexander Hamilton was born a British subject on the island of Nevis in the West Indies. Apparently he fixed the date of his birth as January 11, 1757, but this date is not of record and is now held to be uncertain. Born out of wedlock, he was the son of James Hamilton and Rachel (Fawcett) Levine. Hamilton's mother died in 1768. Even before her death, his father had departed the family. At some date not certainly known—perhaps on the death of his mother—the boy entered the employ of Nicholas Cruger, a merchant of Christianstadt. He learned the business rapidly and was entrusted with considerable responsibility before he left the West Indies (in 1772) to prepare for college at Francis Barber's school in Elizabethtown, New Jersey. In 1773 he matriculated at King's College (now Columbia University) in New York.

As the struggle between the colonies and the British government developed, Hamilton supported the colonial cause first as a pamphleteer and later as an artillery officer, notably at Harlem Heights

---

NOTE: The sources for this essay will be found in the section Suggestions for Further Reading, pp. 157–159, and especially in three works by Bower Aly: *The Rhetoric of Alexander Hamilton*; "Alexander Hamilton," in Marie K. Hochmuth, ed., *A History and Criticism of American Public Address*, Vol. III; and *Alexander Hamilton: Selections Representing His Life, His Thought, and His Style*.

---

[1] Alexander Hamilton, "Remarks on an Act Granting to Congress Certain Imposts and Duties," *The Papers of Alexander Hamilton* (New York: Columbia University Press, 1962), Vol. IV, p. 91.

and in the attack on Trenton and Princeton. On March 1, 1777, Hamilton entered Washington's military family as aide-de-camp and thus began a personal relationship that ended only with Washington's death. Until his resignation as aide-de-camp in 1781, Hamilton was entrusted with much of Washington's military correspondence.

In December 1780, Hamilton married Miss Elizabeth Schuyler, the daughter of General Philip Schuyler of Albany, New York. At the close of the war Hamilton settled down to an intensive study of the law, was admitted to the bar, and after a term in the Continental Congress began to practice law in New York City. Always interested in public affairs, in 1786 he was a delegate to the Annapolis Convention, in January–April 1787, a member of the New York Assembly, during the summer of 1787, a delegate to the Constitutional Convention in Philadelphia, and in 1788, a member of the New York Convention convened in Poughkeepsie to consider the proposed new constitution. On the formation of the federal government, President Washington approved Hamilton's appointment as Secretary of the Treasury. With characteristic energy and management, he assumed his obligations, of which he took a comprehensive view, to establish the new government. He soon found himself at odds with Thomas Jefferson, then Secretary of State; the differences that developed between the two men came to symbolize divergent conceptions of government in the United States.

In January 1795, doubtless in response to the financial requirements of a thriving family, he resigned as Secretary of the Treasury to return to the practice of law, but he remained in touch with members of the cabinet during the remainder of Washington's and most of John Adams' administration. In his practice of the law he was judged to be among the foremost in New York, where he was retained in a number of interesting cases, including *Rutgers v. Waddington*, *People v. Weeks*, and *People v. Croswell*. His steady practice, however, was in equity, chiefly in commercial cases of fraud, insurance, and exchange, and in maritime matters. Hamilton died on July 12, 1804, of a mortal wound suffered in a duel with Aaron Burr.

As the leading author of *The Federalist* and as the composer of state papers, Hamilton's reputation is secure. Less a popular hero than Thomas Jefferson, he is nevertheless recognized by thoughtful persons as one of the principal founders of the American republic. No one contributed more than he to the actual formation of the government of the United States.

THE SPEAKER

Before his life was cut short in the duel with Aaron Burr, Alexander Hamilton did more work and made more speeches than many of his fellows who lived out their three-score years and ten. Nearly all of his speeches of record were delivered either in the practice of his profession of the law or as a member of a parliamentary body. Among Hamilton's notable speeches delivered in the courtroom, two should be cited as examples of political-legal questions in which his practice involved him.

In *Rutgers v. Waddington*, Hamilton held a brief for the defendant, Waddington, in an action for trespass growing out of the tumult of the American Revolution. In this case, even before the adoption of the Constitution of 1787, an issue arose between the enactments of the New York Assembly and the national policy. Hamilton's obligation to his client, as well, doubtless, as his own inclination, set him in opposition to the parochial view.

In the Croswell case, tried a few months before Hamilton's death, Hamilton held a brief for Harry Croswell, editor of *The Wasp*, a newspaper at Hudson, New York. Croswell, who had published a statement attributed to a polemicist named Callender, was indicted for a libel against Thomas Jefferson, then President of the United States. Croswell's attorneys endeavored to subpoena Callender so that he might testify to the truth of the statement. The judge ruled, however, that Callender's evidence would be irrelevant on the ground "the greater the truth the greater the libel." A verdict of guilty was brought in, and Croswell's attorneys appealed to the Court of Errors sitting in Albany.

At this point Hamilton entered the case for Croswell and was chosen to present the final speech to the Court in Croswell's behalf. In the opinion of Chancellor James Kent, eminent jurist, Hamilton's speech—essentially a defense of a free press in a republic—had never "in any case at the bar commanded higher reverence for his principles, or equal admiration of the power and pathos of his eloquence." [2] Although the Court of Errors declined on a divided vote to overrule Croswell's conviction, Hamilton's principle was sustained when the next legislature of the state of New York enacted a statute permitting the truth to serve as sufficient defense against a charge of libel.

Hamilton's career as a parliamentary speaker was unusual in this respect: he abandoned it at an age when many men have hardly begun to speak in public. Prior to his speech "On an Act Granting to Congress Certain Imposts and Duties," he had gained some experience in parliamentary negotiation, if not in debate, in his post as receiver of taxes for the Continental Congress from the state of New York. This post doubtless led to his election as delegate from New York to the Continental Congress, where he was required to consider such important measures as the disbanding of the army, the conclusion of a treaty of peace with Britain, the reduction of the public debt, and the restoration of American credit at home and abroad. Hamilton, as the moving spirit in the Annapolis Convention of 1786, phrased the resolutions leading to the Constitutional Convention that convened in Philadelphia on May 25, 1787. Meanwhile he was elected to the New York Assembly and took his seat in January 1787. Still before him was his election to the Constitutional Convention of 1787 and his membership in the New York Convention that met in Poughkeepsie in 1788 to consider the Constitution drafted in Philadelphia.

As a parliamentary speaker, Hamilton had no superiors and few equals in his own day. Such was the opinion of his contemporaries who considered rhetoric and speechmaking to include not utterance alone—in which Hamilton excelled—but also cogency of argument and sober concern for the probabilities in questions of policy. Ham-

[2] James Kent, "Address before the Law Association," New York, October 21, 1836. Quoted in George Shea, *The Life and Epoch of Alexander Hamilton: A Historical Study* (Boston: Houghton Mifflin, 1881), p. 436.

ilton must be numbered among the few great orators who, like Edmund Burke, were not only eloquent but genuinely inventive.

The Speech

Hamilton's speech chosen for this book, like Adlai Stevenson's last address delivered in Geneva on July 9, 1965, is one that "does work." It presents a case—a sustained chain of reasoning, a cogent line of argument—that suggests Hamilton's acceptance of the Aristotelian dictum: sound law and custom forbid talk about nonessentials. Only in his introduction, when he endeavors to establish his right to be heard, does he depart from his constructive case for the measure and his refutation of opposing argument. In developing a case with minimum digression, Hamilton paid his hearers the compliment of supposing that they were willing and able to follow a closely knit chain of assumptions, reasoning, and evidence. Whether Hamilton's supposition was justified cannot be determined. The failure of his legislative colleagues to answer his argument (for it was not answered) need not be laid to indifference or neglect: shrewd debaters know that sometimes the best defense against a strong argument is silence. Roger Sherman, Hamilton's Connecticut colleague at the Philadelphia Convention, expressed the parliamentarian's wisdom: "When you are in the minority, talk; when you are in a majority, vote." [3] The failure to approve the measure he advocated need not be construed as the consequence of a poor speech: all students of rhetoric know that great speeches are often given in lost causes. An orator may lose a battle and still win a war. In essence, Hamilton did just that with his speech in the New York Assembly on February 15, 1787, for in this remarkably cogent analysis and appeal may be found the antecedents of The Federalist and of Hamilton's persuasive speeches delivered at the New York State Convention in 1788.

Hamilton's speech of February 15, 1787, reveals a keen intelligence hard at work on problems concerning the life of the state. The

[3] Quoted in Robert T. Oliver, History of Public Speaking in America (Boston: Allyn and Bacon, 1965), p. 67.

taste for the study of such speeches, like that for olives or caviar, doubtless must be acquired. But just as some enterprising minds must concentrate on old maps and battle plans and others on human experience with fiscal policies, so some men, if people are wise, will be encouraged to study the inception and development of successful—and even unsuccessful—lines of argument and persuasion in questions of probability.

On an Act
Granting to Congress
Certain Imposts and Duties

⚭

Mr. Chairman,

There appears to me to have been some confusion in the manner of voting on the two preceding clauses of this bill; the first, for granting the impost to the United States,* having been carried by a

From *The Papers of Alexander Hamilton*, edited by Harold C. Syrett and Jacob Cooke (New York: Columbia University Press, 1962), Vol. IV, pp. 71–92. Reprinted by permission. Footnotes supplied by Syrett and Cooke are indicated by an asterisk; in these notes "Hamilton" is abbreviated as "H."

---

* A note printed at the end of this speech reads as follows: "The extreme length of the foregoing speech and an accident which attended the transcribing of the short hand Notes, together with our desire to lay the same before the public, entire and correct, have necessarily delayed the publication of it till this day." The New-York Journal, and Weekly Register, February 22, 1787, recorded that "the lengthy speech" made by H was not "even replied to by the other party, notwithstanding he was one hour and twenty minutes in delivering it."

Consistent with a congressional resolve of April 18, 1783, calling on the states to grant Congress the authority to collect an impost, William Malcom introduced in the Assembly on February 9, 1787, "An act for granting to the United States in Congress assembled, certain Imposts and Duties upon foreign Goods imported into this State, for the purpose of discharging the Debts contracted by the United States, in the Prosecution of the late War with Great-Britain" (New York Assembly Journal, 1787, p. 41). (For information on New York's earlier response to the congressional resolution of April 18, 1783, see "Remarks on the Answer to Governor George Clinton's Message to the Legislature," January 17, 1787.)

The act introduced by Malcom provided that Congress be allowed specified duties on certain goods imported into New York and a five percent ad valorem duty on all other goods. Collectors of the tax, according to the act, were to be appointed by the New York State Council of Appointment, but they were to be accountable to and removable by the United States. The United States was granted authority to make such ordinances and regulations as were considered necessary to levy and collect the tax.

On February 15 the Assembly resolved itself into a committee of the whole to consider the act granting the impost. As stated by H in the first paragraph of his speech, the section of the act containing a grant of the impost to Congress was majority of one, and the last, for making the officers employed in the collection accountable to them, having been lost by a much larger majority. I was induced to hope, from the success of the first question, that the second would have met with equal success; as I presumed gentlemen who meant to adhere to the act of the last session would have opposed the whole of the present bill as unnecessary; and those who meant to depart from it, would be willing to agree substantially to the system recommended by Congress,[1] as it had been adopted and modified by the other states generally. From the complexion of the votes on the first question, I am obliged to conclude either that I was mistaken in my ideas of the intention of the committee, or that there is some misapprehension in part of the members.

It becomes therefore necessary,—to obviate such misapprehension, if any exists, and to discharge my duty at all events,—to lay the subject fully before the committee, and to detail, at large, my reasons for wishing to see the bill in its present form prevail.

It is a common practice in entering upon the discussion of an important subject, to endeavour to conciliate the good-will of the audience to the speaker, by professions of disinterestedness and zeal for the public good. The example, however frequent, I shall no further imitate than by making one or two general observations. If in the public stations I have filled, I have acquitted myself with zeal, fidelity and disinterestedness; if in the private walk of life my conduct

---

carried by a majority of one, but the clause making the collectors accountable to Congress was lost by a majority of nineteen (*New York Assembly* Journal, 1787, 51–52). H's speech, according to *The Daily Advertiser, was made in support of the acceptance of the section of the bill giving Congress authority to enact regulations for levying and collecting the tax.*

[1] Under the Articles of Confederation adopted by Congress on November 15, 1777, the Congress was a legislative-executive body in which each of the thirteen states was entitled to one vote. The Congress depended on the several states for funds and for enforcing its legislation. Since action normally required the approval of every one of the thirteen states, any single state could thwart the wishes of the other twelve. New York alone could (and did) block the establishment of a tariff to be collected by the United States.

The central government ("The League of Friendship") established under the Articles of Confederation was superseded in 1789 by the federal government provided by the Constitution, adopted by the Constitutional Convention of 1787, and ratified by the required number of states by June 21, 1788.

has been unstained by any dishonorable act, if it has been uniformly consistent with the rules of integrity, I have a right to the confidence of those to whom I address myself: They cannot refuse it to me without injustice. I am persuaded they will not refuse it to me.

If, on the other hand, my public conduct has been in any instance marked with perfidy, duplicity, or with sinister views of any kind; if any imputations, founded in fact, can be adduced to the prejudice of my private character, I have no claim to the confidence of the committee, nor should I expect it.

Even these observations I should have spared myself, did I not know that, in the rage of party, gross calumnies have been propagated; some I have traced and detected; there may still be others in secret circulation with which I am unacquainted. Against the influence of such arts, I can have no other shield than the general tenor of my past conduct. If *that* will protect me I may safely confide in the candour of the committee; to that standard I chearfully submit.

But indeed of what importance is it who is the speaker? 'tis his *reasons* only that concern the committee; if these are good they owe it to themselves, and to their constituents to allow them their full weight.

The first objection (and that which is supposed to have the greatest force) against the principles of the bill is, that it would be unconstitutional to delegate legislative power to Congress. If this objection be founded in truth, there is at once an end of the enquiry. God forbid that we should violate that constitution which is the charter of our rights. But it is our duty to examine dispassionately whether it really stands in our way; if it does not, let us not erect an ideal barrier to a measure which the public good may require.

The first ground of the objection is deduced from that clause of the constitution which declares "that no power shall be exercised over the people of this state, but such as is granted by or derived from them."

This, it is plain amounts to nothing more than a declaration of that fundamental maxim of republican government, that all power, mediately, or immediately, is derived from the consent of the people, in opposition to those doctrines of despotism which uphold the divine right of kings, or lay the foundations of government in force, conquest, or necessity. It does not at all effect the question how far the legislature may go in granting power to the United States. A power conferred by the representatives of the people, if warranted by the constitution under which they act, is a power derived from the people. This is not only a plain inference of reason, but the terms of the clause itself, seem to have been calculated to let in the principle. The words "derived from" are added to the words "granted by," as if with design to distinguish an indirect derivation of power from an immediate grant of it. This explanation is even necessary to reconcile the constitution to itself, and to give effect to all its parts, as I hope fully to demonstrate in its proper place.

The next clause of the constitution relied upon is, that which declares that "the supreme legislative power *within this state* shall be vested in a senate and assembly. This, it is said, excludes the idea of any other legislative power operating within the state. But the more obvious construction of this clause, and *that* which best consists with the situation and views of the country at this time, with what has been done before and since the formation of our constitution, and with those parts of the constitution itself which acknowledge the federal government, is this—"In the distribution of the different parts of the sovereignty in the *particular* government of this state the legislative authority shall reside in a senate and assembly," or in other words, "the legislative authority of the particular government of the state of New-York shall be vested in a senate and assembly." The framers of the constitution could have had nothing more in view than to delineate the different departments of power in our own state government, and never could have intended to interfere with the formation of such a constitution for the union as the safety of the whole might require.

The justness of this construction will be further elucidated by that part of the constitution which prescribes that "the supreme executive authority *of the state* shall be vested in a governor." If the former clause excludes the grant of legislative power, this must equally exclude the grant of executive power. And the consequence would be, that there would be no federal government at all.

It will be of no avail to say, that there is a difference in the two cases in the mode of expression; that in one the terms of description are *"within the state,"* in the other *"of the state."* In grammar, or good sense the difference in the phrases constitutes no substantial difference in the meaning, or if it does, it concludes against the objection; for the words, *within this state,* which are applied to the legislative power, have a certain precision that may be supposed to intend a distinction between that legislative power which is to operate *within this state* only, and that which is to operate upon this state in conjunction with the others. But I lay no stress on this observation. In my opinion the legislative power *"within this state,"* or the legislative power "of this state" amount in substance to the same thing. And therefore (as has been already observed) if the constitution prohibits the delegation of legislative power to the union, it equally prohibits the delegation of executive power—and the confederacy must then be at an end: for without legislative or executive power it becomes a nullity.

Unfortunately for the objection, if it proves any thing it proves too much. It proves that the powers of the union in their present form arc an usurpation on the constitution of this state. This will appear not only from the reasoning already adduced, but from this further consideration—that the United States are already possessed of *legislative* as well as *executive* authority. The objects of executive power are of three kinds, to make treaties with foreign nations, to make war and peace, to execute and interpret the laws. This description of the executive power will enable us the more readily to distinguish the legislative; which in general may be defined the power of prescribing rules for the community.

The United States are authorised to require from the several states as much money as they judge necessary for the general purposes of the union, and to limit the time within which it is to be raised: to call for such a number of troops as they deem requisite for the common defence in time of war—to establish rules in all cases of capture by sea or land—to regulate the alloy and value of coin; the standard of weights and measures, and to make all laws for the government of the army and navy of the union. All these are powers of the legislative kind, and are declared by the confederation to be binding upon all the states.

The first is nothing less than a power of taxing the states in gross though not in detail; and the last is the power of disposing of the liberty and lives of the citizens of this state, when in arms for the common defence.

That the powers enumerated are all, or most of them, of a legislative nature, will not be denied by the law members on the other side of the question. If the constitution forbids the grant of legislative power to the union, all those authorities are illegal and unconstitutional, and ought to be resumed.

If, on the contrary, those authorities were properly granted, then it follows that the constitution does not forbid the grant of legislative power, and the objection falls to the ground; for there is nothing in the constitution permitting the grant of one kind of legislative authority, and forbidding that of another. The degree or nature of the powers of legislation which it might be proper to confer upon the federal government, would in this case be a mere question of prudence and expediency—to be determined by general considerations of utility and safety.

The principle of the objection under consideration would not only subvert the foundation of the union as now established—would not only render it impossible that any federal government could exist; but would defeat some of the provisions of the constitution itself. This last idea deserves particular attention.

The nineteenth clause makes it the duty of the governor "to correspond with the continental Congress." The twentieth provides "that the judges and chancellor shall hold no other office than delegate to the general Congress"; and the thirtieth directs that "delegates *to represent* this state in the general Congress of the United States of America shall be annually appointed."

Now, Sir, I ask, if Congress were to have neither executive nor legislative authority, to what purpose were they to exist? To what purpose were delegates to be annually appointed to that body? To what purpose were these delegates *to represent* this state? Or how could they be said to represent it at all?

Is not the plain import of this part of the constitution, that they were *to represent this state* in the general assembly of the United States, for the purpose of managing the common concerns of the union? And does not this necessarily imply that they were to be cloathed with such powers as should be found essential to that object? Does it not amount to a constitutional warrant to the legislature to confer those powers of whatever kind they might be?

To answer these questions in the negative would be to charge the constitution with the absurdity of proposing to itself an *end*, and yet prohibiting the means of accomplishing that end.

The words "to represent this state" are of great latitude, and are of themselves sufficient to convey any power necessary to the conduct and direction of its affairs in connection with the other parts of the confederacy.

In the interpretation of laws it is admitted to be a good rule to resort to the co-existing circumstances and collect from thence the intention of the framers of the law. Let us apply this rule to the present case.

In the commencement of the revolution delegates were sent to meet in Congress with large discretionary powers. In short, generally speaking, with full power "to take care of the republic." In the whole of this transaction the idea of an *union* of the colonies was carefully held up. It pervaded all our public acts.

In the declaration of independence we find it continued and confirmed. That declaration, after setting forth its motives and causes, proceeds thus—"We, therefore, the representatives of the United States of America in general Congress assembled, appealing to the Supreme Judge of the world for the rectitude of our intentions, do in the name and by the authority of the good people of these colonies, solemnly publish and declare, that these United Colonies are and of right ought to be free and independent states; that they are absolved from all allegiance to the British crown, and that all political connection between them and the state of Great-Britain is and ought to be totally dissolved; and that as free and independent states they have full power to levy war, conclude peace, contract alliances, establish commerce, and do all other acts and things that* independent states may of right do."

Hence we see that the union and independence of these states are blended and incorporated in one and the same act; which, taken

* In original, "what."

together clearly, imports, that the United States had in their origin full power to do all acts and things which independent states may of right do; or, in other words, full power of sovereignty.

Accordingly we find that upon the authority of that act only approved by the several states, they did levy war, contract alliances, and exercise other high powers of sovereignty even to the appointment of a dictator prior to the present confederation.*

In this situation, and with this plenitude of power, our constitution knows and acknowledges the United States in Congress assembled, and provides for the annual appointment of delegates to represent this state in that body; which in substance amounts to a constitutional recognition of the union with complete sovereignty.

A government may exist without any formal organization or precise definition of its powers. However improper it might have been that the federal government should have continued to exist with such absolute and undefined authority this does not militate against the position that it did possess such authority. It only proves the propriety of a more regular formation to ascertain its limits. This was the object of the present confederation, which is, in fact, an abridgment of the original sovereignty of the union.

It may be said (for it has been said upon other occasions) that, though the constitution did consider the United States in the light I have described, and left the legislature at liberty in the first instance to have organized the federal government in such a manner as they thought proper, yet that liberty ceased with the establishment of the present confederacy. The discretion of the legislature was then determined.

This upon the face of it is a subtilty, uncountenanced by a single principle of government, or a single expression of the constitution. It is saying that a general authority given to the legislature for the permanent preservation and good of the community, has been exhausted and spent by the exercise of a part of that authority. The position is the more destitute of colour; because the confederation, by the express terms of the compact, preserves and continues this

* *The dictator to whom H alludes cannot be determined. He may have referred to Robert Morris whose powers as Superintendent of Finance were considered by many as dictatorial.*

power. The last clause of it authorises Congress to propose, and the states to agree to such alterations as might be afterwards found necessary or expedient.

We see therefore that the constitution knows and acknowledges the United States in Congress; that it provides for the annual appointment of delegates *to represent this state* in that body without prescribing the objects or limits of that representation: That at the time our constitution was framed, the union existed with full sovereignty; and that therefore the idea of sovereignty in the union is not incompatible with it. We see further, that the doctrine contained in the objection against granting legislative power, would equally operate against granting executive power; would prove that the powers already vested in the union are illegal and unconstitutional; would render a confederacy of the states in any form impracticable and would defeat all those provisions of our own constitution which relate to the United States. I submit it to the committee, whether a doctrine pregnant with such consequences can be true— whether it is not as opposite to our constitution as to the principles of national safety and prosperity—and whether it would not be lamentable if the zeal of opposition to a particular measure should carry us to the extreme of imposing upon the constitution a sense foreign to it; which might embarrass the national councils upon future occasions, when all might agree in the utility and necessity of a different construction.

If the arguments I have used under this head are not well founded, let gentlemen *come forward and shew their fallacy.* Let the subject have a fair and full examination, and let truth, on whatever side it may be, prevail!

Flattering myself it will appear to the committee that the constitution at least offers us no impediment—I shall proceed to other topics of objection. The next that presents itself is a supposed danger to liberty from granting legislative power to Congress.

But before I enter upon this subject, to remove the aspersions thrown upon that body, I shall give a short history of some material facts relating to the origin and progress of the business. To excite the jealousies of the people, it has been industriously represented as an undue attempt to acquire an increase of power. It has been for-

gotten or intentionally overlooked, that considering it in the strongest light as a proposal to alter the confederation, it is only exercising
a power which the confederation has in direct terms reposed in
Congress; who as before observed, are by the 13th article, expressly
authorised to propose alterations.

By so far was the measure from originating in improper views of
that body, that if I am rightly informed, it did not originate there
at all—it was first suggested by a convention of the four Eastern
states, and New-York, at Hartford; and I believe was proposed there
by the deputies of this state.* A gentleman on our bench, uncon-
nected with Congress, who now hears me (I mean judge Hobart) **
was one of them. It was dictated by a principle which *bitter experience then* taught us, and which in peace or war will always be
found true—that adequate supplies to the federal treasury, can never
flow from any system which requires the intervention of thirteen
deliberatives between the *call* and the *execution*.

Congress agreed to the measure and recommended it. This state
complied without hesitation. All parts of the government, senate,
assembly, and council of revision concurred—neither the constitution nor the public liberty presented any obstacle—the difficulties
from these sources are a recent discovery.

So late as the first session of the legislature after the evacuation
of this city, the governor of the state in his speech to both houses,
gave a decided countenance to the measure—this he does, though
not in express terms, yet by implications not to be misunderstood.

The *leading opponents* of the impost, of the present day, have
all of them at other times, either concurred in the measure in its
most exceptionable form, and without the qualifications annexed to
it by the proposed bill, or have by other instances of conduct con-

* *The convention to which H refers was held in Hartford, Connecticut, in November,
1780. It developed from an earlier convention held in Boston in August, 1780, the
proceedings of which were sent to New York with a request for its concurrence. The
New York legislature appointed commissioners to meet with the representatives of
the eastern states in Hartford in November. The convention in Hartford reaffirmed
the recommendations previously made in Boston.*

** *John Sloss Hobart, a justice of the New York Supreme Court, had represented
New York at the Hartford convention.*

tradicted their own hypothesis on the constitution which professedly forms the main prop of their opposition.

The honorable member in my eye, (Mr. Jones,) at the last session brought in a bill for granting to the United States, the power of regulating the trade of the union. This surely includes more ample legislative authority than is comprehended in the mere power of levying a particular duty. It indeed goes to a prodigious extent much farther than on a superficial view can be imagined. Can we believe that the constitutional objection, if well founded would so long have passed undiscovered and unnoticed? or is it fair to impute to Congress criminal motives for proposing a measure which was first recommended to them by five states, or from persisting in that measure after the unequivocal experience they have had of the total inefficacy of the mode provided in the confederation for supplying the treasury of the union?

I leave the answer to these questions to the good sense and candor of the committee and shall return to the examination of the question, how far the power proposed to be conferred upon Congress, would be dangerous to the liberty of the people. And here I ask,

Whence can this danger arise? The members of Congress are annually chosen by the several legislatures—they are removable at any moment at the pleasure of those legislatures. They come together with different habits, prejudices and interests. They are in fact continually changing. How is it possible for a body so composed to be formidable to the liberties of states, several of which are large empires in themselves?

The subversion of the liberty of these states could not be the business of a day. It would at least require time, premeditation and concert. Can it be supposed that the members of a body so constituted would be unanimous in a scheme of usurpation? If they were not, would it not be discovered and disclosed? If we could even suppose this unanimity among one set of men, can we believe that all the new members who are yearly sent from one state or another would instantly enter into the same views? Would there not be found one honest man to warn his country of the danger?

Suppose the worst—suppose the combination entered into and

continued—the execution would at least announce the design; and the means of defence would be easy. Consider the separate power of several of these states, and the situation of all. Consider the extent populousness and resources of Massachusetts, Virginia, Pennsylvania; I might add of New-York, Connecticut, and other states. Where could Congress find means sufficient to subvert the government and liberties of either of these states! or rather where find means sufficient to effect the conquest of all? If an attempt was made upon one, the others from a sense of common danger, would make common cause; and they could immediately unite and provide for their joint defence.

There is one consideration of immense force in this question not sufficiently attended to. It is this, that each state possesses in itself the full powers of government, and can at once in a regular and constitutional way, take measures for the preservation of its rights. In a single kingdom or state, if the rulers attempt to establish a tyranny, the people can only defend themselves by a tumultary insurrection; they must run to arms without concert or plan; while the usurpers cloathed with the forms of legal authority can employ the forces of the state to suppress them in embryo; and before they can have time or opportunity to give system to their opposition. With us the case is widely different, each state has a government completely organized in itself; and can at once enter into a regular plan of defence, with the forces of the community at its command it can immediately form connections with its neighbours, or even with foreign powers, if necessary.

In a contest of this kind the body of the people will always be on the side of the state governments. This will not only result from their love of liberty and regard to their own safety; but from other strong principles of human nature. The state governments operate upon those immediate familiar personal concerns to which the sensibility of individuals is awake. The distribution of private justice belonging to them; they must always appear to the senses of the people as the immediate guardians of their rights—they will of course have the strongest hold on their attachment, respect and obedience. Another circumstance will contribute to the same end: Far the greatest number of offices and employments are in the gift of the states separately—the weight of official influence will therefore be in favor of the state governments; and with all these advantages they cannot fail to carry the people along with them in every contest with the general government in which they are not palpably in the wrong, and often when they are. What is to be feared from the efforts of Congress to establish a tyranny with the great body of the people under the direction of their state governments combined in opposition to their views? Must not their attempts recoil upon themselves, and terminate in their own ruin and disgrace? or rather would not these considerations, if they were insensible to other motives, forever restrain them from making such attempts.

The causes taken notice of as securing the attachment of the people to their local governments, present us with another important truth—the natural imbecility of federal governments, and the danger that they will never be able to exercise power enough to manage the general affairs of the union. Though the states will have a common interest; yet they will also have a particular interest. For example, as a part of the union, it will be the interest of every state, that the general government should be supplied with the revenues necessary for the national purposes; but it will be the particular interest of each state to pay as little itself and to let its neighbours pay as much as possible. Particular interests have always more influence upon men than general. The several states therefore consulting their immediate advantage may be considered as so many eccentric powers tending in a contrary direction to the government of the union; and as they will generally carry the people along with them, the confederacy will be in continual danger of dissolution.[2]

This, Mr. Chairman is the real rock upon which the happiness of this country is likely to split—this is the point to which our fears and cares should be directed—to guard against this and not to terrify ourselves with imaginary dangers from the spectre of power in Congress will be our true wisdom.

But let us examine a little more closely the measure under con-

[2] Hamilton's reasoning at this point—indeed, throughout the speech—forecasts the arguments he presented later in *The Federalist* and at the New York Convention that ratified the new Constitution on July 25, 1788.

sideration. What does the bill before us require us to do? merely to grant certain duties on imposts to the United States for the short period of twenty-five years,—to be applied to the discharge of the principal and interest of the debts contracted for the support of the late war; the collection of which duties, is to be made by officers appointed by the state but accountable to Congress, according to such general regulations as the United States shall establish; subject to these important checks, that no citizen should be carried out of the state for trial; that all prosecutions shall be in our own courts; that no excessive fines or penalties shall be imposed; and that a yearly account of the proceeds and application of the revenue shall be rendered to the legislature, on failure of which, it reserves to itself a right of repealing its grant.

Is it possible for any measure to be better guarded? or is it possible that a grant for such precise objects and with so many checks can be dangerous to the public liberty?

Having now, as I trust, satisfactorily shewn that the constitution offers no obstacle to the measure; and that the liberty of the people cannot be endangered by it; it remains only to consider it in the view of revenue.

The sole question left for discussion, is, whether it be an eligible mode of supplying the federal treasury or not?

The better to answer this question it will be of use to examine how far the mode by quotas and requisitions has been found competent to the public exigencies.

The universal delinquency of the states during the war, shall be passed over with the bare mention of it. The public embarrassments were a plausible apology for that delinquency; and [if] it was hoped the peace would produce greater punctuality the experiment has disappointed that hope to a degree, which confounds the least sanguine. A comparative view of the compliances of the several states, for the five last years will furnish a striking result.

During that period as appears by a statement on our files, New-Hampshire, North-Carolina, South-Carolina and Georgia, have paid nothing. I say nothing because the only actual payment, is the trifling sum of about 7000 dollars, by New-Hampshire. South-Carolina indeed has credits but these are merely by way of discount, on the supplies furnished by her during the war, in consideration of her peculiar sufferings and exertions while the immediate theatre of it.

Connecticut and Delaware, have paid about one third of their requisitions. Massachusetts, Rhode-Island, and Maryland, about one half. Virginia, about three fifths; Pennsylvania, nearly the whole, and New-York, more than her quota.

These proportions are taken on the specie requisitions, the indents have been very partially paid, and in their present state, are of little account.

The payments into the federal treasury have declined rapidly each year. The whole amount for three years past in specie, has not exceeded 1,400,000 dollars, of which New-York has paid 100 per cent, more than her proportion. This sum, little more than 400,000 dollars a year, it will readily be conceived has been exhausted in the support of the civil establishments of the union, and the necessary guards and garrisons at public arsenals, and on the frontiers; without any surplus for paying any part of the debt, foreign or domestic, principal or interest.

Things are continually growing worse, the last year in particular produced less than two hundred thousand dollars, and that from only two or three states. Several of the states have been so long unaccustomed to pay, that they seem no longer concerned even about the appearances of compliance.

Connecticut and Jersey have almost formally declined paying any longer. The ostensible motive is the non-concurrence of this state in the impost system. The real one must be conjectured from the fact.

Pennsylvania, if I understand the scope of some late resolutions, means to discount the interest she pays upon her assumption to her own citizens; in which case, there will be little coming from her to the United States. This seems to be bringing matters to a crisis.

The pecuniary support of the federal government has of late devolved almost entirely upon Pennsylvania and New-York. If Pennsylvania refuses to continue her aid, what will be the situation of New-York? Are we willing to be the Atlas of the union? or are we willing to see it perish?

This seems to be the alternative. Is there not a species of political knight errantry in adhering pertinaciously to a system which throws the whole weight of the confederacy upon this state, or upon one or two more? Is it not our interest on mere calculations of state-policy, to promote a measure which operating under the same regulations in every state, must produce an equal, or nearly equal, effect every where, and oblige all the states to share the common burthen?

If the impost is granted to the United-States, with the power of levying it, it must have a proportional effect in all the states; for the same mode of collection every where, will have nearly the same result every where.

What must be the final issue of the present state of things? Will the few states that now contribute, be willing to contribute much longer? Shall we ourselves be long content with bearing the burthen singly? will not our zeal for a particular system, soon give way to the pressure of so unequal a weight? and if all the states cease to pay, what is to become of the union? It is sometimes asked why do not Congress oblige the states to do their duty; but where are the means? Where are the fleets and armies, where the federal treasury to support those fleets and armies, to enforce the requisitions of the union? All methods short of coertion, have repeatedly been tried in vain.

Let us now proceed to another most important inquiry. How are we to pay our foreign debt?

This I think is estimated at about 7,000,000 of dollars; which will every year increase with the accumulations of interest. It we pay neither principal nor interest, we not only abandon all pretensions to character as a nation; but we endanger the public peace. However, it may be in our power to evade the just demands of our domestic creditors; our foreign creditors must and will be paid.

They have power to enforce their demands, and sooner or later they may be expected to do it. It is not my intention to endeavour to excite the apprehensions of the committee; but I would appeal to their prudence. A discreet attention to the consequences of national measures is no impeachment of our firmness.

The foreign debt, I say, must sooner or later be paid, and the longer provision is delayed, the heavier it must fall at last.

We require about 1,600,000 dollars, to discharge the interest and instalments of the present year; about a million annually upon an average for ten years more, and about 300,000 dollars for another ten years.

The product of the impost, may be computed at about a million of dollars annually. It is an increasing fund—this fund would not only suffice for the discharge of the foreign debt, but important operations might be ingrafted upon it, towards the extinguishment of the domestic debt.

Is it possible to hesitate about the propriety of adopting a resource so easy in itself and so extensive in its effects?

Here I expect I may be told there is no objection to employing this resource; the act of the last session does it. The only dispute is about the mode. We are willing to grant the *money* but not the *power* required from us. Money will pay our debts; power may destroy our liberties. It has been insinuated that nothing but a lust of power would have prevented Congress from accepting the grant in the shape it has already passed the legislature.

This is a severe charge; if true, it ought undoubtedly to prevent our going a step further. But it is easy to show that Congress could not have accepted our grant without removing themselves further from the object, than they now are. To gain one state they must have lost all the others.

The grants of every state are accompanied with a condition, that similar grants be made by the other states. It is not denied that our act is essentially different from theirs. Their acts give the United States the power of collecting the duty—Ours reserves it to the state, and makes it receivable in paper money.

The immediate consequence of accepting our grant would be a relinquishment of the grants of the other states; they must take the matter up anew, and do the work over again, to accommodate it to our standard. In order to anchor one state, would it have been wise to set twelve, or at least eleven others afloat?

It is said that the states which have granted *more* would certainly be willing to grant *less*. They would easily accommodate their acts to that of New-York, as more favorable to their own power and security.

But would Massachusets and Virginia, which have no paper money of their own, accede to a plan that permitted other states to pay in paper while they paid in *specie?* Would they consent that their citizens should pay *twenty* shillings in the pound, while the citizens of Rhode-Island paid only *four,* the citizens of North-Carolina *ten,* and of other states in different degrees of inequality, in proportion to the relative depreciation of their paper? Is it wise in this state to cherish a plan that gives such an advantage to the citizens of other states over its own?

The paper money of the state of New-York, in most transactions is equal to gold and silver—that of Rhode-Island is depreciated to five for one—that of North-Carolina to two for one—that of South-Carolina may perhaps be worth fifteen shillings in the pound.

If the states pay the duties in paper, is it not evident that for every pound of that duty consumed by the citizen of New-York he would pay 20s. while the citizen of South-Carolina would pay 15s. of North-Carolina, 10s and Rhode-Island, only four!

This consideration alone, is sufficient to condemn the plan of our grant of last session, and to prove incontestably, that the states which are averse to emitting a paper currency, or have it in their power to support one when emitted, would never come into it.

Again, would those states which by their public acts demonstrate a conviction that the powers of the union require augmentation; which are conscious of energy in their own administration—would they be willing to concur in a plan, which left the collection of the duties in the hands of each state, and of course subject to all the inequalities which a more or less vigourous system of collection would produce?

This too is an idea which ought to have great weight with us—we have better habits of government than are to be found in some of the states—and our constitution admits of more energy than the constitution of most of the other states—the duties therefore would be more effectually collected with us than in such states, and this would have a similar effect to the depreciation of the money, in imposing a greater burthen on the citizens of this state.

If any state should incline to evade the payment of the duties, having the collection in its own hands, nothing would be easier than to effect it, and without materially sacrificing appearances.

It is manifest from this view of the subject, that we have the strongest reasons as a state, to depart from our own act: and that it would have been highly injudicious in Congress to have accepted it.

If there even had been a prospect of the concurrence of the other states in the plan, how inadequate would it have been to the public exigencies—fettered with the embarrassments of a depreciating paper.

It is to no purpose to say that the faith of the state was pledged by the act, to make the paper equal to gold and silver—and that the other states would be obliged to do the same; what greater dependance can be had on the faith of the states pledged to this measure, than on the faith they pledged in the confederation, sanctioned by a solemn appeal to heaven. If the obligation of faith in one case, have had so little influence upon their conduct in respect to the requisitions of Congress; what hope can there be that they would have greater influence in respect to the deficiencies of the paper money?

There yet remains an important light in which to consider the subject in the view of revenue. It is a clear point that we cannot carry the duties upon imposts to the same extent by separate arrangements as by a general plan—we must regulate ourselves by what we find done in the neighbouring states: while Pennsylvania has only two and a half per cent. on her importations we cannot greatly exceed her—we must content ourselves with the same or nearly the same rate. To go much beyond it would injure our commerce in a variety of ways, and would defeat itself—while the ports of Connecticut and Jersey are open to the introduction of goods, free from duty and the conveyance from them to us is so easy—while they consider our imposts as an ungenerous advantage taken of them, which it would be laudable to elude, the duties must be light or they would be evaded—the facility of doing it, and the temptation to do it would be both so great that we should collect, perhaps less by an increase of the rates than we do now. Already we experience the effects of this situation. But if the duties were to be levied under a common direction, with the same precautions every where to guard against smuggling, they might be carried without prejudice to trade to a much more considerable height.

As things now are, we must adhere to the present standard of duties, without any material alterations. Suppose this to produce fifty thousand pounds a year. The duties to be granted to Congress ought, in proportion, to produce double that sum. To this it appears by a scheme now before us, that additional duties might be imposed for the use of the state, on certain enumerated articles, to the amount of thirty thousand pounds. This would be an augmentation of our national revenue by indirect taxation to the extent of eighty thousand pounds a year; an immense object in a single state, which alone demonstrates the good policy of the measure.

It is no objection to say that a great part of this fund will be dedicated to the use of the United States. Their exigencies must be supplied in some way or other—the more is done towards it by means of the impost, the less will be to be done in other modes. If we do not employ that resource to the best account, we must find others in direct taxation. And to this are opposed all the habits and prejudices of the community. There is not a farmer in the state who would not pay a shilling in the voluntary consumption of articles on which a duty is paid, rather than a penny imposed immediately on his house and land.

There is but one objection to the measure under consideration that has come to my knowledge, which yet remains to be discussed. I mean the effect it is supposed to have upon our paper currency. It is said the diversion of this fund would leave the credit of the paper without any effectual support.

Though I should not be disposed to put a consideration, of this kind in competition with the safety of the union; yet I should be extremely cautious about doing any thing that might affect the credit of our currency. The legislature having thought an emission of paper advisable, I consider it my duty as a representative of the people to take care of its credit. But it appears to me that apprehensions on this score are without foundation.

What has hitherto been the principal support of the credit of the paper? Two things—the universal demand for money, and the immediate interest of the merchants to countenance whatever would facilitate the recovery of his debts. The first cause begat a general clamour in the country for a paper emission, and a disposition to uphold its credit. The farmers appeared willing to exchange their produce for it; the merchant on the other hand, had large debts outstanding; they supposed that giving a free circulation to the paper, would enable their customers in the country to pay, and as they perceived, that they would have it in their power to convert the money into produce, they naturally resolved to give it their support.

These causes combined to introduce the money into general circulation, and having once obtained credit, it will now be able to support itself.

The chief difficulty to have been apprehended in respect to the paper, was to overcome the diffidence which the still recent experience of depreciating paper, had instilled into mens minds. This, it was to have been feared, would have shaken its credit at its outset; and if it had once began to sink, it would be no easy matter to prevent its total decline.

The event has however turned out otherwise and the money has been fortunate enough to conciliate the general confidence. This point gained, there need be no apprehensions of its future fate, unless the government should do something to destroy that confidence.

The causes that first gave it credit, still operate, and will in all probability continue to do so. The demand for money has not lessened, and the merchant has still the same inducement to countenance the circulation of the paper.

I shall not deny that the outlet which the payment of duties furnished to the merchant, was an additional motive to the reception of the paper. Nor is it proposed to take away this motive. There is now before the house a bill, one object of which is, the establishment of a state impost, on certain enumerated articles, in addition to that to be granted to the United States. It is computed on very good grounds that the additional duties would amount to about 30,000 £. and as they would be payable in paper currency, they would create a sufficient demand upon the merchant, to leave him in this respect, substantially the same inducement which he had before. Indeed independent of this, the readiness of the trading people to take the money, can never be doubted, while it will freely command the commodities of the country; for this, to them, is the most important use they can make of it.

But besides the state impost, there must be other taxes; and these will all contribute to create a demand for the money; which is all we now mean, when we talk of funds for its support; for there are none appropriated for the *redemption* of the paper.

Upon the whole the additional duties will be a competent substitute for those now in existence; and the general good will of the community towards the paper, will be the best security for its credit.

Having now shewn, Mr. Chairman, that there is no constitutional impediment to the adoption of the bill; that there is no danger to be apprehended to the public liberty from giving the power in question to the United States; that in the view of revenue the measure under consideration is not only expedient, but necessary. Let us turn our attention to the other side of this important subject. Let us ask ourselves what will be the consequence of rejecting the bill; what will be the situation of our national affairs if they are left much longer to float in the chaos in which they are now involved.

Can our national character be preserved without paying our debts. Can the union subsist without revenue. Have we realized the consequences which would attend its dissolution.

If these states are not united under a federal government, they will infalliably have wars with each other; and their divisions will subject them to all the mischiefs of foreign influence and intrigue. The human passions will never want objects of hospitality. The western territory is an obvious and fruitful source of contest. Let us also cast our eye upon the mass of this state, intersected from one extremity to the other by a large navigable river. In the event of a rupture with them, what is to hinder our metropolis from becoming a prey to our neighbours? Is it even supposeable that they would suffer it to remain the nursery of wealth to a distinct community?

These subjects are delicate, but it is necessary to contemplate them to teach us to form a true estimate of our situation.

Wars with each other would beget standing armies—a source of more real danger to our liberties than all the power that could be conferred upon the representatives of the union. And wars with each other would lead to opposite alliances with foreign powers, and plunge us into all the labyrinths* of European politics.

The Romans in their progress to universal dominion, when they conceived the project of subduing the refractory spirit of the Grecian

* *In original, "laibrynths."*

Republics, which composed the famous Achaian league, began by sowing dissensions among them, and instilling jealousies of each other, and of the common head, and finished by making them a province of the Roman empire.

The application is easy; if there are any foreign enemies, if there are any domestic foes to this country, all their arts and artifices will be employed to effect a dissolution of the union. This cannot be better done than by sowing jealousies of the federal head and cultivating in each state an undue attachment to its own power.

§ Critical Analysis

To what extent does Hamilton draw upon the knowledge and accepted beliefs of his audience? To what extent does he depend on unfamiliar evidence to inform and persuade?

§

In this speech of February 15, 1787, Alexander Hamilton said:

> The application is easy; if there are any foreign enemies, if there are any domestic foes to this country, all their arts and artifices will be employed to effect a dissolution of the union. This cannot be better done than by sowing jealousies of the federal head and cultivating in each state an undue attachment to its own power.

In the (New York) *Daily Advertiser* for November 21, 1787, *The Federalist* No. 9 contained the following language:

> A Firm Union will be of the utmost moment to the peace and liberty of the States as a barrier against domestic faction and insurrection. It is impossible to read the history of the petty Republics of Greece and Italy, without feeling sensations of horror and disgust at the distractions with which they were continually agitated, and at the rapid succession of revolutions, by which they were kept in a state of perpetual vibration, between the extremes of tyranny and anarchy.

What similarities do you observe between the speech of February and *The Federalist* essay of November 1787?

§

In his "Address before the Law Association, New York, October 31, 1836," Chancellor James Kent spoke as follows:

> Among his brethren [at the New York Bar] Hamilton was indisputably preeminent. This was universally conceded. He rose at once to the loftiest heights of professional eminence, by his profound penetration, his power of analysis, the comprehensive grasp and strength of his understanding, and the firmness, frankness, and integrity of his character.[1]

---

[1] In George Shea, *The Life and Epoch of Alexander Hamilton: A Historical Study* (Boston: Houghton Mifflin, 1881), p. 435.

What evidence do you find in Hamilton's speech to confirm or deny Chancellor Kent's appraisal?

§

In a letter addressed to James Duane on September 3, 1780, Hamilton made the following observation:

> The fundamental defect is a want of power in Congress. It is hardly worth while to show in what this consists, as it seems to be universally acknowledged; or to point out how it has happened, as the only question is how to remedy it.[2]

How does Hamilton's observation relate to this speech?

§

William Pierce, who set down his impressions of outstanding persons attending the Federal Convention of 1787, declared that:

> Col. Hamilton . . . is rather a convincing speaker than a blazing orator. Col. Hamilton requires time to think; he inquires into every part of his subject with the searchings of philosophy, and when he comes forward he comes highly charged with interesting matter.[3]

In the text of the address, what would suggest that the Hamilton who spoke on February 15, 1787, justifies these remarks?

§ SUGGESTIONS FOR FURTHER READING

The Works of Alexander Hamilton (New York: Charles S. Francis, 1851) in the seven volumes edited by John C. Hamilton and *The Works of Alexander Hamilton* (New York: G. P. Putnam's, 1904) in the twelve volumes edited by Henry Cabot Lodge are being supplanted by *The Papers of Alexander Hamilton* (New York: Columbia University Press, 1961–), a magnificent scholarly enterprise undertaken by Harold C. Syrett, Jacob E. Cooke, and an obviously able staff. The first eleven volumes of the edition, containing Hamilton's papers through June 1792, are currently available, and others are promised to complete the project initiated in 1955.

[2] Bower Aly, ed., *Alexander Hamilton: Selections Representing His Life, His Thought, and His Style* (New York: Liberal Arts, 1957), p. 43.
[3] *Ibid.*, pp. 86–87.

The first volume of a distinguished ancillary work, *The Law Practice of Alexander Hamilton: Documents and Commentary* (New York: Columbia University Press, 1964), edited by Julius Goebel, Jr., and associates is also available. The endeavors of Syrett, Cooke, Goebel, and their staffs make the accomplishments of Alexander Hamilton known to scholars and to the public in a way that has heretofore been impossible. The net effect of the volumes is to confirm Hamilton in his standing as a brilliant lawyer, political analyst, and administrator and to increase his already formidable reputation as an ambitious and indefatigable architect of the government of the United States.

Hamilton has also been the subject of recent treatises and biographies supplementing and to some degree supplanting earlier ones. As recent studies the following should be cited: John C. Miller, *Alexander Hamilton: Portrait in Paradox* (New York: Harper & Brothers, 1959), and two volumes by Broadus Mitchell, *Alexander Hamilton: Youth to Maturity 1755–1788* (New York: Macmillan, 1957) and *Alexander Hamilton: The National Adventure 1788–1804* (New York: Macmillan, 1962). Also of interest are Broadus Mitchell, *Heritage from Hamilton* (New York: Columbia University Press, 1957); Richard B. Morris, ed., *Alexander Hamilton and the Founding of the Nation* (New York: Dial, 1957); Saul K. Padover, ed., *The Mind of Alexander Hamilton* (New York: Harper & Brothers, 1958); and Samuel McKee, Jr., ed., with an introduction by J. Harvie Williams, *Alexander Hamilton's Papers on Public Credit Commerce and Finance* (New York: Liberal Arts, 1957). *Alexander Hamilton in the American Tradition* (New York: McGraw-Hill, 1957) by Louis M. Hacker is a penetrating reappraisal of Hamilton's place in the development of the American republic. *Alexander Hamilton and the Constitution* (New York: Harcourt, Brace and World, 1964) by Clinton Rossiter develops the thesis that Hamilton is "in plain if not desperate need of a fresh appraisal."

Of the earlier biographies of Hamilton, the following may be mentioned: John T. Morse, Jr., *The Life of Alexander Hamilton*, 2 vols. (Boston: Little, Brown, 1876); Henry Cabot Lodge, *Alexander Hamilton* (Boston: Houghton Mifflin, 1882); William Graham Sumner, *Alexander Hamilton* (New York: Dodd, Mead, 1890); Frederick Scott Oliver, *Alexander Hamilton: An Essay on American Union* (New York: G. P. Putnam's, 1920); Henry Jones Ford, *Alexander Hamilton* (New York: Scribner's, 1925); Ralph Edward Bailey, *An American Colossus: The Singular Career of Alexander Hamilton* (Boston: Lothrop, Lee & Shepard, 1933); David Loth, *Alexander Hamilton: The Portrait of a Prodigy* (New York:

Carrick & Evans, 1939); Johan J. Smertenko, *Alexander Hamilton: Man of Action* (New York: Messner, 1941); Nathan Schachner, *Alexander Hamilton* (New York: Appleton-Century, 1946).

The Federalist has been published in the major European languages and in many editions, of which two may be mentioned: Alexander Hamilton, John Jay, and James Madison, *The Federalist . . . With a Special Introduction by Goldwin Smith, D.C.L.*, rev. ed. (New York: Colonial, 1901) and *The Federalist . . . With an Introduction by Edward Mead Earle* (Washington, D.C.: National Home Library Foundation, 1937). A systematic explication of *The Federalist* can be found in Gottfried Dietze, *The Federalist: A Classic on Federalism and Free Government* (Baltimore: Johns Hopkins, 1960).

Treatises concerning special features of Hamilton's life and thought are well-nigh innumerable, and certainly too numerous to list here. Perhaps, however, those interested in his speechmaking will wish to consult three treatises by Bower Aly: *The Rhetoric of Alexander Hamilton* (New York: Columbia University Press, 1941); *Alexander Hamilton: Selections Representing His Life, His Thought, and His Style* (New York: Liberal Arts, 1957); and "Alexander Hamilton," in Marie K. Hochmuth, ed., *A History and Criticism of American Public Address* (New York: Longmans, Green, 1955), Vol. III, pp. 24–51.

Wendell Phillips

"When Liberty is in danger, Faneuil Hall has the right, it is her duty, to strike the key-note for these United States." [1]
—WENDELL PHILLIPS

BIOGRAPHICAL SKETCH

Wendell Phillips was born on November 29, 1811, and died on February 2, 1884. The son of John and Sarah Walley Phillips, he was descended from the Reverend George Phillips, who settled in Massachusetts in 1630. At the Boston Latin School and at Harvard, from which he graduated (B.A., 1831; LL.B., 1834), Phillips showed unusual proficiency in speechmaking. On completing his studies at Harvard, he was admitted to the bar and opened an office in Boston. Possessed of an independent income, he was not diligent and in 1839 withdrew from practice to devote himself thereafter to lecturing and to worthy causes.

On October 12, 1837, Phillips married Ann Terry Greene, a brilliant young woman who encouraged him to agitate for the abolition of slavery. He contributed to *The Liberator*, attended the Anti-Slavery Convention in London (1840), and carried on a systematic and relentless campaign against slavery. With William Lloyd Garrison, who declared the Constitution of the United States to be "a covenant with death and an agreement with Hell," Phillips opposed the Mexican War and the annexation of Texas and advocated the dissolution of the Union as long as it countenanced slavery. During the Civil War he attacked Lincoln for his failure to eman-

NOTE: The sources for this essay will be found in the section Suggestions for Further Reading, pp. 177–178. Chief reliance is placed in Carlos Martyn's *Wendell Phillips: The Agitator*.

---

[1] Wendell Phillips, "The Murder of Lovejoy," *Speeches, Lectures and Letters by Wendell Phillips* (Boston: Walker, Wise, 1864), p. 10.

cipate the slaves immediately. After the war he succeeded Garrison as president of the American Anti-Slavery Society.

On the adoption of the Fifteenth Amendment enfranchising former slaves, Phillips turned to other causes with almost equal zeal. He was a popular and persuasive lecturer for prohibition, currency reform, the abolition of capital punishment, the rights of women, and the rights of labor. Extreme in his views, immoderate in his proposals, vehement in his attacks, Wendell Phillips was disarmingly gentle in his speech and persuasive in his language. A handsome man of distinguished position and assured bearing, he gained for the causes he adopted a hearing that others might have found difficulty in obtaining.

THE SPEAKER

When Wendell Phillips arose in Faneuil Hall on the morning of December 8, 1837, to deliver his speech "The Murder of Lovejoy," he had just celebrated (on November 29) his twenty-sixth birthday. The son of the first mayor of Boston and scion of the first families of Massachusetts, he appeared to have before him, as predicted by the eminent Judge Story, a career of unprecedented brilliance in the practice of law. Handsome, gifted, highly intelligent, he had the presence of a patrician, the manners of a prince, and the self-confidence of the Boston Brahmin. Why did he forsake the law, alienate his aristocratic friends, and spend his life in agitation for reform? Phillips was influenced chiefly by his parents, by his experience at Harvard, by his wife, and by one striking event that marked a turning point in his life.

John Phillips was a proper Bostonian who endeavored to teach all of his children, including Wendell, the Puritan virtues of self-reliance, of independence of mind and spirit. Wendell Phillips' mother, profoundly religious, taught him as a youth a precept that he remembered all his life: "Wendell," she would say, "be good and do good; this is my whole desire for you. Add other things if you may—these are central." [2] As a child, as a boy, as a young man,

[2] Carlos Martyn, *Wendell Phillips: The Agitator* (New York: Funk & Wagnalls, 1890), p. 30.

Phillips was given every advantage by parents genuinely concerned for his development as a person, in a home a few blocks from Faneuil Hall—the Cradle of Liberty—and not far from Bunker Hill.

When Phillips left his parental home to go to Harvard, he did not leave the environment of freedom but rather extended it in wide reading. During his student days he gave a year to the study of the English Revolution of 1640. He read also the histories of the Dutch struggle for independence. He steeped himself in the literature and law of freedom.[3] He was thus prepared to meet, to understand, and deeply to love Ann Terry Greene, of whom he once said, "My wife made an out and out abolitionist of me. . . ."[4] Both by nature and nurture a believer in freedom and an opponent of slavery, Phillips was ready to be persuaded by his wife formally to declare himself one of the band of abolitionists—a sect despised by the aristocracy of Boston hardly less than by the aristocracy of Charleston, South Carolina—and to be active in the struggle against slavery.

Even before his marriage, however, Phillips had witnessed an event that proved critical in his life. As a young lawyer not yet twenty-four years old, he found the quiet of his office disturbed one day by tumults and shouting down the block on Washington Street. On going to observe, he discovered "a broadcloth mob" including gentlemen of property and standing, his friends and associates on Beacon Hill. This aristocratic mob was dragging William Lloyd Garrison, a printer and editor of *The Liberator*, toward City Hall with cries of "Kill him!" "Lynch him!" Wendell Phillips, astonished and profoundly disturbed, went back to his office, deep in thought. The mobbing of William Lloyd Garrison made an ineradicable impression upon Phillips, not only because of his opposition to slavery but also because of his commitment to freedom of speech. When he came under the influence of that active and fervent abolitionist, his wife, he was thus prepared to respond without reservation to measures for the freeing of the slaves and, as he would have said, to the freeing of their masters from the oppressive crime of slavery. The

[3] Raymond H. Barnard, "The Freedom Speech of Wendell Phillips," *The Quarterly Journal of Speech*, XXV, 4 (December 1939), 596–611. Barnard's article is recommended as an excellent example of rhetorical criticism.

[4] Lorenzo Sears, *Wendell Phillips: Orator and Agitator* (New York: Doubleday, Page, 1909), p. 34.

culminating event in his decision was his reply to Attorney General Austin, in a speech that brought him to the notice of his fellow citizens and marked him as a man henceforth to be respected and feared.

THE OCCASION

"The Murder of Lovejoy" was delivered at a public meeting called to consider resolutions concerning the death at Alton, Illinois, on November 7 of Elijah P. Lovejoy, editor of a journal that consistently attacked slavery. The killing of Lovejoy by a mob outraged many persons in Boston, perhaps not so much because of the issue of slavery as because of the attack upon free speech and a free press. No less a person than Dr. William Ellery Channing applied for the use of Faneuil Hall and obtained it in spite of the reluctance of the city fathers to permit its use. The Honorable Jonathan Phillips, a distant kinsman of Wendell Phillips, presided. The resolutions condemning the actions of the mob at Alton were offered by the Honorable Benjamin F. Hallet, and the motion for their adoption was seconded by George S. Hillard. Immediately thereafter the Honorable James T. Austin, Attorney General of the Commonwealth, gained the floor to speak against the resolutions. A popular leader and politician, Austin expressed views widely held in Boston but contrary to those stated in the resolutions. Austin, while professing his belief in the principles, decried Lovejoy's exercise of free speech:

> We have a menagerie here with lions, tigers, a hyena, an elephant, a jackass or two, and monkeys in plenty. Suppose, now, some new cosmopolite, some man of philanthropic feelings, not only toward men, but animals, who believes that all are entitled to freedom as an inalienable right, should engage in the humane task of giving freedom to the wild beasts of the forest, some of whom are nobler than their keepers; or having discerned some new mode of reaching their understanding, should try to induce them to break their cages and be free. The people of Missouri had as much reason to be afraid of their slaves as we should have to be afraid of the wild beasts of the menagerie. They had the same dread of Lovejoy that we should have of the supposed instigator, if we really believed the bars would be broken and

the caravan let loose to prowl about our streets. . . . He died as the fool dieth. His clerical character is no palliation of his conduct. I have as little sympathy for a minister of the gospel who is found, gun in hand, fighting in a broil with a mob, as I have for one who leaves his pulpit to mingle in the debates of a popular assembly in matters that do not concern his sacred office. In either situation he is marvellously out of place.[5]

The Audience

At the conclusion of his speech, Austin left the gallery from which he spoke, amid cheers and great applause. What kind of audience applauded Austin? Since Faneuil Hall provided no chairs, the members of the audience were standing, and, since the hall was crowded (the number present has been variously estimated at from 2,500 to 5,000), they were presumably standing close together. The audience was probably divided three ways: approximately one-third of the group favored the resolutions and had come prepared to endorse them; another third followed the line of reasoning presented by Austin—for freedom of speech in principle but not in Lovejoy's practice; and still another third were undecided. These people— friendly, neutral, and hostile—made up the group to whom Phillips prepared to speak as, working his way toward the platform and gaining the recognition of the chairman, he began his reply to James Austin.

The Speech

Two facts concerning Phillips' speech are obvious: it was refutatory and it was extempore. Whether or not Phillips went to Faneuil Hall intending to speak is in doubt. Perhaps he did, but certainly he had not prepared to speak in reply to Austin, whose objections had

[5] The text of Austin's speech is found in Ralph Korngold's *Two Friends of Man: The Story of William Lloyd Garrison and Wendell Phillips and Their Relationship with Abraham Lincoln* (Boston: Little, Brown, 1950), p. 129. Austin's closing remark is obviously directed at the Reverend William Ellery Channing, who was Austin's pastor.

not been anticipated. Yet "The Murder of Lovejoy" is word for word, line for line, a reply to Austin's objections to the resolutions. Phillips' refutation, while extempore, was not unprepared. Indeed, it might be said that the whole of his twenty-six years had prepared him for this moment: his manly bearing and persuasive voice; his self-confidence derived from his parents and his assured social position; his genuine devotion to liberty breathed with the air of Massachusetts; his intellectual commitment to free speech and a free press furthered by his studies at Harvard; his acquaintance with the specific questions raised by the resolutions and by Austin's objections. When he spoke, he was thus superbly—perhaps uniquely—prepared to deal with the problems presented by Austin's speech and perhaps to justify the opinion of George William Curtis that "The Murder of Lovejoy" is one of the three greatest speeches ever delivered in America—the other two being Patrick Henry's speech to the Virginia House of Burgesses at Williamsburg and Abraham Lincoln's address at Gettysburg.

Not all great speeches succeed in their immediate purpose for, as Aristotle observed, absolute persuasion is not required of the orator. Yet it is somehow gratifying to know that when, following Phillips' speech, the chairman put the question on the resolutions condemning the murder of Lovejoy and supporting a free press and free speech, he heard a resounding chorus of "Ayes" and not one "Nay." Wendell Phillips was launched on a unique career as reformer, gadfly, chronic objector, public orator, disturber of the peace, and friend and advocate of the slave.

The Murder of Lovejoy

Mr. Chairman:—We have met for the freest discussion of these resolutions, and the events which gave rise to them. [Cries of "Question," "Hear him," "Go on," "No gagging," etc.] I hope I shall be permitted to express my surprise at the sentiments of the last speaker,[1]—surprise not only at such sentiments from such a man, but at the applause they have received within these walls. A comparison has been drawn between the events of the Revolution and the tragedy at Alton.[2] We have heard it asserted here, in Faneuil Hall,[3] that Great Britain had a right to tax the Colonies, and we have heard the mob at Alton, the drunken murderers of Lovejoy,[4] compared to those patriot fathers who threw the tea overboard![5] [Great applause.] Fellow-citizens, is this Faneuil Hall doctrine? ["No, no."] The mob at Alton were met to wrest from a citizen his just rights,—met to resist the laws. We have been told that our fathers did the same; and the glorious mantle of Revolutionary precedent has been thrown over the mobs of our day. To make out their title to such defence, the gentleman says that the British Parliament had a *right* to tax these Colonies. It is manifest that, without this, his parallel

From *Speeches, Lectures and Letters by Wendell Phillips* (Boston: Walker, Wise, 1864), pp. 1–10. Asterisked footnote on p. 172 appeared in this 1864 edition.

[1] The previous speaker was James T. Austin, Attorney General of Massachusetts.

[2] Alton, Illinois, is just across the Mississippi River from Missouri, which in 1837 was a slave state.

[3] Faneuil Hall, used as a public market and meeting place, was given to the city of Boston by Peter Faneuil in 1742. It has been called "the cradle of liberty."

[4] Elijah P. Lovejoy (1802–1837), whose abolitionist views were highly unpopular in Missouri, where he edited *The Observer*, moved in 1836 to Alton, Illinois. On November 7, 1837, while protecting the press of his new abolitionist paper, *The Alton Observer*, he was killed by a mob.

[5] The Boston Tea Party took place on December 16, 1773, as the response of the patriots to the tax on tea, which had been retained by the British ministry as a symbol of the right of Parliament to tax the American colonies. A number of Bostonians, garbed as Indians, boarded the ships in which the tea had been transported and threw the tea into the harbor.

falls to the ground; for Lovejoy had stationed himself within constitutional bulwarks. He was not only defending the freedom of the press, but he was under his own roof, in arms with the sanction of the civil authority. The men who assailed him went against and over the laws. The *mob*, as the gentleman terms it,—mob, forsooth! certainly we sons of the tea-spillers are a marvellously patient generation!—the "orderly mob" which assembled in the Old South[6] to destroy the tea were met to resist, not the laws, but illegal exactions. Shame on the American who calls the tea-tax and stamp-act *laws!* Our fathers resisted, not the King's prerogative, but the King's usurpation. To find any other account, you must read our Revolutionary history upside down. Our State archives are loaded with arguments of John Adams[7] to prove the taxes laid by the British Parliament unconstitutional,—beyond its power. It was not till this was made out that the men of New England rushed to arms. The arguments of the Council Chamber and the House of Representatives preceded and sanctioned the contest. To draw the conduct of our ancestors into a precedent for mobs, for a right to resist laws we ourselves have enacted, is an insult to their memory. The difference between the excitements of those days and our own, which the gentleman in kindness to the latter has overlooked, is simply this: the men of that day went for the right, as secured by the laws. They were the people rising to sustain the laws and constitution of the Province. The rioters of our day go for their own wills, right or wrong. Sir, when I heard the gentleman lay down principles which place the murderers of Alton side by side with Otis and Hancock, with Quincy and Adams,[8] I thought those pictured lips [pointing to

[6] The Old South Meeting House, famed church in Boston, was often a center for the activities of the patriots.

[7] John Adams (1735–1826), a lawyer and leader opposing the measures of the British Parliament that led to the American Revolution, was a member of the Continental Congresses and one of the committee that drafted the Declaration of Independence. Active in public affairs throughout his life, he was Vice-President of the United States from 1789 to 1797 and succeeded Washington as President in 1797.

[8] James Otis (1725–1783) resigned as Advocate General of the Commonwealth of Massachusetts in order to oppose the issuing of Writs of Assistance. John Hancock (1737–1793), Boston merchant and early advocate of colonial resistance to Britain, signed the Declaration of Independence and served as President of the Continental Congress (1775–1777). Josiah Quincy (1744–1775), an outstanding colonial lawyer,

the portraits in the Hall] would have broken into voice to rebuke the recreant American,—the slanderer of the dead. [Great applause and counter applause.] The gentleman said that he should sink into insignificance if he dared to gainsay the principles of these resolutions. Sir, for the sentiments he has uttered, on soil consecrated by the prayers of Puritans and the blood of patriots, the earth should have yawned and swallowed him up.

> [Applause and hisses, with cries of "Take that back." The uproar became so great that for a long time no one could be heard. At length G. Bond, Esq., and Hon. W. Sturgis came to Mr. Phillips's side at the front of the platform. They were met with cries of "Phillips or nobody," "Make him take back 'recreant,'" "He sha'n't go on till he takes it back." When it was understood they meant to sustain, not to interrupt, Mr. Phillips, Mr. Sturgis was listened to, and said: "I did not come here to take any part in this discussion, nor do I intend to; but I do entreat you, fellow-citizens, by everything you hold sacred, —I conjure you by every association connected with this Hall, consecrated by our fathers to freedom of discussion,—that you listen to every man who addresses you in a decorous manner." Mr. Phillips resumed.]

Fellow-citizens, I cannot take back my words. Surely the Attorney-General,[9] so long and well known here, needs not the aid of your hisses against one so young as I am,—my voice never before heard within these walls!

Another ground has been taken to excuse the mob, and throw doubt and discredit on the conduct of Lovejoy and his associates. Allusion has been made to what lawyers understand very well,—the "conflict of laws." We are told that nothing but the Mississippi River rolls between St. Louis and Alton; and the conflict of laws somehow or other gives the citizens of the former a right to find fault with the defender of the press for publishing his opinions so near

---

opposed the Stamp Act and British policies generally. His articles published during the controversy with Britain helped to articulate colonial opinion. Samuel Adams (1722–1803), one of the earliest and most forceful advocates of American independence, helped to organize the Sons of Liberty and to agitate against British policy through the Committees of Correspondence. He was a member of the Continental Congress (1774–1781) and Governor of Massachusetts (1794–1797).

[9] Mr. Austin.

their limits. Will the gentleman venture that argument before lawyers? How the laws of the two States could be said to come into conflict in such circumstances I question whether any lawyer in this audience can explain or understand. No matter whether the line that divides one sovereign State from another be an imaginary one or ocean-wide, the moment you cross it the State you leave is blotted out of existence, so far as you are concerned. The Czar might as well claim to control the deliberations of Faneuil Hall, as the laws of Missouri demand reverence, or the shadow of obedience, from an inhabitant of Illinois.

I must find some fault with the statement which has been made of the events at Alton. It has been asked why Lovejoy and his friends did not appeal to the executive,—trust their defence to the police of the city. It has been hinted that, from hasty and ill-judged excitement, the men within the building provoked a quarrel, and that he fell in the course of it, one mob resisting another. Recollect, Sir, that they did act with the approbation and sanction of the Mayor. In strict truth, there was no executive to appeal to for protection. The Mayor acknowledged that he could not protect them. They asked him if it was lawful for them to defend themselves. He told them it was, and sanctioned their assembling in arms to do so. They were not, then, a mob; they were not merely citizens defending their own property; they were in some sense the *posse comitatus*,[10] adopted for the occasion into the police of the city, acting under the order of a magistrate. It was civil authority resisting lawless violence. Where, then, was the imprudence? Is the doctrine to be sustained here, that it is *imprudent* for men to aid magistrates in executing the laws?

Men are continually asking each other, Had Lovejoy a right to resist? Sir, I protest against the question, instead of answering it. Lovejoy did not resist, in the sense they mean. He did not throw himself back on the natural right of self-defence. He did not cry anarchy, and let slip the dogs of civil war, careless of the horrors which would follow.

Sir, as I understand this affair, it was not an individual protecting his property; it was not one body of armed men resisting another,

[10] That body of men who may be, or have been, summoned by the sheriff of a county to maintain law and order.

and making the streets of a peaceful city run blood with their contentions. It did not bring back the scenes in some old Italian cities,
where family met family, and faction met faction, and mutually
trampled the laws under foot. No; the men in that house were regularly *enrolled,* under the sanction of the Mayor. There being no mili-
tia in Alton, about seventy men were enrolled with the approbation
of the Mayor. These relieved each other every other night. About
thirty men were in arms on the night of the sixth, when the press
was landed. The next evening, it was not thought necessary to sum-
mon more than half that number; among these was Lovejoy. It was,
therefore, you perceive, Sir, the police of the city resisting rioters,—
civil government breasting itself to the shock of lawless men.

Here is no question about the right of self-defence. It is in fact
simply this: Has the civil magistrate a right to put down a riot?

Some persons seem to imagine that anarchy existed at Alton
from the commencement of these disputes. Not at all. "No one of
us," says an eyewitness and a comrade of Lovejoy, "has taken up
arms during these disturbances but at the command of the Mayor."
Anarchy did not settle down on that devoted city till Lovejoy
breathed his last. Till then the law, represented in his person, sustained itself against its foes. When he fell, civil authority was trampled under foot. He had "planted himself on his constitutional
rights,"—appealed to the laws,—claimed the protection of the civil
authority,—taken refuge under "the broad shield of the Constitution. When through that he was pierced and fell, he fell but one
sufferer in a common catastrophe." He took refuge under the banner
of liberty,—amid its folds; and when he fell, its glorious stars and
stripes, the emblem of free institutions, around which cluster so
many heart-stirring memories, were blotted out in the martyr's
blood.

It has been stated, perhaps inadvertently, that Lovejoy or his
comrades fired first. This is denied by those who have the best
means of knowing. Guns were first fired by the mob. After being
twice fired on, those within the building consulted together and de-
liberately returned the fire. But suppose they did fire first. They had
a right so to do; not only the right which every citizen has to defend
himself, but the further right which every civil officer has to resist

violence. Even if Lovejoy fired the first gun, it would not lessen his claim to our sympathy, or destroy his title to be considered a martyr in defence of a free press. The question now is, Did he act within the Constitution and the laws? The men who fell in State Street on the 5th of March, 1770,[11] did more than Lovejoy is charged with. They were the *first* assailants. Upon some slight quarrel they pelted the troops with every missile within reach. Did this bate one jot of the eulogy with which Hancock and Warren[12] hallowed their memory, hailing them as the first martyrs in the cause of American liberty?

If, Sir, I had adopted what are called Peace principles, I might lament the circumstances of this case. But all you who believe, as I do, in the right and duty of magistrates to execute the laws, join with me and brand as base hypocrisy the conduct of those who assemble year after year on the 4th of July, to fight over the battles of the Revolution and yet "damn with faint praise," or load with obloquy, the memory of this man, who shed his blood in defence of life, liberty, property, and the freedom of the press!

Throughout that terrible night I find nothing to regret but this, that within the limits of our country, civil authority should have been so prostrated as to oblige a citizen to arm in his own defence, and to arm in vain. The gentleman says Lovejoy was presumptuous and imprudent,—he "died as the fool dieth." And a reverend clergyman of the city* tells us that no citizen has a right to publish opinions disagreeable to the community! If any mob follows such publication, on *him* rests its guilt! He must wait, forsooth, till the people come up to it and agree with him! This libel on liberty goes on to say that the want of right to speak as we think is an evil inseparable from republican institutions! If this be so, what are they worth? Welcome the despotism of the Sultan, where one knows what he may publish

* *Rev. Hubbard Winslow's discourse on* Liberty! *in which he defined "republican liberty" to be "liberty to say and do what the* prevailing *voice and will of the brotherhood will allow and protect."*

[11] On March 5, 1770, British troops stationed in Boston to enforce the edicts of the British Parliament, on being attacked by some townspeople, fired into the crowd. Five men were killed. In the trial that followed, Robert Treat Paine prosecuted and John Adams and Josiah Quincy defended the soldiers, who were acquitted.

[12] Joseph Warren (1741–1775), a physician, practiced medicine in Boston. In the forefront of resistance to the British, he was killed in the Battle of Bunker Hill.

and what he may not, rather than the tyranny of this many-headed monster, the mob, where we know not what we may do or say, till some fellow-citizen has tried it, and paid for the lesson with his life. This clerical absurdity chooses as a check for the abuses of the press, not the *law*, but the dread of a mob. By so doing, it deprives not only the individual and the minority of their rights, but the majority also, since the expression of *their* opinion may sometimes provoke disturbance from the minority. A few men may make a mob as well as many. The majority, then, have no right, as Christian men, to utter their sentiments, if by any possibility it may lead to a mob! Shades of Hugh Peters and John Cotton,[13] save us from such pulpits!

Imprudent to defend the liberty of the press! Why? Because the defence was unsuccessful? Does success gild crime into patriotism, and the want of it change heroic self-devotion to imprudence? Was Hampden[14] imprudent when he drew the sword and threw away the scabbard? Yet he, judged by that single hour, was unsuccessful. After a short exile, the race he hated sat again upon the throne.

Imagine yourself present when the first news of Bunker Hill battle reached a New England town. The tale would have run thus: "The patriots are routed,—the redcoats victorious,—Warren lies dead upon the field." With what scorn would that *Tory* have been received, who should have charged Warren with *imprudence!* who should have said that, bred a physician, he was "out of place" in that battle, and "died as the *fool dieth*"! [Great applause.] How would the intimation have been received, that Warren and his associates should have waited a better time? But if success be indeed the only criterion of prudence, *Respice finem*,—wait till the end.

Presumptuous to assert the freedom of the press on American

[13] Hugh Peters (1598–1660), Puritan preacher, not conforming to the Anglican Doctrines, left England for Holland and later for Massachusetts, where he was pastor of the church at Salem. In 1641 he returned to England where, during the Puritan revolution, he served in Oliver Cromwell's army and on the restoration of the Stuarts was executed. John Cotton (1584–1652) was Vicar of St. Botolph's Church at Boston, Lincolnshire, when he was summoned to appear before the High Court, presumably to answer charges growing out of his Puritan teaching. Instead of responding to the summons, he fled to Massachusetts, where he was protected and honored.

[14] John Hampden (1594–1643), English statesman, refused to pay ship-money, a tax he believed to be an illegal exaction. A cousin of Oliver Cromwell, Hampden raised a regiment for the parliamentary government. He was killed at the battle of Chalgrove.

ground! Is the assertion of such freedom before the age? So much before the age as to leave one no right to make it because it displeases the community? Who invents this libel on his country? It is this very thing which entitles Lovejoy to greater praise. The disputed right which provoked the Revolution—taxation without representation—is far beneath that for which he died. [Here there was a strong and general expression of disapprobation.] One word, gentlemen. As much as *thought* is better than money, so much is the cause in which Lovejoy died nobler than a mere question of taxes. James Otis thundered in this Hall when the King did but touch his *pocket*. Imagine, if you can, his indignant eloquence, had England offered to put a gag upon his lips. [Great applause.]

The question that stirred the Revolution touched our civil interests. *This* concerns us not only as citizens, but as immortal beings. Wrapped up in its fate, saved or lost with it, are not only the voice of the statesman, but the instructions of the pulpit, and the progress of our faith.

The clergy "marvellously out of place" where free speech is battled for,—liberty of speech on national sins? Does the gentleman remember that freedom to preach was first gained, dragging in its train freedom to print? I thank the clergy here present, as I reverence their predecessors, who did not so far forget their country in their immediate profession as to deem it duty to separate themselves from the struggle of '76,—the Mayhews and Coopers,[15] who remembered they were citizens before they were clergymen.

Mr. Chairman, from the bottom of my heart I thank that brave little band at Alton for resisting. We must remember that Lovejoy had fled from city to city,—suffered the destruction of three presses patiently. At length he took counsel with friends, men of character, of tried integrity, of wide views, of Christian principle. They thought the crisis had come: it was full time to assert the laws. They saw around them, not a community like our own, of fixed habits, of character moulded and settled, but one "in the gristle, not yet hardened into the bone of manhood." The people there, children of our

---

[15] Jonathan Mayhew (1720–1766) and Samuel Cooper (1725–1783), prominent preachers in New England, were outspoken in defense of the rights of the colonists against the British.

older States, seem to have forgotten the blood-tried principles of their fathers the moment they lost sight of our New England hills. Something was to be done to show them the priceless value of the freedom of the press, to bring back and set right their wandering and confused ideas. He and his advisers looked out on a community, staggering like a drunken man, indifferent to their rights and confused in their feelings. Deaf to argument, haply they might be stunned into sobriety. They saw that of which we cannot judge, the *necessity* of resistance. Insulted law called for it. Public opinion, fast hastening on the downward course, must be arrested.

Does not the event show they judged rightly? Absorbed in a thousand trifles, how has the nation all at once come to a stand? Men begin, as in 1776 and 1640, to discuss principles, to weigh characters, to find out where they are. Haply we may awake before we are borne over the precipice.

I am glad, Sir, to see this crowded house. It is good for us to be here. When Liberty is in danger, Faneuil Hall has the right, it is her duty, to strike the key-note for these United States. I am glad, for one reason, that remarks such as those to which I have alluded have been uttered here. The passage of these resolutions, in spite of this opposition, led by the Attorney-General of the Commonwealth, will show more clearly, more decisively, the deep indignation with which Boston regards this outrage.

§ Critical Analysis

Any speaker has the problem of commanding and sustaining the attention of the audience, even when the audience is disposed to agree with his proposition. The problem of the speaker who faces a hostile audience is even more severe; he must overcome resistance even to gain a hearing, and he must find acceptable premises from which to argue his case. Phillips' speech on the murder of Lovejoy is a remarkable example of overcoming the hostility of the audience. Lorenzo Sears wrote that the speech "set a thousand minds in a new direction and recalled thousands more from momentary deviation back to the principles of free speech and personal liberty." [1] How does Phillips "set minds in a new direction" at the outset of the speech? How does the first sentence help to do this? To what principles does he "recall" the audience in his first paragraphs?

§

After the interruption when he was urged to take back the charge "recreant," and at other points in the speech, how does Phillips demonstrate the ability to turn audience comments to advantage in making effective refutation? How does he use Austin's own arguments as a basis for his reply? In refuting the arguments, how effective is his method of focusing on single words or phrases—*mob; conflict of laws; imprudent; presumptuous; died as the fool dieth*? In arguing that Lovejoy's cause was greater than the taxation-without-representation dispute, how does he convert angry objection to approval?

§

In the course of the address, Phillips makes various references to the setting—to Faneuil Hall itself, to a painting on the wall—and to "our fathers" who participated in the famous tea party and ensuing war. How did such references suggest the speaker's understanding of his audience? Consider the date of the events and of the speech about Lovejoy. Would these references be likely to affect an audience today with equal force?

[1] *Wendell Phillips: Orator and Agitator* (New York: Doubleday, Page, 1909), p. 61.

§

Carlos Martyn, in his biography of Phillips, reported that when he arose, the "classic beauty of his face," his "masterful bearing," and his "marvellous voice, sweet as a song, clear as a flute" produced an immediate effect on the audience.[2] What evidence do you see in the text of the speech to suggest that the delivery contributed to the effect? Where, for example, does Phillips seem to speak with confidence and force? Can you identify climactic points?

§ SUGGESTIONS FOR FURTHER READING

Wendell Phillips is the subject of two doctoral dissertations, one by John William Sattler, "Wendell Phillips: Speaker and Agitator" (Evanston, Illinois: Northwestern University, 1943) and another by Oscar Sherwin, "Prophet of Liberty: A Biography of Wendell Phillips" (New York: New York University, 1940). Sherwin's dissertation was followed by his book *Prophet of Liberty: The Life and Times of Wendell Phillips* (New York: Bookman Associates, 1958). Frankly partisan in favor of Phillips and his position toward abolition, the book contains copious documentation and an extensive bibliography. It relies heavily and sometimes closely on Carlos Martyn's *Wendell Phillips: The Agitator* (New York: Funk & Wagnalls, 1890), a work that quotes extensively from Phillips and includes in an appendix three of Phillips' major addresses: "The Lost Arts," "Daniel O'Connell," and "The Scholar in a Republic."

An earlier volume, published the year Phillips died, is George Lowell Austin's *The Life and Times of Wendell Phillips* (Boston: B. B. Russell, 1884), which contains a final chapter of eulogies and tributes. Lorenzo Sears' *Wendell Phillips: Orator and Agitator* (New York: Doubleday, Page, 1909), a circumstantial account of the life and labor of Wendell Phillips, includes a chapter (IV) on "The Murder of Lovejoy" and a chapter of critical commentary (XXV) on Phillips' oratory. Two more recent books present Phillips sympathetically but not eulogistically: Irving H. Bartlett's *Wendell Phillips: Brahmin Radical* (Boston: Beacon, 1961) and Ralph Korngold's *Two Friends of Man: The Story of William Lloyd Garrison and Wendell Phillips and Their Relationship with Abraham*

[2] *Wendell Phillips: The Agitator* (New York: Funk & Wagnalls, 1890), p. 95.

Lincoln (Boston: Little, Brown, 1950). Korngold's book is particularly useful for its account of the relations between Garrison and Phillips and contains a selected bibliography for Garrison as well as for Phillips.

Wendell Phillips' papers have been published in two series, the first, edited by James Redpath under the title *Speeches, Lectures and Letters by Wendell Phillips* (Boston: Lee and Shepard, 1892), includes the text of "The Murder of Lovejoy"; the second, edited by Theodore C. Pease and offered by the same publisher in 1891, includes the text of his famous lyceum lecture, "The Lost Arts," as well as his tributes to Theodore Parker, Francis Jackson, Abraham Lincoln, William Lloyd Garrison, and others. Wendell Phillips' eulogy of Garrison may be found also in the *Old South Leaflets,* Vol. IV, No. 79 (Boston: Directors of the Old South Work, 1879).

Charles Edward Russell in *The Story of Wendell Phillips: Soldier of the Common Good* (Chicago: Charles H. Kerr & Company Cooperative, 1914) presents Phillips as a socialist in a war against privilege. George Edward Woodberry in *Wendell Phillips: The Faith of an American* (New York: printed for the Woodberry Society, 1912) offers an address delivered to mark the one hundredth anniversary of the birth of Wendell Phillips. Wendell Phillips Stafford delivered a similar address, *A Centennial Oration Delivered at Park Street Church, Boston, November 28, 1911* (Boston: National Association for the Advancement of Colored People, W. B. Clarke Company, n. d.). The volume includes photographs and facsimiles. An interesting account of Phillips' platform appearance by one who heard him speak is incorporated in Elbert Hubbard's *Little Journeys to the Homes of the Great,* Vol. XIII, No. 6 (December 1903), 153–184.

For a systematic account of Phillips' oratory, the best single source is Willard Hayes Yeager, "Wendell Phillips," in William Norwood Brigance, ed., *A History and Criticism of American Public Address* (New York: McGraw-Hill, 1943), Vol. I, pp. 329–362.

George William Curtis

ॐ | ⑤

> "To say that in this country the rogues must rule, is to defy history
> and to despair of the republic." [1] —GEORGE WILLIAM CURTIS

BIOGRAPHICAL SKETCH

George William Curtis, essayist, critic, editor, and lecturer, was born
in Providence, Rhode Island, on February 24, 1824, the son of George
and Elizabeth Burrill Curtis. When he was two years old, his mother
died, and in 1835 his father married Julia Bridgham, a young woman
of unusual accomplishments, who gave to George William Curtis,
to his brother, and to the four sons born to her, both care and com-
panionship. The Bridghams, like the Curtises and the Burrills, were
descended from early settlers in New England. George William
Curtis attended boarding school in Jamaica Plain, Massachusetts,
from 1830 until his father's second marriage, when he joined the
family, then living in Providence but soon (1840) to move to New
York. Curtis' education, extensive but informal and undisciplined,
was obtained by independent study and by residence at Brook Farm.
In 1838 he failed the entrance examination at Brown, a university
that sixteen years later conferred an honorary degree on him.

At Brook Farm and, later, during an extended stay in Concord,
Massachusetts, George William Curtis and his brother Burrill met
and learned from some of the leading men of their day: Ralph Waldo
Emerson, William Henry Channing, Henry David Thoreau, and
others. Following these experiences, Curtis began an extended tour

NOTE: The sources for this essay will be found in the section Suggestions for Further
Reading, pp. 204–205, and in the editors' discursive reading, particularly of Emerson
and Thoreau.

[1] George William Curtis, "The Public Duty of Educated Men," in Charles Eliot
Norton, ed., Orations and Addresses of George William Curtis (New York: Harper &
Brothers, 1894), p. 268.

of Europe and the Near East. He drew on this experience for a series of travel essays that achieved a measure of acclaim, and in 1852 he was employed by Harper & Brothers, publishers. He assumed the editorship of *Harper's Magazine* and from 1853 to 1892—except for a short period of illness—was the sole author of essays published in the column called "The Easy Chair." These urbane essays furthered his reputation and helped to establish him as a lyceum lecturer and popular speaker.

Throughout his career, Curtis' receipts from lectures were a substantial part of his income. With his marriage on Thanksgiving Day, 1856, to Anna Shaw, and with the responsibilities of a family, the additional source of income was welcome. Moreover, the lectures gave him a splendid opportunity to advance ideas on good government, women's suffrage, and abolition of slavery to audiences that were usually responsive. An early opponent of slavery, although not as extreme in his views as Phillips and Garrison, Curtis was a leader in the Republican Party at its origin and for many years thereafter. In 1884, however, disappointed by the nomination of James G. Blaine, he helped to organize Republican support for Grover Cleveland, the Democratic nominee. Curtis consistently attacked machine politics, the spoils system, and corruption in public office. A believer in civil service reform, he was for many years one of its most effective advocates. In 1890, after long service on the Board of Regents of the University of the State of New York, he was chosen Chancellor. He died at his home on Staten Island on August 31, 1892.

THE SPEAKER

To profit from the study of a speech one should examine the orator's ideas, his ability to adapt these ideas to his hearers, his command of language, his habits of preparation, and his characteristic manner of talking to an audience.

The Ideas

In his youth George William Curtis went to school, in a sense, to Ralph Waldo Emerson. His education under Emerson, although informal, was nevertheless significant, for Curtis never forgot his master's teaching. Like Emerson, Curtis was the protagonist of the honest, the honorable, the responsible course of action. Like Emerson, Curtis was the American optimist, the true believer in the destiny of a great Republic. Like Emerson, Curtis expounded a social gospel that assumed the perfectibility of man. Significantly, Curtis once declared that Emerson "was the philosopher Proteus, and he spoke through all the more popular mouths." [2] Ralph Waldo Emerson spoke also through the mouth of George William Curtis, and although Curtis, as journalist and orator, sometimes ventured into fields where Emerson did not go, his ideas were consistently Emersonian. Indeed, although one can find much in Emerson that would not have come from Curtis, it would be difficult to discover in the lectures and speeches of Curtis any complete train of thought that could not have been derived from Emerson. Self-reliance, duty, spiritual independence—all Emersonian concepts—furnished the discourse of George William Curtis.

The range of Curtis' ideas may thus be considered, perhaps justly, as narrow, as somewhat parochial. Yet to dismiss Curtis with this observation would be a mistake. The intellectual as orator is a rare person; although Curtis was no dominating intellectual, he was nevertheless an orator. Indeed the orator *as* orator is not required to create ideas: he finds them and adapts them. In his speeches and lectures from 1856 to 1892, with the one Emersonian string to his bow of ideas, Curtis yet managed to speak eloquently in his own time to his own special audience: an American genteel middle class. Perhaps he succeeded because the single theme that governed his discourse is as old as conscience in mankind; as old as Plato observing that wise men who decline to take part in public affairs must be governed by fools; as old as Cromwell appealing to the rectitude of the Puritan Commonwealth; as old as George Washington founding a nation on principles of responsible citizenship. Yet Curtis' theme, expressed in today's idiom, is as current as the morning paper. Is it not found in General MacArthur's stirring words to the young men at West Point: "Always there echoes and re-echoes: Duty, Honor, Coun-

---

[2] Edward Cary, *George William Curtis* (Boston: Houghton Mifflin, 1894), p. 328.

try"?[3] Is it not found in President Kennedy's appeal to all his countrymen: "And so, my fellow Americans, ask not what your country can do for you: Ask what you can do for your country"?[4]

The Adaptation

In his speechmaking, George William Curtis avoided rather than solved the problem of adapting his ideas to a particular group. The audience he addressed at the Commencement of Union College in 1877 did not present problems greatly different from those he met at Wesleyan University in 1856. Its members were able to buy lyceum tickets, interested in the kind of adult education the lyceum provided, and not expecting to be roused to action. Even in his political activities, as in the New York State Constitutional Convention in 1867–1868, though Curtis met opposition, he did not meet hostility. Perhaps the greatest test of his ability to adapt his discourse occurred at the dinner of the New England Society of New York, on December 22, 1876, when he succeeded marvelously in employing an after-dinner occasion for a suasive purpose. Some national leaders believed that his counsel of moderation in the election disputed between Hayes and Tilden went far toward encouraging a peaceful rather than a violent settlement of the issue. But such opportunities were exceptional for Curtis: ordinarily his audiences expected to be pleased, edified, uplifted, perhaps challenged a bit. He met the requirements with only minor variations in his central theme.

The Language

In considering a speaker's style, one does well to remember Aristotle's dictum that the hearer is the speech's end and object. A certain presumption must be permitted, therefore, in favor of the style of a speaker so uniformly acceptable to his audiences as Curtis came to be. Yet it may be observed that his spoken language seems sometimes

[3] Douglas MacArthur, "Duty, Honor, Country," in Vorin E. Whan, Jr., ed., *A Soldier Speaks: Public Papers and Speeches of General of the Army Douglas MacArthur* (New York: Praeger, 1965), p. 358.

[4] See below, p. 275.

to be at a remove—perhaps a literary remove—from his hearers. Is it because, like Emerson, he put his speeches into his essays and his essays into his speeches?

To be sure, in "The Public Duty of Educated Men," Curtis speaks some passages, as the following, that are forthright, clear, direct, quite as vigorous in style as any phrases of Wendell Phillips:

> Public duty in this country is not discharged, as is so often supposed, by voting. A man may vote regularly and still fail essentially of his political duty, as the Pharisee, who gave tithes of all that he possessed and fasted three times in the week, yet lacked the very heart of religion. When an American citizen is content with voting merely, he consents to accept what is often a doubtful alternative.[5]

In other language, however, perhaps just as characteristic, Curtis backs reflexively into his ideas:

> It was under the forms of the republic that Julius Cæsar made himself emperor of Rome. It was while professing reverence for the national traditions that James II. was destroying religious liberty in England.[6]

From a more vigorous orator—Phillips, perhaps, or Chatham—one would expect to find at least this modification:

> Under the forms of the republic Julius Cæsar made himself emperor of Rome. While professing reverence for the national traditions, James II destroyed religious liberty in England.

At its best, however, Curtis' style is as manifestly oral as that of Edmund Burke and as concrete:

> Thieves welcome him to the polls and offer him a choice, which he has done nothing to prevent, between Jeremy Diddler and Dick Turpin. The party-cries for which he is responsible are, "Turpin and Honesty," "Diddler and Reform." And within a few years, as a result of this indifference to the details of public duty, the most powerful politician in the Empire State of the Union was Jonathan Wild the Great, the captain of a band of plunderers.[7]

[5] See below, p. 188.
[6] See below, p. 187.
[7] See below, p. 188.

Perhaps Curtis' style was admirably suited to his genteel audiences and to his suasive purpose to keep the home fires burning rather than to burn down the city.

The Preparation

Curtis' most important speeches were written out and read, but read so well that the manuscript was not a barrier to communication. Sometimes he committed a speech to memory but when he did so his command of language was so perfect that he spoke without hesitation. The great majority of the occasions on which he spoke permitted him to avoid impromptu or extempore speaking and to prepare every item of the speech to the level of excellence that he sought. Perhaps this opportunity encouraged the tendency observed by Edward Cary, his biographer:

> If he did not cling to the usual forms of authorship, he was continually under the spell of the literary spirit; and he gave to all his productions unstintingly and almost unconsciously that which makes books literature,—absolute and loving fidelity to the best thought. His addresses are full of his love of scholarship and of the fruits of that love, and his ideal of the citizen was the citizen who regarded and performed his duties as a scholar should.[8]

The Delivery

The accounts of Curtis' speechmaking agree that he owed his effectiveness in large measure to his personal charm. Lacking the rugged virtues of a Phillips, or Sumner, or Benton, he spoke nevertheless with grace and dignity. He had the manly presence of an orator, the appearance of a man of quality, and a deep and musical voice that responded to every need for inflectional variety. He was not given to gestures nor to the studied action of the elocutionist. As he spoke he seemed to be absorbed by his ideas and by his audience. Indeed, to deny George William Curtis the rank of orator would be difficult, for he was indubitably a good man and one who spoke well.

[8] Cary, *op. cit.*, p. 331.

The Public Duty of
Educated Men

⚬⚬⚬

It is with diffidence that I rise to add any words of mine to the music
of these younger voices. This day, gentlemen of the graduating class,
is especially yours. It is a day of high hope and expectation, and the
counsels that fall from older lips should be carefully weighed, lest
they chill the ardor of a generous enthusiasm or stay the all-conquer-
ing faith of youth that moves the world. To those who, constantly
and actively engaged in a thousand pursuits, are still persuaded that
educated intelligence moulds States and leads mankind, no day in
the year is more significant, more inspiring, than this of the College
Commencement. It matters not at what college it may be celebrated.
It is the same at all. We stand here indeed beneath these college
walls, beautiful for situation, girt at this moment with the perfumed
splendor of midsummer, and full of tender memories and joyous
associations to those who hear me. But on this day, and on other
days, at a hundred other colleges, this summer sun beholds the same
spectacle of eager and earnest throngs. The faith that we hold, they
also cherish. It is the same God that is worshipped at the different
altars. It is the same benediction that descends upon every reverent
head and believing heart. In this annual celebration of faith in the
power and the responsibility of educated men, all the colleges in the
country, in whatever State, of whatever age, of whatever religious
sympathy or direction, form but one great Union University.

But the interest of the day is not that of mere study, of sound
scholarship as an end, of good books for their own sake, but of education as a power in human affairs, of educated men as an influence in
the commonwealth. "Tell me," said an American scholar of Goethe,[1]

From *Orations and Addresses of George William Curtis*, edited by Charles Eliot
Norton (New York: Harper & Brothers, 1894), Vol. I, pp. 261–285. Asterisked footnote on p. 187 is by Charles Eliot Norton.

[1] Johann Wolfgang von Goethe (1749–1832), German poet, dramatist, novelist, sci-

the many-sided, "what did he ever do for the cause of man?" The scholar, the poet, the philosopher, are men among other men. From these unavoidable social relations spring opportunities and duties. How do they use them? How do they discharge them? Does the scholar show in his daily walk that he has studied the wisdom of ages in vain? Does the poet sing of angelic purity and lead an unclean life? Does the philosopher peer into other worlds and fail to help this world upon its way? Four years before our civil war the same scholar—it was Theodore Parker[2]—said sadly, "If our educated men had done their duty, we should not now be in the ghastly condition we bewail." The theme of to-day seems to me to be prescribed by the occasion. It is the festival of the departure of a body of educated young men into the world. This company of picked recruits marches out with beating drums and flying colors to join the army. We who feel that our fate is gracious which allowed a liberal training, are here to welcome and to advise. On your behalf, Mr. President and gentlemen, with your authority, and with all my heart, I shall say a word to them and to you of the public duty of educated men in America.

I shall not assume, gentlemen graduates, for I know that it is not so, that what Dr. Johnson[3] says of the teachers of Rasselas and the princes of Abyssinia can be truly said of you in your happy valley— "The sages who instructed them told them of nothing but the miseries of public life, and described all beyond the mountains as regions of calamity where discord was always raging, and where man preyed upon man." The sages who have instructed you are American citizens. They know that patriotism has its glorious opportunities and its sacred duties. They have not shunned the one, and they have well performed the other. In the sharpest stress of our awful conflict, a clear voice of patriotic warning was heard from these peaceful academic shades, the voice of the venerated teacher whom this Uni-

---

entist, and philosopher. As the protégé of Charles Augustus, Duke of Saxe-Weimar, who ennobled him, Goethe spent most of his life (after 1775) at the court of Saxe-Weimar.

[2] Theodore Parker (1810–1860), theologian, was a reformer and leader in the anti-slavery movement who preached and wrote in liberal causes until his death.

[3] Samuel Johnson (1709–1784), author of *Rasselas* and other works, lexicographer, critic, and inspired conversationalist, dictated the standards of taste in literary London during the latter half of the eighteenth century.

versity still freshly deplores,* drawing from the wisdom of experience stored in his ample learning a lesson of startling cogency and power from the history of Greece for the welfare of America.

This was the discharge of a public duty by an educated man. It illustrated an indispensable condition of a progressive republic, the active, practical interest in politics of the most intelligent citizens. Civil and religious liberty in this country can be preserved only through the agency of our political institutions. But those institutions alone will not suffice. It is not the ship so much as the skilful sailing that assures the prosperous voyage. American institutions presuppose not only general honesty and intelligence in the people, but their constant and direct application to public affairs. Our system rests upon all the people, not upon a part of them, and the citizen who evades his share of the burden betrays his fellows. Our safety lies not in our institutions, but in ourselves. It was under the forms of the republic that Julius Cæsar made himself emperor of Rome. It was while professing reverence for the national traditions that James II.[4] was destroying religious liberty in England. To labor, said the old monks, is to pray. What we earnestly desire we earnestly toil for. That she may be prized more truly, heaven-eyed Justice flies from us, like the Tartar maid from her lovers, and she yields her embrace at last only to the swiftest and most daring of her pursuers.

By the words public duty I do not necessarily mean official duty, although it may include that. I mean simply that constant and active practical participation in the details of politics without which, upon the part of the most intelligent citizens, the conduct of public affairs falls under the control of selfish and ignorant, or crafty and venal men. I mean that personal attention—which, as it must be incessant, is often wearisome and even repulsive—to the details of politics, attendance at meetings, service upon committees, care and trouble and expense of many kinds, patient endurance of rebuffs,

---

* Professor Tayler Lewis died on May 11, 1877. The work referred to was his "Heroic Periods in a Nation's History."

[4] James II (1633–1701) served briefly (1685–1688) as king of England, Scotland, and Ireland. After the Glorious Revolution (1688) he was succeeded by William and Mary. His declarations of tolerance for the Catholic religion were construed by Anglican bishops—and others—as an attempt to subvert the Protestant religion in England.

chagrins, ridicules, disappointments, defeats—in a word, all those duties and services which, when selfishly and meanly performed, stigmatize a man as a mere politician; but whose constant, honorable, intelligent, and vigilant performance is the gradual building, stone by stone and layer by layer, of that great temple of self-restrained liberty which all generous souls mean that our government shall be.

Public duty in this country is not discharged, as is so often supposed, by voting. A man may vote regularly and still fail essentially of his political duty, as the Pharisee,[5] who gave tithes of all that he possessed and fasted three times in the week, yet lacked the very heart of religion. When an American citizen is content with voting merely, he consents to accept what is often a doubtful alternative. His first duty is to help shape the alternative. This, which was formerly less necessary, is now indispensable. In a rural community such as this country was a hundred years ago, whoever was nominated for office was known to his neighbors, and the consciousness of that knowledge was a conservative influence in determining nominations. But in the local elections of the great cities of to-day, elections that control taxation and expenditure, the mass of the voters vote in absolute ignorance of the candidates. The citizen who supposes that he does all his duty when he votes places a premium upon political knavery. Thieves welcome him to the polls and offer him a choice, which he has done nothing to prevent, between Jeremy Diddler and Dick Turpin.[6] The party-cries for which he is responsible are, "Turpin and Honesty," "Diddler and Reform." And within a few years, as a result of this indifference to the details of public duty, the most powerful politician in the Empire State of the Union was Jonathan Wild the Great,[7] the captain of a band of plunderers. I know it is said that the knaves have taken the honest men in a

---

[5] See Luke, XVIII, 10–13.

[6] In James Kenney's farce *Raising the Wind*, Jeremy Diddler was a small-time cheat who obtained money under false pretenses. Dick Turpin (1706–1739) was an English criminal, noted for horse-stealing.

[7] New York is known as the Empire State. Jonathan Wild (1683–1725), an English receiver of stolen goods and an entrepreneur of crime, was hanged at Tyburn. The reference to Wild, doubtless metaphorical, is probably intended to suggest William Marcy (Boss) Tweed (1823–1878), who plundered the city of New York.

188

net, and have contrived machinery which will inevitably grind only the grist of rascals. The answer is, that when honest men did once what they ought to do always, the thieves were netted and their machine was broken. To say that in this country the rogues must rule, is to defy history and to despair of the republic. It is to repeat the imbecile executive cries of sixteen years ago, "Oh, dear! the States have no right to go?" and, "Oh, dear! the nation has no right to help itself." Let the Union, stronger than ever and unstained with national wrong, teach us the power of patriotic virtue—and Ludlow Street jail console those who suppose that American politics must necessarily be a game of thieves and bullies.

If ignorance and corruption and intrigue control the primary meeting and manage the convention and dictate the nomination, the fault is in the honest and intelligent workshop and office, in the library and the parlor, in the church and the school. When these are as constant and faithful to their political rights as the slums and the grog-shops, the pool-rooms and the kennels; when the educated, industrious, temperate, thrifty citizens are as zealous and prompt and unfailing in political activity as the ignorant and venal and mischievous, or when it is plain that they cannot be roused to their duty, then, but not until then—if ignorance and corruption always carry the day—there can be no honest question that the republic has failed. But let us not be deceived. While good men sit at home, not knowing that there is anything to be done, nor caring to know; cultivating a feeling that politics are tiresome and dirty, and politicians vulgar bullies and bravoes; half persuaded that a republic is the contemptible rule of a mob, and secretly longing for a splendid and vigorous despotism—then remember it is not a government mastered by ignorance, it is a government betrayed by intelligence; it is not the victory of the slums, it is the surrender of the schools; it is not that bad men are brave, but that good men are infidels and cowards.[8]

But, gentlemen, when you come to address yourselves to these primary public duties, your first surprise and dismay will be the dis-

---

[8] The two paragraphs preceding have been much employed as exercises in the study of delivery of speeches. See, for example, James A. Winans, *Public Speaking*, rev. ed. (New York: Century, 1917), pp. 462–463.

covery that, in a country where education is declared to be the hope of its institutions, the higher education is often practically held to be almost a disadvantage. You will go from these halls to hear a very common sneer at college-bred men; to encounter a jealousy of education, as making men visionary and pedantic and impracticable; to confront a belief that there is something enfeebling in the higher education, and that self-made men, as they are called, are the sure stay of the State. But what is really meant by a self-made man? It is a man of native sagacity and strong character, who was taught, it is proudly said, only at the plough or the anvil or the bench. He was schooled by adversity, and was polished by hard attrition with men. He is Benjamin Franklin, the printer's boy, or Abraham Lincoln, the rail-splitter. They never went to college, but nevertheless, like Agamemnon,[9] they were kings of men, and the world blesses their memory.

So it does; but the sophistry here is plain enough, although it is not always detected. Great genius and force of character undoubtedly make their own career. But because Walter Scott was dull at school, is a parent to see with joy that his son is a dunce? Because Lord Chatham was of a towering conceit, must we infer that pompous vanity portends a comprehensive statesmanship that will fill the world with the splendor of its triumphs? Because Sir Robert Walpole gambled and swore and boozed at Houghton, are we to suppose that gross sensuality and coarse contempt of human nature are the essential secrets of a power that defended liberty against Tory intrigue and priestly politics? [10] Was it because Benjamin Franklin was not college-bred that he drew the lightning from heaven and tore the sceptre from the tyrant? Was it because Abraham Lincoln had little schooling that his great heart beat true to God and man, lifting him

[9] Benjamin Franklin (1706–1790), statesman, scientist, writer, publisher, and philosopher, was a self-taught printer. Abraham Lincoln (1809–1865), whose formal schooling amounted to less than one year, educated himself in literature, law, and politics before becoming President of the United States (1861). Agamemnon was, in legend, the leader of the Greek armies against Troy.

[10] Walter Scott (1771–1832), novelist and poet, was the author of *Ivanhoe* and *The Lady of the Lake*. William Pitt, first Earl of Chatham (1708–1778), British statesman, was an orator of the first rank. Robert Walpole, first Earl of Orford (1676–1745), became, in practice, the first Prime Minister in British history.

to free a race and die for his country? Because men naturally great have done great service in the world without advantages, does it follow that lack of advantage is the secret of success? Was Pericles a less sagacious leader of the State, during forty years of Athenian glory, because he was thoroughly accomplished in every grace of learning? Or, swiftly passing from the Athenian agora to the Boston town-meeting, behold Samuel Adams, tribune of New England against Old England, of America against Europe, of liberty against despotism.[11] Was his power enfeebled, his fervor chilled, his patriotism relaxed, by his college education? No, no; they were strengthened, kindled, confirmed. Taking his Master's degree one hundred and thirty-four years ago, thirty-three years before the Declaration of Independence, Samuel Adams, then twenty-one years old, declared in a Latin discourse—the first flashes of the fire that blazed afterwards in Faneuil Hall [12] and kindled America—that it is lawful to resist the supreme magistrate if the commonwealth cannot otherwise be preserved. In the very year that Jefferson[13] was born, the college boy, Samuel Adams, on a Commencement day like this, on an academical platform like this on which we stand, struck the key-note of American independence, which still stirs the heart of man with its music.

Or, within our own century, look at the great modern statesmen who have shaped the politics of the world. They were educated men; were they therefore visionary, pedantic, impracticable? Cavour, whose monument is United Italy—one from the Alps to Tarentum, from the lagoons of Venice to the gulf of Salerno; Bismarck, who has raised the German empire from a name to a fact; Gladstone, to-day the incarnate heart and conscience of England,[14]—they are the per-

[11] Pericles (495?–429 B.C.) was notable not only as a statesman but also as a patron of the arts. Samuel Adams (1722–1803), American patriot, drafted a protest against the Stamp Act.

[12] Faneuil Hall, Boston, was the meeting place of the American patriots who resisted the British rule.

[13] Thomas Jefferson (1743–1826), third President of the United States, was the principal author of the Declaration of Independence.

[14] Camillo Benso, Conte di Cavour (1810–1861), statesman primarily responsible for the unification of Italy under the house of Savoy, was scion of a noble family of Piedmont; Otto von Bismarck (1815–1898), German statesman, studied at the universities of Göttingen and Berlin before entering into a career of politics and diplomacy;

petual refutation of the sneer that high education weakens men for practical affairs. Trained themselves, such men know the value of training. All countries, all ages, all men, are their teachers. The broader their education, the wider the horizon of their thought and observation; the more affluent their resources, the more humane their policy. Would Samuel Adams have been a truer popular leader had he been less an educated man? Would Walpole the less truly have served his country had he been, with all his capacities, a man whom England could have revered and loved? Could Gladstone so sway England with his fervent eloquence, as the moon the tides, were he a gambling, swearing, boozing squire like Walpole? There is no sophistry more poisonous to the State, no folly more stupendous and demoralizing, than the notion that the purest character and the highest education are incompatible with the most commanding mastery of men and the most efficient administration of affairs.

Undoubtedly a practical and active interest in politics will lead you to party association and co-operation. Great public results—the repeal of the corn-laws[15] in England, the abolition of slavery in America—are due to that organization of effort and concentration of aim which arouse, instruct, and inspire the popular heart and will. This is the spring of party, and those who earnestly seek practical results instinctively turn to this agency of united action. But in this tendency, useful in the State as the fire upon the household hearth, lurks, as in that fire, the deadliest peril. Here is our republic—it is a ship with towering canvas spread, sweeping before the prosperous gale over a foaming and sparkling sea; it is a lightning train darting with awful speed along the edge of dizzy abysses and across bridges that quiver over unsounded gulfs. Because we are Americans, we have no peculiar charm, no magic spell, to stay the eternal laws. Our safety lies alone in cool self-possession, directing the forces of wind and wave and fire. If once the madness to which the excitement tends

---

William E. Gladstone (1809–1898), British statesman, graduated from Oxford University, where he achieved the rare eminence of a double first prize in classics and in mathematics.

[15] The corn laws in England represented an effort to revive agriculture by forbidding the importation of grain from abroad. The increase in the price of bread attributed to the corn laws worked hardships on the poor in manufacturing towns and gave rise to the Anti-Corn-Law League.

usurps control, the catastrophe is inevitable. And so deep is the conviction that sooner or later this madness must seize every republic that the most plausible suspicion of the permanence of the American government is founded in the belief that party spirit cannot be restrained. It is indeed a master passion, but its control is the true conservatism of the republic and of happy human progress; and it is men made familiar by education with the history of its ghastly catastrophes, men with the proud courage of independence, who are to temper by lofty action, born of that knowledge, the ferocity of party spirit.

The first object of concerted political action is the highest welfare of the country. But the conditions of party association are such that the means are constantly and easily substituted for the end. The sophistry is subtle and seductive. Holding the ascendency of his party essential to the national welfare, the zealous partisan merges patriotism in party. He insists that not to sustain the party is to betray the country, and against all honest doubt and reasonable hesitation and reluctance he vehemently urges that quibbles of conscience must be sacrificed to the public good; that wise and practical men will not be squeamish; that every soldier in the army cannot indulge his own whims; and that if the majority may justly prevail in determining the government, it must not be questioned in the control of a party.

This spirit adds moral coercion to sophistry. It denounces as a traitor him who protests against party tyranny, and it makes unflinching adherence to what is called regular party action the condition of the gratification of honorable political ambition. Because a man who sympathizes with the party aims refuses to vote for a thief, this spirit scorns him as a rat and a renegade. Because he holds to principle and law against party expediency and dictation, he is proclaimed as the betrayer of his country, justice, and humanity. Because he tranquilly insists upon deciding for himself when he must dissent from his party, he is reviled as a popinjay and a visionary fool. Seeking with honest purpose only the welfare of his country, the hot air around him hums with the cry of "the grand old party," "the traditions of the party," "loyalty to the party," "future of the party," "servant of the party"; and he sees and hears the gorged and portly money-changers in the temple usurping the very divinity of the God. Young hearts! be not dismayed. If ever any one of you shall be the man so denounced, do not forget that your own individual convictions are the whip of small cords which God has put into your hands to expel the blasphemers.

The same party spirit naturally denies the patriotism of its opponents. Identifying itself with the country, it regards all others as public enemies. This is substantially revolutionary politics. It is the condition of France, where, in its own words, the revolution is permanent. Instead of regarding the other party as legitimate opponents —in the English phrase, His Majesty's Opposition—lawfully seeking a different policy under the government, it decries that party as a conspiracy plotting the overthrow of the government itself. History is lurid with the wasting fires of this madness. We need not look to that of other lands. Our own is full of it. It is painful to turn to the opening years of the Union, and see how the great men whom we are taught to revere, and to whose fostering care the beginning of the republic was intrusted, fanned their hatred and suspicion of each other. Do not trust the flattering voices that whisper of a Golden Age behind us, and bemoan our own as a degenerate day. The castles of hope always shine along the horizon. Our fathers saw theirs where we are standing. We behold ours where our fathers stood. But pensive regret for the heroic past, like eager anticipation of the future, shows only that the vision of a loftier life forever allures the human soul. We think our fathers to have been wiser than we, and their day more enviable. But eighty years ago the Federalists abhorred their opponents as Jacobins,[16] and thought Robespierre and Marat[17] no worse than Washington's Secretary of State.[18] Their opponents

[16] The Federalists, under the leadership of Alexander Hamilton, organized the first party government in the United States. The Anti-Federalists, under Thomas Jefferson, became known as the Democratic-Republican and eventually as the Democratic Party. In party strife, the Federalists referred to Jefferson and his followers as "Jacobins" to suggest a supposed link with the French revolutionists.

[17] Maximilien François Marie Isidore de Robespierre (1758–1794), one of the leaders of the Reign of Terror during the French Revolution, died on the guillotine. Jean Paul Marat (1743–1793), French revolutionist and "friend of the people," was murdered by Charlotte Corday.

[18] Thomas Jefferson.

retorted that the Federalists were plotting to establish a monarchy by force of arms. The New England pulpit anathematized Tom Jefferson as an atheist and a satyr. Jefferson denounced John Jay[19] as a rogue, and the chief newspaper of the opposition, on the morning that Washington retired from the Presidency, thanked God that the country was now rid of the man who was the source of all its misfortunes. There is no mire in which party spirit wallows to-day with which our fathers were not befouled; and how little sincere the vituperation was, how shallow a fury, appears when Jefferson and Adams had retired from public life. Then they corresponded placidly and familiarly, each at last conscious of the other's fervent patriotism; and when they died, they were lamented in common by those who in their names had flown at each other's throat, as the patriarchal Castor and Pollux[20] of the pure age of our politics, now fixed as a constellation of hope in our heaven.

The same brutal spirit showed itself at the time of Andrew Johnson's[21] impeachment. Impeachment is a proceeding to be instituted only for great public reasons, which should, presumptively, command universal support. To prostitute the power of impeachment to a mere party purpose would readily lead to the reversal of the result of an election. But it was made a party measure. The party was to be whipped into its support; and when certain senators broke the party yoke upon their necks, and voted according to their convictions, as honorable men always will whether the party whips like it or not, one of the whippers-in exclaimed of a patriotism, the struggle of obedience to which cost one senator, at least, his life, "If there is anything worse than the treachery, it is the cant which pretends that it is the result of conscientious conviction; the pretence of a conscience is quite unbearable." This was the very acridity of

[19] John Jay (1745–1829), American statesman, was a member of the Continental Congresses. He held many important posts under both the Articles of Confederation and the Constitution, notably as the first Chief Justice of the United States Supreme Court (1789–1795).

[20] Castor and Pollux, in the Greek and Roman religions, were twins who could not be parted. Devoted to each other, they were immortalized by Zeus, who transformed them into the heavenly constellation Gemini.

[21] Andrew Johnson (1808–1875), seventeenth President of the United States, was impeached and acquitted on charges growing out of political controversy.

bigotry, which in other times and countries raised the cruel tribunal of the Inquisition[22] and burned opponents for the glory of God. The party madness that dictated these words, and the sympathy that approved them, were treason not alone to the country, but to well-ordered human society. Murder may destroy great statesmen, but corruption makes great States impossible, and this was an attempt at the most insidious corruption. The man who attempts to terrify a senator of the United States into casting a dishonest vote, by stigmatizing him as a hypocrite and devoting him to party hatred, is only a more plausible rascal than his opponent who gives Pat O'Flanagan a fraudulent naturalization paper or buys his vote with a dollar or a glass of whiskey. Whatever the offences of the President may have been, they were as nothing when compared with the party spirit which declared that it was tired of the intolerable cant of honesty. So the sneering Cavalier was tired of the cant of the Puritan conscience; but the conscience of which plumed Injustice and coroneted Privilege were tired has been for three centuries the invincible body-guard of civil and religious liberty.

Gentlemen, how dire a calamity the same party spirit was preparing for the country within a few months we can now perceive with amazement and with hearty thanksgiving for a great deliverance. The ordeal of last winter was the severest strain ever yet applied to republican institutions. It was a mortal strain along the very fibre of our system. It was not a collision of sections, nor a conflict of principles of civilization. It was a supreme and triumphant test of American patriotism. Greater than the declaration of independence by colonies hopelessly alienated from the crown and already in arms; greater than emancipation, as a military expedient, amid the throes of civil war, was the peaceful and reasonable consent of two vast parties—in a crisis plainly foreseen and criminally neglected, a crisis in which each party asserted its solution to be indisputable —to devise a lawful settlement of the tremendous contest, a settlement which, through furious storms of disappointment and rage, has been religiously respected. We are told that our politics are

[22] During the thirteenth century, the Inquisition originated in France where it was employed to root out the Albigensian heresy. Established in Spain (1478) under Torquemada, the Inquisition gained a reputation for monstrous cruelty.

mean—that already, in its hundredth year, the decadence of the American republic appears and the hope of the world is clouded. But tell me, scholars, in what high hour of Greece, when, as DeWitt Clinton[23] declared, "the herb-woman of Athens could criticise the phraseology of Demosthenes, and the meanest artisan could pronounce judgment on the works of Apelles and Phidias," [24] or at what proud epoch of imperial Rome, or millennial moment of the fierce Italian republics, was ever so momentous a party difference so wisely, so peacefully, so humanely composed? Had the sophistry of party prevailed; had each side resolved that not to insist upon its own claim at every hazard was what the mad party spirit of each side declared it to be—a pusillanimous surrender; had the spirit of Marius mastered one party and that of Sylla the other, this waving valley of the Mohawk[25] would not to-day murmur with the music of industry, these tranquil voices of scholars blending with its happy harvest-song; it would have smoked and roared with fraternal war, and this shuddering river would have run red through desolated meadows and by burning homes.

It is because these consequences are familiar to the knowledge of educated and thoughtful men that such men are constantly to assuage this party fire and to take care that party is always subordinated to patriotism. Perfect party discipline is the most dangerous weapon of party spirit, for it is the abdication of the individual judgment: it is the application to political parties of the Jesuit principle of implicit obedience.

It is for you to help break this withering spell. It is for you to

---

[23] DeWitt Clinton (1769–1828) was a founder and president (1817) of the New York Historical Society. He held many political offices in New York, including the governorship (1817–1821, 1825–1828).

[24] Apelles, active in the fourth century B.C., was court painter to Philip of Macedonia and to Alexander the Great; Phidias (500?–432? B.C.) is credited by tradition with the greatest sculpture of ancient Greece. Demosthenes (384?–322 B.C.) is often regarded as the greatest of orators.

[25] Caius Marius (155?–86 B.C.), plebeian general of Rome; Lucius Cornelius Sylla (138–78 B.C.), Roman general who defeated the forces of Marius, executed the captives, and systematically sought out and destroyed his opponents. Union College, where Curtis delivered this address, is located in Schenectady, New York, within the Mohawk Valley. Curtis' reference here is to the hard fought and contested election (1876) between Hayes and Tilden.

assert the independence and the dignity of the individual citizen, and to prove that party was made for the voter, not the voter for party. When you are angrily told that if you erect your personal whim against the regular party behest, you make representative government impossible by refusing to accept its conditions, hold fast by your own conscience and let the party go. There is not an American merchant who would send a ship to sea under the command of Captain Kidd, however skilful a sailor he might be. Why should he vote to send Captain Kidd to the legislature or to put him in command of the ship of state because his party directs? The party which to-day nominates Captain Kidd will to-morrow nominate Judas Iscariot,[26] and to-morrow, as to-day, party spirit will spurn you as a traitor for refusing to sell your master. "I tell you," said an ardent and well-meaning partisan, speaking of a closely contested election in another State—"I tell you it is a nasty State, and I hope we have done nasty work enough to carry it." But if your State has been carried by nasty means this year, success will require nastier next year, and the nastiest means will always carry it. The party may win, but the State will have been lost, for there are successes which are failures. When a man is sitting upon the bough of a tree and diligently sawing it off between himself and the trunk, he may succeed, but his success will break his neck.

The remedy for the constant excess of party spirit lies, and lies alone, in the courageous independence of the individual citizen. The only way, for instance, to procure the party nomination of good men, is for every self-respecting voter to refuse to vote for bad men. In the mediæval theology the devils feared nothing so much as the drop of holy water and the sign of the cross, by which they were exorcised. The evil spirits of party fear nothing so much as bolting and scratching. *In hoc signo vinces.*[27] If a farmer would reap a good crop, he scratches the weeds out of his field. If we would have good men upon the ticket, we must scratch bad men off. If the scratching breaks down the party, let it break; for the success of the party by

[26] William Kidd (1645?–1701), British privateer, convicted—perhaps wrongfully—of piracy; Judas Iscariot, who betrayed Jesus for thirty pieces of silver.
[27] "By this sign shalt thou conquer."

such means would break down the country. The evil spirits must be taught by means that they can understand. "Them fellers," said the captain of a canal-boat of his men—"them fellers never think you mean a thing until you kick 'em. They feel that, and understand."

It is especially necessary for us to perceive the vital relation of individual courage and character to the common welfare, because ours is a government of public opinion, and public opinion is but the aggregate of individual thought. We have the awful responsibility as a community of doing what we choose, and it is of the last importance that we choose to do what is wise and right. In the early days of the antislavery agitation a meeting was called at Faneuil Hall, in Boston, which a good-natured mob of sailors was hired to suppress. They took possession of the floor and danced breakdowns and shouted choruses and refused to hear any of the orators upon the platform. The most eloquent pleaded with them in vain. They were urged by the memories of the Cradle of Liberty, for the honor of Massachusetts, for their own honor as Boston boys, to respect liberty of speech. But they still laughed and sang and danced, and were proof against every appeal. At last a man suddenly arose from among themselves and began to speak. Struck by his tone and quaint appearance, and with the thought that he might be one of themselves, the mob became suddenly still. "Well, fellow-citizens," he said, "I wouldn't be quiet if I didn't want to." The words were greeted with a roar of delight from the mob, which supposed it had found its champion, and the applause was unceasing for five minutes, during which the strange orator tranquilly awaited his chance to continue. The wish to hear more hushed the tumult, and when the hall was still he resumed, "No, I certainly wouldn't stop if I hadn't a mind to; but then, if I were you, I *would* have a mind to!" The oddity of the remark and the earnestness of the tone held the crowd silent, and the speaker continued: "Not because this is Faneuil Hall, nor for the honor of Massachusetts, nor because you are Boston boys, but because you are men, and because honorable and generous men always love fair play." The mob was conquered. Free speech and fair play were secured. Public opinion can do what it has a mind to in this country. If it be debased and demoralized, it is the most odious of tyrants. It is Nero and Caligula[28] multiplied by millions. Can there then be a more stringent public duty for every man—and the greater the intelligence the greater the duty—than to take care, by all the influence he can command, that the country, the majority, public opinion, shall have a mind to do only what is just and pure and humane?

Gentlemen, leaving this college to take your part in the discharge of the duties of American citizenship, every sign encourages and inspires. The year that is now ending, the year that opens the second century of our history, has furnished the supreme proof that in a country of rigorous party division the purest patriotism exists. That and that only is the pledge of a prosperous future. No mere party fervor or party fidelity or party discipline could fully restore a country torn and distracted by the fierce debate of a century and the convulsions of civil war; nothing less than a patriotism all-embracing as the summer air could heal a wound so wide. I know—no man better—how hard it is for earnest men to separate their country from their party, or their religion from their sect. But nevertheless the welfare of the country is dearer than the mere victory of party, as truth is more precious than the interest of any sect. You will hear this patriotism scorned as an impracticable theory, as the dream of a cloister, as the whim of a fool. But such was the folly of the Spartan Leonidas, staying with his three hundred the Persian horde and teaching Greece the self-reliance that saved her. Such was the folly of the Swiss Arnold von Winkelried, gathering into his own breast the host of Austrian spears, making his dead body the bridge of victory for his countrymen. Such was the folly of the American Nathan Hale, gladly risking the seeming disgrace of his name, and grieving that he had but one life to give for his country.[29] Such are the beacon-

---

[28] Nero Claudius Caesar (A.D. 37–68), Roman emperor execrated for his cruelty, said to have fiddled while Rome burned; Caligula (A.D. 12–41), Roman emperor, probably insane, noted for irresponsible cruelty, said to have made his horse a Roman Consul.

[29] Leonidas (d. 480 B.C.), king of Sparta, died bravely with his soldiers at Thermopylae; Arnold von Winkelried (d. 1386) is credited with a heroic and self-sacrificial action that enabled the Swiss to defeat the Austrians at Sempach; Nathan Hale (1755–1776), American schoolmaster who volunteered to obtain information concerning enemy forces, is remembered for the statement he is reputed to have made on the gallows: "I only regret that I have but one life to lose for my country."

lights of a pure patriotism that burn forever in men's memories and answer each other through the illuminated ages. And of the same grandeur, in less heroic and poetic form, was the patriotism of Sir Robert Peel [30] in recent history. He was the leader of a great party and the prime minister of England. The character and necessity of party were as plain to him as to any man. But when he saw that the national welfare demanded the repeal of the corn-laws which he had always supported, he did not quail. Amply avowing the error of a life and the duty of avowing it—foreseeing the probable overthrow of his party and the bitter execration that must fall upon him, he tranquilly did his duty. With the eyes of England fixed upon him in mingled amazement, admiration, and indignation, he rose in the House of Commons to perform as great a service as any English statesman ever performed for his country, and in closing his last speech in favor of the repeal, describing the consequences that its mere prospect had produced, he loftily exclaimed: "Where there was dissatisfaction, I see contentment; where there was turbulence, I see there is peace; where there was disloyalty, I see there is loyalty. I see a disposition to confide in you, and not to agitate questions that are the foundations of your institutions." When all was over, when he had left office, when his party was out of power and the fury of party execration against him was spent, his position was greater and nobler than it had ever been. Cobden said of him, "Sir Robert Peel has lost office, but he has gained a country"; and Lord Dalling[31] said of him, what may truly be said of Washington, "Above all parties, himself a party, he had trained his own mind into a disinterested sympathy with the intelligence of his country."

A public spirit so lofty is not confined to other ages and lands. You are conscious of its stirrings in your souls. It calls you to courageous service, and I am here to bid you obey the call. Such pa-

[30] Sir Robert Peel (1788–1850), British statesman, in his day achieved a dubious reputation as a turncoat. His actions in gaining Catholic emancipation and repeal of the corn laws are now generally thought to have been both wise and courageous.

[31] Richard Cobden (1804–1865) devoted himself to the Anti-Corn-Law League. A friend of John Bright, Cobden is said to have persuaded Robert Peel to favor repeal of the corn laws. William Henry Lytton Earle Bulwer, Baron Dalling and Bulwer (1801–1872), statesman and diplomat, had a distinguished career in Parliament and as Ambassador to the United States.

triotism may be ours. Let it be your parting vow that it shall be yours. Bolingbroke[32] described a patriot king in England; I can imagine a patriot president in America. I can see him indeed the choice of a party, and called to administer the government when sectional jealousy is fiercest and party passion most inflamed. I can imagine him seeing clearly what justice and humanity, the national law and the national welfare require him to do, and resolved to do it. I can imagine him patiently enduring not only the mad cry of party hate, the taunt of "recreant" and "traitor," of "renegade" and "coward," but what is harder to bear, the amazement, the doubt, the grief, the denunciation, of those as sincerely devoted as he to the common welfare. I can imagine him pushing firmly on, trusting the heart, the intelligence, the conscience of his countrymen, healing angry wounds, correcting misunderstandings, planting justice on surer foundations, and, whether his party rise or fall, lifting his country heavenward to a more perfect union, prosperity, and peace. This is the spirit of a patriotism that girds the commonwealth with the resistless splendor of the moral law—the invulnerable panoply of States, the celestial secret of a great nation and a happy people.

[32] Henry St. John, Viscount Bolingbroke (1678–1751), English statesman, orator, and writer, is thought to have influenced George III through his *Idea of a Patriot King.*

∫ Critical Analysis

One of the signs of the practiced orator is the ability to use the situation itself to lend immediacy to the idea. How does Curtis demonstrate this ability in his address to a graduating class? What is the effect of his introductory comments on commencement exercises? How does he use national events to find a common ground with the audience?

∫

The commencement occasion imposes unusual requirements on a speaker because of the double audience—the graduates themselves and the friends and relatives who have come to witness the conferring of the degrees. How has Curtis sought to reach both of these audiences in his selection of thesis and his development of the idea? What assumptions about the audience seem to underlie his choice of subject and selection of material?

∫

In advancing a positive thesis a speaker may recognize the advisability of counteracting misconceptions that could interfere with the response of the audience to the idea. To what extent does Curtis use refutation to dispose of possible misapprehensions? Does he depend chiefly on direct attacks on premises (denial) and on the pointing out of logical fallacies, or does he rely on indirect refutation? In several places he uses the word *sophistry* in introducing an argument. In these instances, what kind of refutation does he employ? Does the total effect of the speech seem refutative, or does the constructive argument dominate?

∫

In his setting forth of arguments, how careful is Curtis to define terms? How does he, for example, define *public duty? educated men? party loyalty?* To what extent are these definitions intrinsic to his idea? What kind of support does he offer? How well does he bear out Aristotle's statement that a convincing speaker rests his arguments on sound reasons and examples?

§

Fashions in speaking style change with time. What evidence in the commencement address suggests that audience tastes in 1877 differ from those of today? What differences in syntax and vocabulary do you observe? in the length and rhythm of the sentences? in the use of allusions? in the metaphor? Would you say that the ideas developed seem equally "dated," or are the differences chiefly in style of expression?

§

Gordon Milne states the gist of "The Public Duty of Educated Men" as follows: "One's public duty is not discharged by voting only. The college-bred man must enter the political arena and strive to rid it of thieves and bullies and incompetents." [1] What would you add to this summary statement?

§

In his essay on Curtis, Carroll C. Arnold opines that in "The Public Duty of Educated Men" Curtis did not ". . . adequately support the basic inference that wisdom and righteousness in public policy are peculiarly dependent upon the influence exerted by educated men." [2] What are your grounds for agreement—or disagreement—with Arnold?

§ SUGGESTIONS FOR FURTHER READING

As an essayist and littérateur, George William Curtis dealt with a wide range of topics relevant in his time but less so today. His *Literary and Social Essays* (New York: Harper & Brothers, 1895) deals with nineteenth-century authors, including Emerson, Hawthorne, Longfellow, Holmes, and Irving. For the current generation of students perhaps the most readable of his legacies is *Ars Recti Vivendi* (New York: Harper & Brothers, 1898). This publication, a collection of essays from the "Easy Chair"

[1] *George William Curtis: The Genteel Tradition* (Bloomington: Indiana University Press, 1956), pp. 169–170.
[2] In Marie Kathryn Hochmuth, ed., A *History and Criticism of American Public Address* (New York: Longmans, Green, 1955), Vol. III, p. 163.

column of *Harper's Magazine,* offers to college students admonitions and observations on such topics as women's dress, tobacco, and extravagance that will doubtless seem quaint to undergraduates today. Other essays from the "Easy Chair" are perhaps more relevant to current interests. See, for example, "Wendell Phillips at Harvard: 1881" in *From the Easy Chair,* First Series (New York: Harper & Brothers, 1891), or "National Nominating Convention," *From the Easy Chair,* Second Series (New York: Harper & Brothers, 1894), or "Beecher in His Pulpit after the Death of Lincoln," *From the Easy Chair,* Third Series (New York: Harper & Brothers, 1894). Other essays by Curtis appear in *The Potiphar Papers* (New York: Harper & Brothers, 1858).

His novels, never remarkably well received, are still available. Doubtless the best single source for George William Curtis' work, however, will be found in Charles Eliot Norton's three-volume edition of *Orations and Addresses of George William Curtis* (New York: Harper & Brothers, 1894). These volumes include the texts of Curtis' major speeches from 1856 to 1892, the year of his death. His speeches on the value of higher education and the leadership of educated men are found in Volume I. His eulogies on Charles Sumner, James A. Garfield, and Wendell Phillips in Volume II will repay time and thought expended. The final volume contains his addresses concerning patronage, the spoils system, and machine politics, which, taken together, constitute his case for civil service reform.

The best single book concerning George William Curtis, and the most useful, is Gordon Milne's *George William Curtis: The Genteel Tradition* (Bloomington: Indiana University Press, 1956). It contains an excellent bibliography. Some students may wish to consult *George William Curtis* (Boston: Houghton Mifflin, 1894) by Edward Cary; and *Early Letters of George William Curtis to John S. Dwight* (New York: Harper & Brothers, 1898) edited by George Willis Cooke. The latter volume includes an account of Curtis' life at Brook Farm and his attitude toward transcendentalism (pp. 1–103). The authoritative treatise on Curtis' speechmaking is Carroll C. Arnold, "George William Curtis," in Marie Kathryn Hochmuth, ed., *A History and Criticism of American Public Address* (New York: Longmans, Green, 1955), Vol. III, pp. 133–174.

Franklin Delano Roosevelt

℈ | ℈

> "So, first of all, let me assert my firm belief that the only thing we have to fear is fear itself—nameless, unreasoning, unjustified terror which paralyzes needed efforts to convert retreat into advance." [1]
> —FRANKLIN DELANO ROOSEVELT

BIOGRAPHICAL SKETCH

Franklin Delano Roosevelt, thirty-first President of the United States, was born January 30, 1882, and died April 12, 1945. As the only son of James and Sara Delano Roosevelt, members of the Hudson Valley aristocracy, Roosevelt received his early education under private tutors, with occasional trips abroad. He attended Groton and then Harvard, from which he graduated in 1904. He also studied at the Columbia University Law School. In 1905 he married Anna Eleanor Roosevelt, his distant cousin and a niece of Theodore Roosevelt. Five children (Anna, James, Elliott, Franklin D., Jr., and John) were born to the marriage. After passing his bar examination in 1907, Roosevelt began to practice law in New York City. In 1910 he entered a career in politics that was to absorb the rest of his life, except for the years spent in the struggle to recover from poliomyelitis, with which he was stricken in 1921.

Roosevelt was elected to the New York State Senate in 1910, in opposition to Tammany Hall, and in 1912, likewise in opposition to Tammany Hall, he helped to organize Democrats in support of Woodrow Wilson's candidacy for the presidency. From 1913 to 1920

NOTE: The sources for this essay will be found in the section Suggestions for Further Reading, pp. 219–221, and in the contemporary newspaper accounts. The editors have also drawn on their own recollections of events and observations made at the time.

---

[1] Franklin D. Roosevelt, "First Inaugural Address, March 4, 1933," *Inaugural Addresses of the Presidents of the United States from George Washington 1789 to Lyndon Baines Johnson 1965*, 89th Congress, 1st Session, House Document No. 51 (Washington, D.C.: Government Printing Office, 1965), p. 235.

he served in Wilson's cabinet as Assistant Secretary of the Navy, and in 1920 he was defeated as the candidate of the Democratic Party for Vice-President. With the devoted assistance of his wife and Louis M. Howe, he maintained a flourishing correspondence during convalescence from the attack of poliomyelitis. His nominating speeches for Governor Alfred E. Smith at the Democratic Conventions in 1924 and 1928 kept him in the public eye; and his election as Governor of New York made him an obvious possibility for the Democratic presidential nomination in 1932. He was elected in 1932 and again in 1936, 1940, and 1944 for an unprecedented four terms.

In his first hundred days in office, Roosevelt sponsored much of the basic legislation known as the New Deal. With the outbreak of World War II in Europe, domestic issues were overshadowed by foreign policy; and with the Japanese attack on Pearl Harbor (December 7, 1941), Roosevelt—and the nation—devoted full energy to the prosecution of the war. Roosevelt, a strong wartime leader, employed all the dramatic appeal of his persuasion to keep the country in solid support of the war effort. He worked in close collaboration with Winston Churchill and the British, in spite of differences in policy, and rallied support for the organization of the United Nations. Although Roosevelt attempted to achieve similar collaboration with the Russians, he was not successful; in consequence, his hopes for a peaceful world order with cooperation between the Soviet Union and the West following World War II were largely frustrated.

Franklin Roosevelt was a remarkable national leader, both in peace and in war. At least partly through his speeches, he captured the loyalty of the great majority of the American people and kept it throughout his years in office. This loyalty he was able so to translate into electoral votes that out of the total of 531, his opposition was able to claim only 59 in 1932, 8 in 1936, 82 in 1940, and 99 in 1944. As a master of the art of politics, Roosevelt has not been surpassed in the United States.

THE SPEAKER

Franklin D. Roosevelt was the first great master of the microphone. Some of the orators of the old school—those inclined to wave their arms and shout—found themselves lost in the new era of radio; but Franklin Roosevelt from the first found broadcasting a comfortable medium. More handicapped physically by his paralysis than most Americans realized, nevertheless he did not spare himself in campaigning. As he reported,[2] on his re-entering politics, even before he began speaking in his own campaign for Governor of New York in 1928, he had made speeches in behalf of Alfred E. Smith's candidacy for the presidency in Atlanta, Manchester, and Columbus, Georgia; in Cleveland, Ohio; in Boston; and in New York City. In October 1928, during his campaign for the governorship,[3] Roosevelt, according to his own account, made twenty-one speeches in the towns and cities of New York.

That Roosevelt was a vigorous campaigner can hardly be questioned; but formal speechmaking is not the whole of a campaign. Owing to his handicap, he was not able, as other candidates were, to go out and meet people in the shops, in the factories, and in the streets. He could never have followed the schedule that Estes Kefauver, for example, was later to maintain in his candidacies. The microphone, sending Roosevelt's warm and friendly voice over the nation's airwaves, created an illusion of intimacy that politicians in other days could obtain only by the handshake and the look in the eye. People throughout the United States —and later, during World War II, in other countries as well—thought, "I know that man. He is talking to me." Through his voice he became a living presence in millions of homes. It is thus possible to suppose that Franklin Roosevelt as a politician, or statesman, was made, or saved, by the microphone; for neither Roosevelt nor the Democratic Party leaders failed to exploit the advantage of his persuasive voice. From the first "Fireside Chat" on March 12, 1933, until his last appearance, he

---

[2] Samuel I. Rosenman, compiler, *The Public Papers and Addresses of Franklin D. Roosevelt* (Vols. 1–5, New York: Random House, 1938; Vols. 6–9, New York: Macmillan, 1941; Vols. 10–13, New York: Harper & Brothers, 1950), Vol. I, p. 11.

[3] *Ibid.*, p. 12.

was intimately in contact with the American people in a way unknown to any of his predecessors in the presidency. During the Roosevelt years—1933–1945—speechmaking changed. It was never to be the same again. Today the dominant medium is television, and indubitably the medium affects the message.

THE AUDIENCE AND THE OCCASION

On March 4, 1933, when Roosevelt addressed the people of the United States by radio on taking his oath of office as President of the United States, the nation was beset by ills that can hardly be comprehended by young people today. A long continuing economic depression on the farms had overtaken all areas of the economy with the dramatic stock market crash in 1929. As Roosevelt spoke, all banks were closed. Stores, well stocked with groceries, would not accept bank checks in payment for them. Practically all financial transactions had ceased. As one old gentleman said, on the day before the inauguration, "A millionaire today is anybody who has got as much as five honest-to-God dollars in his pocket." Strong, able, competent men were out of work—either because, like many young men coming out of the colleges, they could not find jobs; or because their employers, bankrupt or faced with bankruptcy, had discharged them. Nationwide social security did not exist; unemployment insurance, except in a few isolated instances, was unknown. Men stood for blocks waiting to be fed at soup kitchens. Men and women sold apples on the street corners of the cities and begged for customers. A sick humor developed concerning Wall Street brokers jumping out of skyscraper windows. The task facing the new President of the United States was thus twofold: first, so to speak to the people that a level of confidence would be invited; and, second, to take long-range measures that would restore the economy. Some of President Roosevelt's critics aver that he was more successful with the first task than with the second. Be that as it may, no one who heard him speak in March 1933 and observed the changes wrought in the public psychology is likely to express doubts concerning the power of the spoken word.

THE SPEECH

Roosevelt, already a practiced politician and public speaker, knew very well what his speech must accomplish. As he explained, "I sought principally in the . . . Inaugural Address to banish, so far as possible, the fear of the present and of the future which held the American people and the American spirit in its grasp." According to Judge Samuel I. Rosenman, Roosevelt wrote the first draft of the first inaugural address in his own hand at Hyde Park on February 27, 1933. Only a few changes were made. The first sentence Roosevelt himself added at the last minute while waiting to deliver the speech. The most famous sentence: "So, first of all, let me assert my firm belief that the only thing we have to fear is fear itself—nameless, unreasoning, unjustified terror which paralyzes needed efforts to convert retreat into advance" [4] was also interpolated after the first draft was written.

Perhaps the most striking—and to some listeners the most reassuring—words in the speech, however, were those that came later:

> But in the event that the Congress shall fail to take one of these two courses, and in the event that the national emergency is still critical, I shall not evade the clear course of duty that will then confront me. I shall ask the Congress for the one remaining instrument to meet the crisis—broad Executive power to wage a war against the emergency, as great as the power that would be given to me if we were in fact invaded by a foreign foe.[5]

President Roosevelt closed his address with three sentences that pious folk took to be a prayer. Perhaps it was: "In this dedication of a Nation we humbly ask the blessing of God. May He protect each and every one of us. May He guide me in the days to come." [6]

Destined to be an energetic president, Franklin D. Roosevelt did not depend on speeches, or even on prayer, alone. On the day following the inaugural address, he called the Congress into Extraordinary Session.

[4] See below, p. 212.
[5] See below, p. 216.
[6] See below, p. 217.

First Inaugural Address

I am certain that my fellow Americans expect that on my induction into the Presidency I will address them with a candor and a decision which the present situation of our Nation impels.[1] This is preeminently the time to speak the truth, the whole truth, frankly and boldly. Nor need we shrink from honestly facing conditions in our country to-day. This great Nation will endure as it has endured, will revive and will prosper. So, first of all, let me assert my firm belief that the only thing we have to fear is fear itself—nameless, unreasoning, unjustified terror which paralyzes needed efforts to convert retreat into advance.[2] In every dark hour of our national life a leadership of frankness and vigor has met with that understanding and support of the people themselves which is essential to victory. I am convinced that you will again give that support to leadership in these critical days.

In such a spirit on my part and on yours we face our common difficulties. They concern, thank God, only material things. Values have shrunken to fantastic levels; taxes have risen; our ability to pay has fallen; government of all kinds is faced by serious curtailment of income; the means of exchange are frozen in the currents of trade; the withered leaves of industrial enterprise lie on every side; farmers find no markets for their produce; the savings of many years in thousands of families are gone.

More important, a host of unemployed citizens face the grim

From *Inaugural Addresses of the Presidents of the United States from George Washington 1789 to Lyndon Baines Johnson 1965*, 89th Congress, 1st Session, House Document No. 51 (Washington, D.C.: Government Printing Office, 1965), pp. 235–239.

---

[1] As Roosevelt delivered his first inaugural address on March 4, 1933, he confronted an economic crisis unprecedented in the history of the United States. The great depression that began with the stock market crash on "Black Friday" in October 1929 had continued unabated for more than three years.

[2] The phrase "the only thing we have to fear is fear itself" has been much quoted since 1933.

problem of existence, and an equally great number toil with little return. Only a foolish optimist can deny the dark realities of the moment.

Yet our distress comes from no failure of substance. We are stricken by no plague of locusts. Compared with the perils which our forefathers conquered because they believed and were not afraid, we have still much to be thankful for. Nature still offers her bounty and human efforts have multiplied it. Plenty is at our doorstep, but a generous use of it languishes in the very sight of the supply. Primarily this is because the rulers of the exchange of mankind's goods have failed, through their own stubbornness and their own incompetence, have admitted their failure, and abdicated. Practices of the unscrupulous money changers stand indicted in the court of public opinion, rejected by the hearts and minds of men.

True they have tried, but their efforts have been cast in the pattern of an outworn tradition. Faced by failure of credit they have proposed only the lending of more money. Stripped of the lure of profit by which to induce our people to follow their false leadership, they have resorted to exhortations, pleading tearfully for restored confidence. They know only the rules of a generation of self-seekers. They have no vision, and when there is no vision the people perish.

The money changers have fled from their high seats in the temple of our civilization.[3] We may now restore that temple to the ancient truths. The measure of the restoration lies in the extent to which we apply social values more noble than mere monetary profit.

Happiness lies not in the mere possession of money; it lies in the joy of achievement, in the thrill of creative effort. The joy and moral stimulation of work no longer must be forgotten in the mad chase of evanescent profits. These dark days will be worth all they cost us if they teach us that our true destiny is not to be ministered unto but to minister to ourselves and to our fellow men.

Recognition of the falsity of material wealth as the standard of success goes hand in hand with the abandonment of the false belief that public office and high political position are to be valued only by the standards of pride of place and personal profit; and there must be an end to a conduct in banking and in business which too often

[3] See Mark, XI, 15.

has given to a sacred trust the likeness of callous and selfish wrong-doing. Small wonder that confidence languishes, for it thrives only on honesty, on honor, on the sacredness of obligations, on faithful protection, on unselfish performance; without them it can not live.

Restoration calls, however, not for changes in ethics alone. This Nation asks for action, and action now.

Our greatest primary task is to put people to work. This is no un-solvable problem if we face it wisely and courageously. It can be accomplished in part by direct recruiting by the Government itself, treating the task as we would treat the emergency of a war, but at the same time, through this employment, accomplishing greatly needed projects to stimulate and reorganize the use of our natural resources.

Hand in hand with this we must frankly recognize the overbalance of population in our industrial centers and, by engaging on a national scale in a redistribution, endeavor to provide a better use of the land for those best fitted for the land. The task can be helped by definite efforts to raise the values of agricultural products and with this the power to purchase the output of our cities. It can be helped by pre-venting realistically the tragedy of the growing loss through fore-closure of our small homes and our farms. It can be helped by in-sistence that the Federal, State, and local governments act forthwith on the demand that their cost be drastically reduced. It can be helped by the unifying of relief activities which to-day are often scattered, uneconomical, and unequal. It can be helped by national planning for and supervision of all forms of transportation and of communica-tions and other utilities which have a definitely public character. There are many ways in which it can be helped, but it can never be helped merely by talking about it. We must act and act quickly.

Finally, in our progress toward a resumption of work we require two safeguards against a return of the evils of the old order; there must be a strict supervision of all banking and credits and invest-ments; there must be an end to speculation with other people's money, and there must be provision for an adequate but sound cur-rency.[4]

[4] One of Roosevelt's first acts as President was to close all banks and to assure the public that only those that were financially sound would be permitted to open their

There are the lines of attack. I shall presently urge upon a new Congress in special session detailed measures for their fulfillment, and I shall seek the immediate assistance of the several States.[5]

Through this program of action we address ourselves to putting our own national house in order and making income balance outgo. Our international trade relations, though vastly important, are in point of time and necessity secondary to the establishment of a sound national economy. I favor as a practical policy the putting of first things first. I shall spare no effort to restore world trade by international economic readjustment, but the emergency at home can not wait on that accomplishment.

The basic thought that guides these specific means of national recovery is not narrowly nationalistic. It is the insistence, as a first consideration, upon the interdependence of the various elements in all parts of the United States—a recognition of the old and permanently important manifestation of the American spirit of the pioneer. It is the way to recovery. It is the immediate way. It is the strongest assurance that the recovery will endure.

In the field of world policy I would dedicate this Nation to the policy of the good neighbor—the neighbor who resolutely respects himself and, because he does so, respects the rights of others—the neighbor who respects his obligations and respects the sanctity of his agreements in and with a world of neighbors.

If I read the temper of our people correctly, we now realize as we have never realized before our interdependence on each other; that we can not merely take but we must give as well; that if we are to go forward, we must move as a trained and loyal army willing to sacrifice for the good of a common discipline, because without such discipline no progress is made, no leadership becomes effective. We are, I know, ready and willing to submit our lives and property to

doors again. Banking laws were tightened, but not until 1934 did Congress enact legislation establishing the Securities and Exchange Commission.

[5] Immediately after his inauguration, President Roosevelt called Congress into a special session in which he urged the enactment of legislation designed to combat the depression and to set in motion the reforms known as the "New Deal." The special session of Congress established a number of emergency organizations, including the National Recovery Administration, the Civilian Conservation Corps, and the Public Works Administration.

such discipline, because it makes possible a leadership which aims at a larger good. This I propose to offer, pledging that the larger purposes will bind upon us all as a sacred obligation with a unity of duty hitherto evoked only in time of armed strife.

With this pledge taken, I assume unhesitatingly the leadership of this great army of our people dedicated to a disciplined attack upon our common problems.

Action in this image and to this end is feasible under the form of government which we have inherited from our ancestors. Our Constitution is so simple and practical that it is possible always to meet extraordinary needs by changes in emphasis and arrangement without loss of essential form. That is why our constitutional system has proved itself the most superbly enduring political mechanism the modern world has produced. It has met every stress of vast expansion of territory, of foreign wars, of bitter internal strife, of world relations.

It is to be hoped that the normal balance of executive and legislative authority may be wholly adequate to meet the unprecedented task before us. But it may be that an unprecedented demand and need for undelayed action may call for temporary departure from that normal balance of public procedure.

I am prepared under my constitutional duty to recommend the measures that a stricken nation in the midst of a stricken world may require. These measures, or such other measures as the Congress may build out of its experience and wisdom, I shall seek, within my constitutional authority, to bring to speedy adoption.

But in the event that the Congress shall fail to take one of these two courses, and in the event that the national emergency is still critical, I shall not evade the clear course of duty that will then confront me. I shall ask the Congress for the one remaining instrument to meet the crisis—broad Executive power to wage a war against the emergency, as great as the power that would be given to me if we were in fact invaded by a foreign foe.

For the trust reposed in me I will return the courage and the devotion that befit the time. I can do no less.

We face the arduous days that lie before us in the warm courage of the national unity; with the clear consciousness of seeking old and precious moral values; with the clean satisfaction that comes from the stern performance of duty by old and young alike. We aim at the assurance of a rounded and permanent national life.

We do not distrust the future of essential democracy. The people of the United States have not failed. In their need they have registered a mandate that they want direct, vigorous action. They have asked for discipline and direction under leadership. They have made me the present instrument of their wishes. In the spirit of the gift I take it.

In this dedication of a Nation we humbly ask the blessing of God. May He protect each and every one of us. May He guide me in the days to come.

§ Critical Analysis

Roosevelt states in the "First Inaugural Address" that

> Our greatest primary task is to put people to work. This is no unsolvable problem if we face it wisely and courageously. It can be accomplished in part by direct recruiting by the Government itself, treating the task as we would treat the emergency of a war. . . .

To what extent is the analogy between the peacetime and a wartime emergency acceptable and convincing?

§

At his first press conference, on March 8, 1933, President Roosevelt described the policy he would follow with the press. He said, "There will be a great many questions you will ask that I don't know enough about to answer." [1] As you read the "First Inaugural Address," do you discover any questions that President Roosevelt appeared not to approach with confidence?

§

In the field of foreign policy, President Roosevelt dedicated "this Nation to the policy of the good neighbor." Can you discover, from your study of American history for the period 1933–1945, whether the policy was carried out as announced?

§

Was it wise, was it proper, for the President of the United States to conclude his address with an appeal for "the blessing of God"?

§

President Roosevelt declared, "Happiness lies not in the mere possession of money; it lies in the joy of achievement, in the thrill of creative effort." What support can be found for the statement?

[1] Samuel I. Rosenman, compiler, *The Public Papers and Addresses of Franklin D. Roosevelt* (Vols. 1–5, New York: Random House, 1938; Vols. 6–9, New York: Macmillan, 1941; Vols. 10–13, New York: Harper & Brothers, 1950), Vol. II, p. 30.

§ SUGGESTIONS FOR FURTHER READING

In *Franklin D. Roosevelt: The Apprenticeship* (Boston: Little, Brown, 1952), Frank Freidel, whose three volumes are the obvious first and best reading concerning Roosevelt, sets forth in a bibliographical note (Vol. I, p. 373) a problem that vexes anyone endeavoring to deal with this subject: "No career in American history could be more amply documented than that of Franklin D. Roosevelt, the number of memoirs concerning him is so large, and the body of manuscripts he left so enormous and full. . . . There are an estimated forty tons of paper."

From this embarrassment of riches, the student of Roosevelt's speech-making must necessarily make choices. Excluding certain waspish and unsupported attacks on Roosevelt, the student will do well to examine a selection of the many personal reminiscences, including some by newspaper reporters, who are often the most perceptive observers. A list of such books might well include the following: Gerald W. Johnson, *Roosevelt: Dictator or Democrat?* (New York: Harper & Brothers, 1941); Ernest K. Lindley, *Halfway with Roosevelt* (New York: Viking, 1936); Merriman Smith, *Thank You, Mr. President: A White House Notebook* (New York: Harper & Brothers, 1946); Jonathan Daniels, *The End of Innocence* (Philadelphia: Lippincott, 1954); William D. Hassett, with an introduction by Jonathan Daniels, *Off the Record with F. D. R.: 1942–1945* (New Brunswick, N.J.: Rutgers University Press, 1958); and Michael F. Reilly as told to William J. Slocum, *Reilly of the White House* (New York: Simon and Schuster, 1947).

Three books—two by Roosevelt's sons and one by his wife—call for special mention: Elliott Roosevelt, *As He Saw It* (New York: Duell, Sloan and Pearce, 1946); James Roosevelt and Sidney Shalett, *Affectionately, F. D. R.: A Son's Story of a Lonely Man* (New York: Harcourt, Brace, 1959); and Eleanor Roosevelt, *This I Remember* (New York: Harper & Brothers, 1949). Those interested in Roosevelt's antecedents may consult Allen Churchill, *The Roosevelts* (New York: Harper & Row, 1965).

The relations of Roosevelt with certain persons around him were close, and their accounts are helpful to a proper understanding of the man. Among such accounts, the following should be included: Alfred B. Rollins, Jr., *Roosevelt and Howe* (New York: Knopf, 1962); Grace G. Tully, *F. D. R.: My Boss*, with a foreword by William O. Douglas (New York: Scribner's, 1949); Samuel I. Rosenman, *Working with Roosevelt*

(New York: Harper & Brothers, 1952); Frances Perkins, *The Roosevelt I Knew* (New York: Viking, 1946); Vice-Admiral Ross T. McIntire, in collaboration with George Creel, *White House Physician* (New York: G. P. Putnam's, 1946); Raymond Moley, *After Seven Years* (New York: Harper & Brothers, 1939); Robert E. Sherwood, *Roosevelt and Hopkins: An Intimate History* (New York: Harper & Brothers, 1950); and Charles Michelson, *The Ghost Talks* (New York: G. P. Putnam's, 1944).

Roosevelt's presidency and the policies he enunciated have had the attention of some scholars. As one of his last endeavors, Charles A. Beard wrote *President Roosevelt and the Coming of the War 1941: A Study in Appearances and Realities* (New Haven: Yale University Press, 1948). James MacGregor Burns' *Roosevelt: The Lion and the Fox* (New York: Harcourt, Brace, 1956) treats Roosevelt in the context of politics and partisan leadership. The book is a study of politics in the United States as well as of Roosevelt. *The Roosevelt Leadership 1933–1945* (Philadelphia: Lippincott, 1955) by Edgar Eugene Robinson focuses on Roosevelt as a leader of men in times of crisis.

Among other scholarly studies of Roosevelt's policies and politics, in the context of his times, these should be noted: Denis W. Brogan, *The Era of Franklin D. Roosevelt: A Chronicle of the New Deal and Global War* (New Haven: Yale University Press, 1950); Bernard Bellush, *Franklin D. Roosevelt as Governor of New York* (New York: Columbia University Press, 1955); Dexter Perkins, *The New Age of Franklin Roosevelt: 1932–45* (Chicago: University of Chicago Press, 1957); Mario Einaudi, *The Roosevelt Revolution* (New York: Harcourt, Brace, 1959); Thomas H. Greer, *What Roosevelt Thought: The Social and Political Ideas of Franklin D. Roosevelt* (East Lansing: Michigan State University Press, 1958); and Willard Range, *Franklin D. Roosevelt's World Order* (Athens: University of Georgia Press, 1959).

Arthur M. Schlesinger's *The Age of Roosevelt* (Boston: Houghton Mifflin, 1957, 1959, 1960) is a history of Roosevelt's era rather than a biography of the man, but it provides a description of the climate and country in which Roosevelt's speeches were delivered. George N. Crocker's *Roosevelt's Road to Russia* (Chicago: Regnery, 1959) discloses a distrust of Roosevelt somewhat akin to that of Charles A. Beard, albeit in different context.

Roosevelt's letters, speeches, and state papers are almost innumerable. Elliott Roosevelt has edited four volumes of his father's correspondence: *F. D. R.: His Personal Letters* (New York: Duell, Sloan and Pearce, 1947, 1948, 1950). Some of Roosevelt's letters and speeches are found conveniently in Donald Day, ed., *Franklin D. Roosevelt's Own Story* (Boston: Little, Brown, 1951). The major source for Roosevelt's speeches is Samuel I. Rosenman, compiler, *The Public Papers and Addresses of Franklin D. Roosevelt,* 13 vols. (Vols. 1–5, New York: Random House, 1938; Vols. 6–9, New York: Macmillan, 1941; Vols. 10–13, New York: Harper & Brothers, 1950). Volume 1 has a special introduction and explanatory notes by President Roosevelt. A scholarly critique of Roosevelt's speechmaking is offered by Earnest Brandenburg and Waldo W. Braden, "Franklin Delano Roosevelt," in Marie Kathryn Hochmuth, ed., *A History and Criticism of American Public Address,* Vol. III (New York: Longmans, Green, 1955), pp. 458–530.

Winston Churchill

❧|☙

"In my country, as in yours, public men are proud to be the servants of the state, and would be ashamed to be its masters." [1]
—WINSTON CHURCHILL

BIOGRAPHICAL SKETCH

Sir Winston Leonard Spencer Churchill, British publicist, orator, and statesman, was born at Blenheim Palace on November 30, 1874, and died in London on January 24, 1965. Grandson of the seventh Duke of Marlborough, he was the son of Lord Randolph Churchill and Jennie Jerome, daughter of Leonard W. Jerome, of New York. Churchill was educated at Harrow, where he was something of a problem, and at Sandhurst. In 1895 he entered the British army as a subaltern. On leave from the army, he went to Cuba, where he served as a newspaper correspondent; then to India, where (after a tour of duty in the south) he went to Northwest India as a correspondent to cover the fighting on the frontier. He continued his practice of combining journalism and soldiering in Egypt and in South Africa.

On returning to England in 1900, Churchill was elected to Parliament as a Conservative from Oldham. In 1908 he married Miss Clementine Hozier and, as he said, "lived happily ever after." He left the Conservative Party and in 1906 was returned to the House of Commons as a Liberal from Manchester. In the same year he became Undersecretary for the colonies, the first of a long line of cabi-

NOTE: The sources for this essay will be found in the section Suggestions for Further Reading, pp. 240–241, and in electronic transcriptions of Churchill's speeches. The editors heard Sir Winston speak and were present in the galleries during his last appearance in the House of Commons.

[1] "Address of the Right Honorable Winston Churchill, delivered before the Congress of the United States, on December 26, 1941," *Congressional Record, Senate* (December 26, 1941), p. 10117.

net posts he was to hold. He was successively President of the Board of Trade (1908), Home Secretary (1910), and First Lord of the Admiralty (1911).

During World War I, Churchill was active as a policy-maker. On assuming the blame for the disaster to the British forces at the Dardanelles, he resigned from the cabinet and shortly thereafter went into the trenches with the British forces on the Western front. On Lloyd George's formation of a coalition government, Churchill was called back to England (1917) to serve as Minister of Munitions, a post he filled with distinction. In 1919 Churchill became Secretary of State for War and Air Minister and held the post until he took the Colonial Office in 1921. With the fall of Lloyd George's government in 1922, Churchill was out of office. In 1924, however, he was elected to the House of Commons from Epping. Returning to the Conservative Party, he was soon thereafter made Chancellor of the Exchequer in Baldwin's cabinet. When the Labour Party came to power in 1929, Churchill retired to his home, as he had done before when out of office, to write his books and to observe with growing apprehension the rise of Communist Russia and Nazi Germany.

A frequent and outspoken critic of Neville Chamberlain's government, Churchill continued to warn Britain of approaching danger; but not until Britain's declaration of war on September 3, 1939, was he called to his former position as First Lord of the Admiralty. When Chamberlain was forced to resign, Churchill became Prime Minister and formed a coalition government. He directed the mobilization of Britain's wartime economy and the warfare on land and sea, always with outward confidence and hope manifested in stirring speeches that upheld the spirits of men and women not only in Britain but throughout the Free World. With the entrance of the United States into World War II (December 7, 1941), he sought to achieve a firm and lasting alliance between the United States and Britain.

Following the general elections of 1945, the Labour Party came to power and Churchill assumed the leadership of the loyal opposition. In the elections of October 1951, the Conservative Party again returned to power and Churchill served as Prime Minister until April 1955, when he resigned. He had previously declined a peerage, since it would have made him ineligible for a seat in the House of Commons, but he was knighted by Queen Elizabeth II in 1953.

Sir Winston Churchill died on January 24, 1965. On January 28 a memorial service was held for him in the National Cathedral in Washington, D.C., where Adlai Stevenson, in phrases worthy of Winston Churchill, delivered the memorial address. In the course of his address Stevenson recalled:

> I remember once years ago during a long visit at his country house he talked proudly of his American Revolutionary ancestors and happily of his boyhood visits to the United States. As I took my leave I said I was going back to London to speak to the English Speaking Union and asked if he had any message for them. "Yes," he said, "tell them that you bring greetings from an English Speaking Union." And I think that perhaps it was to the relations of the United Kingdom and the United States that he made his finest contribution.[2]

Winston Churchill was greatly beloved in the United States, his mother's native land. Americans generally heard him with respect and with a certain empathy projected toward his human foibles, his prejudices, and his stubborn belief, even when the clouds were darkest, that the ultimate victory must come to his compatriots who fought for their island home.

THE SPEAKER

Churchill was a man of great versatility: journalist, novelist, historian, soldier, statesman, artist, parliamentarian—and the greatest orator of his time. He had two teachers of speechmaking: the Ciceronian discipline of writing and the British House of Commons.

In *De Oratore* Cicero observed:

[2] Adlai E. Stevenson, "Address at the Memorial Service for Sir Winston Churchill," in Lester Thonssen, ed., *Representative American Speeches: 1964–65*, The Reference Shelf, Vol. 37, No. 4 (New York: H. W. Wilson, 1965), pp. 103–107. From a text furnished by Margaret L. Gerstle, Public Affairs Officer, United States Mission to the United Nations. An excerpt from Stevenson's address, with some of the circumstances, is provided in Lillian Ross, *Adlai Stevenson* (Philadelphia: Lippincott, 1966), pp. 46–48.

Writing is said to be the best and most excellent modeller and teacher of oratory, and not without reason; for if what is meditated and considered easily surpass extempore speech, a constant and diligent habit of writing will surely be of more effect than meditation and consideration itself.

Cicero had in mind, of course, the sober discourse that befits a statesman. That kind of discourse, with the inimitable Churchillian touch of humor or turn of phrase, is what Churchill learned to write and to speak. For, as he acknowledged, he was a child of the House of Commons, of which he was a member from youth to old age.

Churchill had a bad beginning in the House that was to know him well and eventually to call him not child but father. When he entered the House at the turn of the century, he had two bad habits: a lisp of the kind that nowadays sends students to a speech clinic, and a chip on his shoulder. The lisp, mocked by some ill-mannered colleagues, eventually lapsed into a trace, a Churchillian trademark; and as he lived and grew in the House of Commons, the chip on the shoulder disappeared—except for occasional acerbity under control. Churchill never forgot how to read the riot act in such a way as to make the opposition beware. In this respect, as in some others, he resembled his great predecessor William Pitt, the Earl of Chatham. But there was more compassion in Churchill.

In every speech Churchill delivered during World War II can be found examples of eloquence seldom equaled and never surpassed in the English language. The secret, if it be a secret, is twofold: it lies in the utter simplicity of vigorous and felicitous communication and in the indomitable John Bull behind the phrase. For example:

Death and Sorrow will be the companions of our journey; hardship our garment; constancy and valour our only shield. We must be united, we must be undaunted, we must be inflexible. Our qualities and deeds must burn and glow through the gloom of Europe until they become the veritable beacon of its salvation.

We shall not fail or falter; we shall not weaken or tire. Neither the sudden shock of battle, nor the long-drawn trials of vigilance and exertion will wear us down. Give us the tools, and we will finish the job.

Come then: let us to the task, to the battle, to the toil—each to our part, each to our station. Fill the armies, rule the air, pour out the munitions, strangle the U-boats, sweep the mines, plough the land, build the ships, guard the streets, succour the wounded, uplift the downcast, and honour the brave.

Churchill was debater as well as orator. In his years in the House of Commons, he mastered the special idiom of the House and gained the praise even of the opposition for his ability to provide the quick and telling reply. In the anxious days of 1940–1941, when Britain stood alone, Churchill spoke in secret sessions of the House of Commons with the vital force, if without the stirring phrase, that marked his public utterances. For example:

We should, of course, expect to drown a great many on the way over, and to destroy a large proportion of their vessels.

The Almighty in His infinite wisdom did not see fit to create Frenchmen in the image of Englishmen.

Nothing will stir them [the Americans] like fighting in England.[3]

As an orator, Churchill's greatest gift was in the phrasing, the forming of the discourse, an art in which his great teacher, the House of Commons, perfected him. To be sure, he was more than adequate in his delivery; but his command of the language of oratory was incomparable. Time after time, he found the supremely right words to encourage the timid, comfort the stricken, praise the brave—and defy the wicked "Narzis." As long as the English language is spoken, and even thereafter, the language of Winston Churchill will remain to tell men what speech can do in the service of free men.

[3] Of the six quotations given above, the first three are to be found in Churchill's war speeches, widely available in newspapers and on tapes and, like many other Churchillian phrases, so widely disseminated that they have passed into the language. The latter three quotations will be easily located in Charles Eade, compiler, *Winston Churchill's Secret Session Speeches* (New York: Simon and Schuster, 1946).

THE SPEECH

On December 7, 1941, the Japanese attacked Pearl Harbor. Within a fortnight Churchill was on his way to Washington for a series of conferences with President Roosevelt. On December 26, 1941, he delivered his "Address to the Congress of the United States." This address, like Churchill's other war speeches, includes notable examples of lucid, felicitous, and vigorous phrasing.

The object of Churchill's speech is obvious: it is to consummate for their mutual advantage a union between two peoples beset by common enemies. The rhetorical means, perhaps not quite so obvious, on the highest level of simplicity brings to mind their common interests, common ground, common purpose—and common enemies. Churchill's initial reference to "my American forebears" is not merely sentimental. It is a reminder to those who know and information to those who do not that his mother was Miss Jennie Jerome of New York City. Yet he does not make claims for his American heritage: "and that here I am, an Englishman, welcomed in your midst . . ." he says. And shortly he is captivating his congressional audience—and perhaps others—with a typical Churchillian touch that brings appreciative laughter from the Congress:

> By the way, I cannot help reflecting that if my father had been American and my mother British, instead of the other way round, I might have got here on my own. In that case, this would not have been the first time you would have heard my voice. In that case, I should not have needed any invitation; but, if I had, it is hardly likely that it would have been unanimous. So perhaps things are better as they are.[4]

Churchill, wise in the ways of argument, does not attempt to prove his proposition by a frontal assault, for he knows that *formal* argument is a last resort. His entire speech is a witness to the special unity in diversity of the British and American peoples. The speech consistently suggests mutuality without arguing identity:

> We in Britain had the same feeling in our darkest days. We, *too*, were sure that in the end all would be well.

[4] See below, p. 230.

You do not, I am certain, underrate the severity of the ordeal to which *you and we* have still to be subjected.

For the best part of 20 years the youth of *Britain and America* have been taught that war was evil, which is true, and that it would never come again, which has been proved false.

Provided that every effort is made, that nothing is kept back, that the whole manpower, brainpower, virility, valour, and civic virtue of the *English-speaking world*, with all its galaxy of loyal, friendly, or associated communities and states, are bent unremittingly to the simple but supreme task, I think it would be reasonable to hope that the end of 1942 will see *us* quite definitely in a better position than we are now. . . .[5]

Only at the very close of his address does the eloquent speaker state his major thesis:

It is not given to us to peer into the mysteries of the future; still I avow my hope and faith, sure and inviolate, that in days to come the *British and American peoples* will for their own safety and for the good of all, walk together side by side in majesty, in justice, and in peace.[6]

---

[5] See below, *passim*. Italics supplied.
[6] See below, p. 238. Italics supplied.

Address to the Congress
of the United States

❧

Members of the Senate and of the House of Representatives of the United States, I feel greatly honored that you should have invited me to enter the United States Senate Chamber and address the representatives of both branches of Congress.

The fact that my American forebears have for so many generations played their part in the life of the United States,[1] and that here I am, an Englishman, welcomed in your midst, makes this experience one of the most moving and thrilling in my life, which is already long and has not been entirely uneventful. [Laughter.]

I wish indeed that my mother, whose memory I cherish across the vale of years, could have been here to see.[2] By the way, I cannot help reflecting that if my father had been American and my mother British, instead of the other way round, I might have got here on my own. [Laughter and applause.] In that case, this would not have been the first time you would have heard my voice. In that case, I should not have needed any invitation; but, if I had, it is hardly likely that it would have been unanimous. [Laughter.] So perhaps things are better as they are.

I may confess, however, that I do not feel quite like a fish out of water in a legislative assembly where English is spoken. I am a child of the House of Commons.[3] I was brought up in my father's

From *Congressional Record, Senate* (December 26, 1941), pp. 10117–10119.

[1] Leonard W. Jerome, Winston Churchill's American grandfather, was the son of a New York farmer. Going into the newspaper business, he acquired control of the Rochester *Native American* and later of an interest in *The New York Times*. Having made a fortune, he lived comfortably in New York City, where he was active in all kinds of enterprises. Another of Churchill's American forebears was an American Indian. Thus it was well said, "Winston is half American and *all* British."

[2] Churchill's mother was Miss Jennie Jerome of New York, a famous beauty who became after her marriage a leader in London society. She died in 1921.

[3] Winston Churchill was first elected to Parliament as a Conservative (Tory) in 1900. Thereafter, he was never out of public affairs and seldom out of office.

house to believe in democracy.[4] "Trust the people"—that was his message. I used to see him cheered at meetings and in the streets by crowds of workingmen away back in those aristocratic Victorian days when, as Disraeli [5] said, the world was for the few, and for the very few. Therefore I have been in full harmony all my life with the tides which have flowed on both sides of the Atlantic against privilege and monopoly and have steered confidently toward the Gettysburg ideal of "government of the people, by the people, for the people." [Applause.]

I owe my advancement entirely to the House of Commons, whose servant I am. In my country, as in yours, public men are proud to be the servants of the state, and would be ashamed to be its masters. On any day, if they thought the people wanted it, the House of Commons could by a simple vote remove me from my office. But I am not worrying about it at all. [Laughter.] As a matter of fact, I am sure they will approve very highly of my journey here —for which I obtained the King's permission[6]—in order to meet the President of the United States[7] [applause] and to arrange with him for all that mapping out of our military plans, and for all those intimate meetings of the high officers of the armed services of both countries which are indispensable to the successful prosecution of the war.

I should like to say, first of all, how much I have been impressed and encouraged by the breadth of view and sense of proportion which I have found in all quarters over here to which I have had access. Anyone who did not understand the size and solidity of the foundations of the United States might easily have expected to find an excited, disturbed, self-centered atmosphere, with all minds fixed upon the novel, startling, and painful episodes of sudden war as they

[4] Lord Randolph Henry Spencer Churchill (1849–1895) entered the House of Commons as a Conservative in 1874. He endeavored to make the Tory Party initiate popular reforms.

[5] Benjamin Disraeli, first Earl of Beaconsfield (1804–1881), British statesman, led the Tory Party into measures that created the "Tory democracy." Lord Randolph Churchill supported Disraeli, both in and out of the House of Commons.

[6] The reference to the king (George VI) is in keeping with Churchill's consistent respect for the monarchy.

[7] Franklin D. Roosevelt.

hit America. After all, the United States has been attacked and set upon by three most powerfully armed dictator states, the greatest military power in Europe, and the greatest military power in Asia. Japan, Germany, and Italy have all declared and are making war upon you, and a quarrel is opened which can only end in their overthrow or yours. But here in Washington, in these memorable days, I have found an Olympian fortitude which, far from being based upon complacency, is only the mask of an inflexible purpose and the proof of a sure and well-grounded confidence in the final outcome. [Applause.] We in Britain had the same feeling in our darkest days. We, too, were sure that in the end all would be well.

You do not, I am certain, underrate the severity of the ordeal to which you and we have still to be subjected. The forces ranged against us are enormous; they are bitter; they are ruthless. The wicked men and their factions who have launched their peoples on the path of war and conquest know that they will be called to terrible account if they can not beat down by force of arms the peoples they have assailed. They will stop at nothing. They have a vast accumulation of war weapons of all kinds; they have highly-trained and disciplined armies, navies, and air services; they have plans and designs which have long been contrived and matured; they will stop at nothing that violence or treachery can suggest.

It is quite true that on our side our resources in manpower and in materials are far greater than theirs; but only a portion of your resources are as yet mobilized and developed, and we have both of us much to learn in the cruel art of war. We have, therefore, without doubt, a time of tribulation before us. In this time some ground will be lost which it will be hard and costly to regain. Many disappointments and unpleasant surprises await us. Many of them will afflict us before the full marshalling of our latent and total power can be accomplished.

For the best part of 20 years the youth of Britain and America have been taught that war was evil, which is true, and that it would never come again, which has been proved false.[8]

For the best part of 20 years the youth of Germany, Japan, and

[8] Churchill served as Chancellor of the Exchequer from 1924–1929; for ten years

Italy have been taught that aggressive war is the noblest duty of the citizen, and that it should be begun as soon as the necessary weapons and organization have been made. We have performed the duties and tasks of peace. They have plotted and planned for war. This naturally has placed us in Britain, and now places you in the United States, at a disadvantage which only time, courage, and straining, untiring exertions can correct.

We have, indeed, to be thankful that so much time has been granted to us. If Germany had tried to invade the British Isles after the French collapse in June 1940, and if Japan had declared war on the British Empire and the United States at about the same date, no one can say what disasters and agonies might not have been our lot. But now, at the end of December 1941, our transformation from easygoing peace to total-war efficiency has made very great progress. The broad flow of munitions in Great Britain has already begun. Immense strides have been made in the conversion of American industry to military purposes, and now that the United States is at war, it is possible for orders to be given every day which a year or 18 months hence will produce results in war power beyond anything which has yet been seen or foreseen in the dictator states. Provided that every effort is made, that nothing is kept back, that the whole manpower, brainpower, virility, valour, and civic virtue of the English-speaking world, with all its galaxy of loyal, friendly, or associated communities and states, are bent unremittingly to the simple but supreme task, I think it would be reasonable to hope that the end of 1942 will see us quite definitely in a better position than we are now [applause], and that the year 1943 will enable us to assume the initiative upon an ample scale. [Applause.]

Some people may be startled or momentarily depressed when, like your President, I speak of a long and a hard war. Our peoples would rather know the truth, sombre though it be; and, after all, when we are doing the noblest work in the world, not only defending our hearths and homes but the cause of freedom in every land, the question of whether deliverance comes in 1942, or 1943, or 1944,

thereafter, until the outbreak of World War II, while he held no cabinet post, he inveighed in season and out against the policy of appeasement.

falls into its proper place in the grand proportions of human history. [Applause.] Sure I am that this day, now, we are the masters of our fate; that the task which has been set for us is not above our strength, and that its pangs and toils are not beyond our endurance. As long as we have faith in our cause and unconquerable will power, salvation will not be denied us. In the words of the Psalmist:

> He shall not be afraid of evil tidings: his heart is fixed, trusting in the Lord. [9]

Not all the tidings will be evil. On the contrary, mighty strokes of war have already been dealt against the enemy. The glorious defense of their native soil by the Russian Armies and people have inflicted wounds upon the Nazi tyranny and system which have bitten deep, and will fester and inflame not only in the Nazi body but in the Nazi mind. [Applause.]

The boastful Mussolini [laughter] has crumpled already.[10] He is now but a lackey and serf, the merest utensil of his master's will. [Laughter and applause.] He has inflicted great suffering and wrong upon his own industrious people. He has been stripped of all his African empire. Abyssinia has been liberated. Our armies of the east, which were so weak and ill equipped at the moment of French desertion, now control all the regions from Teheran to Benghazi, and from Aleppo to Cyprus and the sources of the Nile. [Applause.]

For many months we devoted ourselves to preparing to take the offensive in Libya. The very considerable battle which has been proceeding for the last 6 weeks in the desert has been most fiercely fought on both sides. Owing to the difficulties of supply on the desert flank we were never able to bring numerically equal forces to bear upon the enemy. Therefore we had to rely upon a superiority in the numbers and quality of tanks and aircraft, British and American. Aided by these, for the first time we have fought the enemy with equal weapons. For the first time we have made the Hun feel the sharp edge of those tools with which he has enslaved Europe. The

[9] Psalms, CXII, 7.

[10] Benito Mussolini (1883–1945), Italian dictator known as "Il Duce," brought Italy into World War II in June 1940 as France was falling to the German armies. By December 1941, Mussolini became increasingly subject to the dictation of Adolf Hitler.

armed force of the enemy in Cyrenaica amounted to 150,000 men, of whom about a third were Germans. General Auchinleck[11] set out to destroy totally that armed force; and I have every reason to believe that his aim will be fully accomplished. [Applause.]

I am so glad to be able to place before you, Members of the Senate and of the House of Representatives, at this moment when you are entering the war, proof that, with proper weapons and proper organization, we are able to beat the life out of the savage Nazi. [Applause.] What Hitler is suffering in Libya is only a sample and a foretaste of what we must give him and his accomplices wherever this war shall lead us, in every quarter of the globe.

There are good tidings also from blue water. The life line of supplies which joins our two nations across the ocean, without which all might fail, is flowing steadily and freely, in spite of all the enemy can do. It is a fact that the British Empire, which many thought 18 months ago was broken and ruined, is now incomparably stronger and is growing stronger with every month. [Applause.]

Lastly, if you will forgive me for saying it, to me the best tiding of all, the United States—united as never before—has drawn the sword for Freedom, and cast away the scabbard. [Applause.]

All these tremendous facts have led the subjugated peoples of Europe to lift up their heads again in hope. They have put aside forever the shameful temptation of resigning themselves to the conqueror's will. Hope has returned to the hearts of scores of millions of men and women, and with that hope there burns the flame of anger against the brutal, corrupt invader, and still more fiercely burn the fires of hatred and contempt for the filthy Quislings[12] whom he has suborned. In a dozen famous ancient states, now prostrate under the Nazi yoke, the masses of the people, all classes and creeds, await

---

[11] Sir Claude John Eyre Auchinleck (1884–   ), British Field Marshal, held various commands in World War II. In July 1941 he succeeded General Wavell in the Middle East and in November 1941 mounted an offensive into Libya. Churchill's expectations, however, were not met, for in June 1942 the British were pushed back into Egypt, and Auchinleck was replaced by General Sir Harold Alexander, who gave command of the British forces in North Africa to General Bernard L. Montgomery.

[12] Vidkun Quisling (1887–1945), Norwegian army officer, was convicted of high treason and executed for the betrayal of his country to the Nazis. His name has become a synonym for "traitor."

the hour of liberation, when they, too, will be able once again to play their part and strike their blows like men. That hour will strike, and its solemn peal will proclaim that the night is passed and that the dawn has come.

The onslaught upon us, so long and so secretly planned by Japan, has presented both our countries with grievous problems for which we could not be fully prepared. If people ask me, as they have a right to ask me in England, "Why is it that you have not got ample equipment of modern aircraft and army weapons of all kinds in Malaya and in the East Indies" I can only point to the victories General Auchinleck has gained in the Libyan campaign. Had we diverted and dispersed our gradually growing resources between Libya and Malaya, we should have been found wanting in both theatres. If the United States has been found at a disadvantage at various points in the Pacific Ocean, we know well that it is to no small extent because of the aid which you have been giving to us in munitions for the defense of the British Isles and for the Libyan campaign, and, above all, because of your help in the battle of the Atlantic, upon which all depends, and which has in consequence been successfully and prosperously maintained.

Of course, it would have been much better, I freely admit, if we had had enough resources of all kinds to be at full strength at all threatened points; but, considering how slowly and reluctantly we brought ourselves to large-scale preparations, and how long such preparations take, we had no right to expect to be in such a fortunate position. The choice of how to dispose of our hitherto limited resources had to be made by Britain in time of war, and by the United States in time of peace; and I believe that history will pronounce that upon the whole—and it is upon the whole that these matters must be judged—the choice made was right.

Now that we are together, now that we are linked in a righteous comradeship of arms, now that our two considerable nations, each in perfect unity, have joined all their life energies in a common resolve, a new scene opens upon which a steady light will glow and brighten.

Many people have been astonished that Japan should, in a single day, have plunged into war against the United States and the British

Empire. We all wonder why, if this dark design, with all its labourious and intricate preparations, had been so long filling their secret minds, they did not choose our moment of weakness 18 months ago. Viewed quite dispassionately, in spite of the losses we have suffered and the further punishment we shall have to take, it certainly appears to be an irrational act. It is, of course, only prudent to assume that they have made very careful calculation and think they see their way through. Nevertheless, there may be another explanation.

We know that for many years past the policy of Japan has been dominated by secret societies of subaltern and junior officers of the Army and Navy who have enforced their will upon successive Japanese cabinets and parliaments by the assassination of any Japanese statesman who opposed or who did not sufficiently further their aggressive policy. It may be that these societies, dazzled and dizzy with their own schemes of aggression and the prospect of early victories, have forced their country, against its better judgment, into war. They have certainly embarked upon a very considerable undertaking [laughter]; for, after the outrages they have committed upon us at Pearl Harbor, in the Pacific islands, in the Philippines, in Malaya, and the Dutch East Indies, they must now know that the stakes for which they have decided to play are mortal. When we consider the resources of the United States and the British Empire, compared to those of Japan, when we remember those of China, which has so long and valiantly withstood invasion [great applause], and when also we observe the Russian menace which hangs over Japan, it becomes still more difficult to reconcile Japanese action with prudence, or even with sanity. What kind of people do they think we are? Is it possible they do not realize that we shall never cease to persevere against them until they have been taught a lesson which they and the world will never forget? [Prolonged applause.]

Members of the Senate and Members of the House of Representatives, I turn for one moment more from the turmoil and convulsions of the present to the broader spaces of the future.

Here we are together, facing a group of mighty foes who seek our ruin. Here we are together, defending all that to freemen is dear. Twice in a single generation the catastrophe of world war has fallen upon us; twice in our lifetimes has the long arm of Fate reached out across the oceans to bring the United States into the forefront of the battle. If we had kept together after the last war; if we had taken common measures for our safety, this renewal of the curse need never have fallen upon us. [Applause.] Do we not owe it to ourselves, to our children, to tormented mankind, to make sure that these catastrophes do not engulf us for the third time?

It has been proved that pestilences may break out in the Old World which carry their destructive ravages into the New World, from which, once they are afoot, the New World cannot by any means escape. Duty and prudence alike command, first, that the germ centres of hatred and revenge should be constantly and vigilantly surveyed and treated in good time; and, secondly, that an adequate organization should be set up to make sure that the pestilence can be controlled at its earliest beginnings before it spreads and rages throughout the entire earth. [Applause.]

Five or six years ago it would have been easy, without shedding a drop of blood, for the United States and Great Britain to have insisted on fulfillment of the disarmament clauses of the treaties which Germany signed after the Great War. That also would have been the opportunity for assuring to Germans those raw materials which we declared in the Atlantic Charter should not be denied to any nation, victor or vanquished.

Prodigious hammer strokes have been needed to bring us together today; or, if you will allow me to use other language, I will say that he must, indeed, have a blind soul who cannot see that some great purpose and design is being worked out here below, of which we have the honour to be the faithful servants.

It is not given to us to peer into the mysteries of the future; still I avow my hope and faith, sure and inviolate, that in days to come the British and American peoples will for their own safety and for the good of all, walk together side by side in majesty, in justice, and in peace.

[Prolonged applause, the Members of the Senate and their guests rising.]

§ Critical Analysis

To whom, in your judgment, was Churchill's speech addressed?

§

Churchill was a student and writer of biography and of history. What evidence can you find in the "Address to the Congress of the United States" of Churchill's indebtedness to his study of history?

§

In the introduction to Churchill's speech to the Congress, the editors have cited a number of examples demonstrating the speaker's endeavor to gain common ground with the audience. What other examples can you find?

§

The British and the American peoples are sometimes said to be *divided* by a common language. How does Churchill's speech bear on this saying?

§

Lillian Ross, in her monograph on Adlai Stevenson, relates that following the memorial address at the service for Churchill, Stevenson remarked about his own speech preparation, "I'm afraid I sit up scribbling until the last minute. Churchill was always rewriting his speeches until he had to give them. . . . But that's where my similarity to Churchill ends." [1] Why would you agree (or disagree) with Stevenson's evaluation of the similarity between himself and Churchill?

§

It is said that Prince Otto von Bismarck (1815–1898), Chancellor of the German Reich, on being asked to state the most important fact for the twentieth century, replied, "That North America speaks the English language." What evidence do you find in Churchill's speech to confirm or deny the Bismarckian reply?

[1] *Adlai Stevenson* (Philadelphia: Lippincott, 1966), p. 49.

§ SUGGESTIONS FOR FURTHER READING

Sir Winston Churchill's son, Randolph S. Churchill, who at times in the past served as editor for his father, is now engaged in editing his father's papers and writing his biography. It is to be hoped that he will do as well with Sir Winston's biography as Sir Winston did with *Lord Randolph Churchill* (London: Macmillan, 1907) and with *Marlborough: His Life and Times*, 6 vols. (New York: Scribner's, 1933–1938). Meanwhile there is no lack of reading matter concerning Sir Winston Churchill. Indeed, much of it was contributed by Sir Winston himself in ninety-one years of energetic versatility. In A *Bibliography of the Works of Sir Winston Churchill, KG, OM, CH, MP* (Toronto: University of Toronto Press, 1960) running to 340 pages, Frederick Woods calculates (p. 9) that the total sale of Churchill's books in the English language alone is in the region of four million copies.

Of Churchill's own published works, the following should be mentioned: A *Roving Commission: My Early Life* (New York: Scribner's, 1930) and *Frontiers and Wars: His Four Early Books Covering His Life as a Soldier and War Correspondent Edited into One Volume* (London: Eyre and Spottiswoode, 1962). Churchill was much given to editing and revising: *Frontiers and Wars* is a revision in handsome format with numerous illustrations of A *Roving Commission*. Perhaps Churchill's best-known work is *While England Slept: A Survey of World Affairs: 1932–1938* (New York: G. P. Putnam's, 1938). *Great Contemporaries* (New York: G. P. Putnam's, 1937) reports Churchill's opinion of the men of that day, including Adolf Hitler. More formidable works are *The Second World War*, 6 vols. (Boston: Houghton Mifflin, 1948–1953), and A *History of the English-Speaking Peoples*, 4 vols. (London: Cassell, 1956–1958).

Churchill's speeches are available in texts edited by his son, Randolph, two of which are *Europe Unite: Speeches 1947 and 1948* (Boston: Houghton Mifflin, 1950) and *In the Balance: Speeches 1949 and 1950* (Boston: Houghton Mifflin, 1952). Another source for his speeches is the volumes compiled by Charles Eade, for example, *The Dawn of Liberation: War Speeches by the Right Hon. Winston Churchill, C.H., M.P.* (Boston: Little, Brown, 1945). *Winston Churchill's Secret Session Speeches* (New York: Simon and Schuster, 1946), also compiled by Charles Eade, should be of special interest to students of speechmaking since it contains Churchill's notes for one and the texts of four major speeches made in secret session of the House of Commons during World War II.

Of the books about Churchill, two offer what may be called literary, rhetorical, or political criticism: Herbert Leslie Stewart, *Sir Winston Churchill as Writer and Speaker* (London: Sidgwick and Jackson, 1954), and Stephen R. Graubard, *Burke, Disraeli, and Churchill* (Cambridge: Harvard University Press, 1961). In editing *Churchill by His Contemporaries* (London: Hutchinson, 1953), Charles Eade has included a chapter (pp. 329–342) by Lord Birkett on Churchill as an orator. Other accounts of Churchill's life providing more continuity, though necessarily incomplete, are *Winston Churchill: A Biography* (Philadelphia: Lippincott, 1941) by René Kraus and *The Life and Times of Winston Churchill* (London: Odhams, 1945) by Malcolm Thomson.

Perhaps the liveliest Churchillian narrative currently available is Robert Lewis Taylor's *Winston Churchill: An Informal Study of Greatness* (Garden City, N.Y.: Doubleday, 1952). A close second, however, is Walter Henry Thompson's *Assignment Churchill* (New York: Farrar, Straus and Young, 1955). Inspector Thompson of Scotland Yard was Churchill's bodyguard for almost twenty years. Princess Marthe Bibesco praises Churchill's central virtue in *Sir Winston Churchill: Master of Courage* (New York: John Day, 1959). Peter de Mendelssohn tells the story of Churchill's early life in *The Age of Churchill: Heritage and Adventure 1874–1911* (New York: Knopf, 1961). Lewis Broad carries Churchill's life to 1963 in two volumes—*Winston Churchill: The Years of Preparation* and *Winston Churchill: The Years of Achievement* (New York: Hawthorn, 1958, 1963).

Douglas MacArthur

"In war, indeed, there can be no substitute for victory." [1]
—DOUGLAS MacARTHUR

BIOGRAPHICAL SKETCH

Douglas MacArthur, General of the Army of the United States, was born in Little Rock, Arkansas, on January 20, 1880, and died in New York City on April 5, 1964. He was the son of General Arthur MacArthur, who served with distinction on the side of the North during the Civil War, and of Mary Pinkney Hardy of Virginia, whose brothers fought for the South. Since Douglas MacArthur's early schooling was subject to the interruptions occasioned by his father's assignments to army posts, his capacities were not fully realized until he received a congressional appointment to the United States Military Academy, where he graduated (1903) as first captain, the highest military honor, as well as first in his class in scholarship. He was commissioned second lieutenant of engineers, assigned to the Philippines, transferred to San Francisco, and then (1905) appointed aide to his father, who was United States Army Observer of the Russo-Japanese War.

In 1906 Douglas MacArthur served as aide to President Theodore Roosevelt. During the years prior to World War I, MacArthur rose

NOTE: For this essay the editors have relied on the references in the section Suggestions for Further Reading, pp. 262–263, particularly on Spanier's *The Truman–MacArthur Controversy and the Korean War* and on certain other works listed in Spanier's bibliography (pp. 298–306). In addition, the editors have followed contemporary newspaper accounts and have consulted their own recollections, correspondence, and notes concerning General MacArthur's speech, which they witnessed by television.

[1] Douglas MacArthur, "Address of General of the Army Douglas MacArthur, delivered before the Congress of the United States on April 19, 1951," *Congressional Record, House* (April 19, 1951), p. 4125.

steadily in rank and with the entry of the United States into the war, he was appointed (September 1917) colonel and Chief of Staff of the 42nd Infantry Division. In June 1918, he was made brigadier general, and as commanding officer led the 84th Infantry Brigade in action. Following World War I, MacArthur was appointed (June 1919) superintendent of the Academy at West Point, where he proceeded to make much-needed changes, both in the curriculum and in the procedures. While at West Point he met Henrietta Louise Cromwell Brooks and entered into a marriage, later dissolved. At the close of his tour of duty at West Point (1922), he was assigned to the Philippines for three years, then (1925) to be commander of the Third Corps Area in Baltimore. Following his assignment in Baltimore, he was appointed commanding general of the Department of the Philippines, a post once held by his father. He returned to the United States and shortly thereafter was named by President Herbert Hoover to be Chief of Staff of the Army, with the rank of general. After serving five depression years (1930–1935) as Chief of Staff, MacArthur accepted appointment by President of the Philippines Manuel Quezon to be military adviser to his government.

In 1937 General MacArthur married Jean Faircloth. One son was born to them. Retiring from the United States Army, MacArthur remained in the Philippines, and in July 1941, as war seemed imminent, he was recalled to active duty in the United States Army and appointed to head United States forces in the Far East. With the Japanese invasion of the Philippines, MacArthur was ordered to Australia, where (1942) he was named Supreme Commander in the Southwest Pacific. Following his return, as promised, to Manila, he was made a five-star general of the army and given command of all United States armies in the Pacific. With the surrender of Japan, he was named Supreme Commander for the Allied Powers and flew to Tokyo (September 2, 1945) to receive the Japanese surrender. Until he was dismissed by President Truman on April 11, 1951, MacArthur ruled Japan with—it is generally agreed—firmness, moderation, and sagacity.

In June 1950, while serving as Supreme Commander for the Allied Powers, MacArthur had to deal with the problems created by the Korean War, a responsibility he undertook as Commander of United Nations forces, in the defense of South Korea. The forces of the United Nations were able, under MacArthur's direction, to repulse the invaders and move into North Korea, when the intervention of Chinese troops forced the armies of the United Nations back across the 38th Parallel. The Chinese offensive was halted, however, and a peace of sorts concluded. During the last five years of his life, Douglas MacArthur was the senior officer in the United States Army, with the rank of General of the Army. During a long and brilliant career in the armed forces, he accumulated a profusion of medals, honors, and decorations, all in tribute to his acknowledged abilities as a strategist and to his qualities of leadership.

THE OCCASION

At one o'clock on the morning of April 11, 1951, the White House held a press conference during which reporters learned that President Harry S. Truman had relieved General Douglas MacArthur of all his duties, including that of Supreme Commander for the Allied Powers. When the news of the President's action reached the American people, the tumult and the shouting might have been heard, it seemed, as far as Tokyo, where General MacArthur was preparing to leave for a triumphal journey across the United States and a hero's welcome in the nation's capital. President Truman was booed to his face; Senator Richard Nixon recommended that the Senate censure the President; Senator Joseph McCarthy, with characteristic delicacy, called the President of the United States a "son of a bitch"; Senator William E. Jenner urged that the President be impeached; the leaders of the Republican Party in the Congress including Senator Robert Taft, Senator Kenneth Wherry, and Congressman Joseph W. Martin, Jr., convened and agreed that Congress should investigate the foreign and military policy of the Truman administration and, in addition, as Congressman Martin—the minority leader —disclosed, "discussed possible impeachments."

On April 16 the general made a farewell trip through Tokyo. It is said that more than 200,000 people lined the streets. In Honolulu, where MacArthur first landed on the soil of the United States, 100,000 people observed the MacArthur parade. On the evening of

April 17, General MacArthur and his wife and son arrived in San Francisco to find an estimated 500,000 people ready to greet them. On the following day a cheering crowd observed the general's tour of the city of San Francisco. Shortly after midnight on April 19, General MacArthur and his party arrived in Washington, to be met at the airport not only by an official party that included Secretary of Defense George Marshall and the Joint Chiefs of Staff but also by thousands of people eager to see him.

Following the tumultuous welcome at the airport, General MacArthur responded at noon on the same day, April 19, 1951, to an invitation to address a joint meeting of the Senate and the House of Representatives.

THE AUDIENCE

As General MacArthur entered the House chamber, escorted by Congressmen McCormack, Martin, Vinson, Halleck, and Brooks and by Senators McFarland, Connally, Russell, Wherry, Bridges, and Wiley, the members of the Congress and the citizens in the galleries rose and applauded. When the general was introduced by Speaker Rayburn and took his place at the Clerk's desk, the audience broke forth in a tremendous demonstration. Thereafter, the speaker was received in a perfect quiet—save for occasional bursts of applause— and with as nearly complete attention as any person is ever likely to command. When the joint session of the two Houses was adjourned at 1:15 P.M., the excited audience continued in absorbed concern with the event they had just witnessed.

Those present in the House chamber constituted only one of the audiences MacArthur had that day. Other groups heard him, although they could not see him, on radio broadcasts. Still others watched the spectacle on television. And another audience of readers followed his speech in the newspapers.

THE SPEAKER

On April 19, 1951, General MacArthur, at seventy-one years, was vigorous, erect, and dignified. His bearing was that of a man accustomed by fifty-two years of military career to command obedience. Yet to those who followed the broadcasts, he did not convey the impression of arrogance. Rather he seemed to be gravely concerned and genuinely sincere in his apprehension for the nation that had granted him the highest military honors. With the possible exception of the peroration, which some hearers thought "corny," the speech was accepted as a legitimate appeal addressed in high drama to the handsomer passions of his fellow citizens.

THE SPEECH

As Professor Henry Lee Ewbank observed, it would be "difficult to imagine a more dramatic speech situation." [2] Professor Ewbank and twelve other persons—five congressional leaders, three journalists, and five academicians—were invited to contribute to a symposium of critical comment edited by Professor Frederick W. Haberman and published in *The Quarterly Journal of Speech*. The judgments expressed did not even approach consensus. Joseph W. Martin, Jr., Republican minority leader, believed the address of General Mac-Arthur to surpass ". . . the first Roosevelt Inaugural speech in 1933 and the Winston Churchill address to the Joint Session of Congress in 1942." Robert S. Kerr, Democratic senator from Oklahoma, was not of the same opinion. "I listened earnestly and carefully," he said, "to General MacArthur's speech. I looked for unity. I didn't find it. . . . I listened for words which would promote cooperation between this nation and our allies for collective security. Those words were not spoken." Karl E. Mundt, Republican senator from South Dakota, reported that ". . . by general agreement of most of us who had heard all four of them [Churchill, Roosevelt, Madame Chiang Kai-shek, and MacArthur] in person, Douglas MacArthur stood out spectacularly above them all." Hubert H. Humphrey, Democratic senator from Minnesota, however, viewed the speech in a different context and concluded that ". . . with the fading away of emotions

[2] The matter quoted from the congressional critics, the journalists, and the academicians will be found in Frederick W. Haberman, ed., "General MacArthur's Speech: A Symposium of Critical Comment," *The Quarterly Journal of Speech*, XXXVII, 3 (October 1951), 321–331.

and the supremacy of reason, the American people will come to see that President Truman was correct in removing General MacArthur."

Among the journalists there was a measure of agreement. Richard Rovere, declining to view the speech from the point of view of oratory, thought that it failed to come to grips with the issues. Quincy Howe asserted that General MacArthur stands out "as perhaps the greatest actor of them all" but estimated his position as a statesman to be "measurably lower than that of Harry S. Truman." William T. Evjue declared that "an injustice is being done to Abraham Lincoln by those who are claiming that General MacArthur's speech to the Congress is 'another Gettysburg address.' "

The academicians did not reach agreement. W. Norwood Brigance declared that "By this speech MacArthur had seized the initiative even as he had done by the audacious landing at Inchon." Professor Herbert A. Wichelns saw ". . . the picture of a masterful man of unique experience and global outlook, wearing authority as to the manner born." Professor Wilbur Samuel Howell was disappointed in MacArthur's logic; Professor Henry Lee Ewbank thought that it would not ". . . find an enduring place in our literature as a model of speech composition"; and Professor A. Craig Baird declared that "General Douglas MacArthur will be ranked as one of America's outstanding military orators."

With the passing of the years General MacArthur's speech remains for those who heard it in person or by television an unforgettable experience. Indubitably the speech provided General MacArthur with a vast stage from which he spoke in accents that made him credible to millions of his fellow Americans and gained for him their respect, if not their allegiance. If, however, the speech be judged by the criterion set forth by Congressman Joseph W. Martin, Jr., it cannot be called effective, for Martin said that "In politics, the effectiveness of a speech is measured by its ability to strengthen friendships and win converts." Although General MacArthur's speech doubtless strengthened some friendships, and surely presented him as a strong man, no evidence suggests that it produced many lasting converts to his cause. The hearings held before the Senate Foreign Relations Committee and the Senate Armed Forces Committee, combined under the chairmanship of Senator Richard Russell, failed to confirm MacArthur's assumption that his views were supported by the Joint Chiefs of Staff. The American people confirmed their tradition of civilian rather than military responsibility in matters of high policy.

It may be that in the rural areas, in the small towns, the people had never been quite so enraptured with General MacArthur, quite so disgusted with President Truman, as the urban demonstrations suggested city dwellers to be. Perhaps their point of view was expressed by the Missouri farmer who was heard to say, "The General is O.K.; but he ain't the boss—Harry is the boss." In any event, although General MacArthur did not quite fade away after his masterful speech, he never again appeared in the limelight that illuminated the House chamber at noon on April 19, 1951, perhaps his grandest hour.

Old Soldiers Never Die

Mr. President, Mr. Speaker, and distinguished Members of the Congress, I stand on this rostrum with a sense of deep humility and great pride—humility in the wake of those great American architects of our history who have stood here before me, pride in the reflection that this forum of legislative debate represents human liberty in the purest form yet devised. [Applause.] Here are centered the hopes, and aspirations, and faith of the entire human race.

I do not stand here as advocate for any partisan cause, for the issues are fundamental and reach quite beyond the realm of partisan consideration. They must be resolved on the highest plane of national interest if our course is to prove sound and our future protected. I trust, therefore, that you will do me the justice of receiving that which I have to say as solely expressing the considered viewpoint of a fellow American. I address you with neither rancor nor bitterness in the fading twilight of life with but one purpose in mind—to serve my country. [Applause.]

The issues are global and so interlocked that to consider the problems of one sector, oblivious to those of another, is but to court disaster for the whole.

While Asia is commonly referred to as the gateway to Europe, it is no less true that Europe is the gateway to Asia, and the broad influence of the one cannot fail to have its impact upon the other.

There are those who claim our strength is inadequate to protect on both fronts—that we cannot divide our effort. I can think of no greater expression of defeatism. [Applause.] If a potential enemy can divide his strength on two fronts, it is for us to counter his effort.

The Communist threat is a global one. Its successful advance in one sector threatens the destruction of every other sector. You cannot appease or otherwise surrender to communism in Asia without simultaneously undermining our efforts to halt its advance in Europe. [Applause.]

From *Congressional Record, House* (April 19, 1951), pp. 4123–4125.

Beyond pointing out these general truisms, I shall confine my discussion to the general areas of Asia. Before one may objectively assess the situation now existing there, he must comprehend something of Asia's past and the revolutionary changes which have marked her course up to the present. Long exploited by the so-called colonial powers, with little opportunity to achieve any degree of social justice, individual dignity, or a higher standard of life such as guided our own noble administration of the Philippines,[1] the peoples of Asia found their opportunity in the war just past to throw off the shackles of colonialism, and now see the dawn of new opportunity, a heretofore unfelt dignity and the self-respect of political freedom.

Mustering half of the earth's population and 60 percent of its natural resources, these peoples are rapidly consolidating a new force, both moral and material, with which to raise the living standard and erect adaptations of the design of modern progress to their own distinct cultural environments. Whether one adheres to the concept of colonization or not, this is the direction of Asian progress and it may not be stopped. It is a corollary to the shift of the world economic frontiers, as the whole epicenter of world affairs rotates back toward the area whence it started. In this situation it becomes vital that our own country orient its policies in consonance with this basic evolutionary condition rather than pursue a course blind to the reality that the colonial era is now past and the Asian peoples covet the right to shape their own free destiny. What they seek now is friendly guidance, understanding, and support, not imperious direction [applause]; the dignity of equality, not the shame of subjugation. Their prewar standards of life, pitifully low, is infinitely lower now in the devastation left in war's wake. World ideologies play little part in Asian thinking and are little understood. What the peoples strive for is the opportunity for a little more food in their stomachs, a little better clothing on their backs, a little firmer roof over their heads, and the realization of the normal nationalist urge for political freedom. These political-social conditions have but an indirect bearing

---

[1] General Arthur MacArthur (1845–1912), father of General Douglas MacArthur, served in the Philippines during the Spanish-American War and was military governor of the Philippines in 1900–1901. On his graduation from West Point and again in 1922–1925, Douglas MacArthur also served in the Philippines.

upon our own national security, but do form a backdrop to contemporary planning which must be thoughtfully considered if we are to avoid the pitfalls of unrealism.

Of more direct and immediate bearing upon our national security are the changes wrought in the strategic potential of the Pacific Ocean in the course of the past war. Prior thereto, the western strategic frontier of the United States lay on the littoral line of the Americas with an exposed island salient extending out through Hawaii, Midway, and Guam to the Philippines. That salient proved not an outpost of strength but an avenue of weakness along which the enemy could and did attack. The Pacific was a potential area of advance for any predatory force intent upon striking at the bordering land areas.

All this was changed by our Pacific victory. Our strategic frontier then shifted to embrace the entire Pacific Ocean which became a vast moat to protect us as long as we hold it. Indeed, it acts as a protective shield for all of the Americas and all free lands of the Pacific Ocean area. We control it to the shores of Asia by a chain of islands extending in an arc from the Aleutians to the Mariannas[2] held by us and our free allies.

From this island chain we can dominate with sea and air power every Asiatic port from Vladivostok to Singapore[3] and prevent any hostile movement into the Pacific. Any predatory attack from Asia must be an amphibious effort. No amphibious force can be successful without control of the sea lanes and the air over those lanes in its avenue of advance. With naval and air supremacy and modest ground elements to defend bases, any major attack from continental Asia toward us or our friends of the Pacific would be doomed to

[2] The Aleutian chain of islands ranges southwest from Alaska toward Japan and the continent of Asia. The Marianas, a group of islands some 1,500 miles east of the Philippines, extend approximately 500 miles north and south. The Marianas include Guam and Saipan.

[3] Vladivostok, a city of approximately 300,000, capital of Territory in Far Eastern Siberia, is the major Russian port on the Pacific Ocean and the Pacific base for Russian fleets. Singapore, a city of approximately 1,000,000 and one of the world's great ports, is located on an island at the very end of the Malay Peninsula. The British naval base at Singapore was completed in 1938.

failure. Under such conditions the Pacific no longer represents menacing avenues of approach for a prospective invader—it assumes instead the friendly aspect of a peaceful lake. Our line of defense is a natural one and can be maintained with a minimum of military effort and expense. It envisions no attack against anyone nor does it provide the bastions essential for offensive operations, but properly maintained would be an invincible defense against aggression.

The holding of this littoral defense line in the western Pacific is entirely dependent upon holding all segments thereof, for any major breach of that line by an unfriendly power would render vulnerable to determined attack every other major segment. This is a military estimate as to which I have yet to find a military leader who will take exception. [Applause.]

For that reason I have strongly recommended in the past as a matter of military urgency that under no circumstances must Formosa[4] fall under Communist control. [Applause.] Such an eventuality would at once threaten the freedom of the Philippines and the loss of Japan, and might well force our western frontier back to the coasts of California, Oregon, and Washington.

To understand the changes which now appear upon the Chinese mainland, one must understand the changes in Chinese character and culture over the past 50 years. China up to 50 years ago was completely nonhomogeneous, being compartmented into groups divided against each other. The war-making tendency was almost nonexistent, as they still followed the tenets of the Confucian ideal of pacifist culture.[5] At the turn of the century, under the regime of Chan So Lin,[6] efforts toward greater homogeneity produced the start of a nationalist urge. This was further and more successfully devel-

[4] Formosa (Taiwan), an island separated from the mainland of China by the Formosa Strait, is the seat of the Chinese Nationalist government. It is presumed to be subject to attack by the Communist regime on the mainland.

[5] Confucius (551?–479? B.C.), Chinese philosopher, taught through his *Analects* certain ethical precepts, including the wisdom of nonviolence in human relationships.

[6] Chang Tso-lin (1873–1928), Chinese military leader, became military governor of Fengtien in 1911. Loyal to the new republic, he obtained control of certain Manchurian provinces. His attempts to bring about administrative changes at Peking were unsuccessful.

oped under the leadership of Chiang Kai-shek[7] but has been brought to its greatest fruition under the present regime, to the point that it has now taken on the character of a united nationalism of increasingly dominant aggressive tendencies. Through these past 50 years, the Chinese people have thus become militarized in their concepts and in their ideals. They now constitute excellent soldiers with competent staffs and commanders. This has produced a new and dominant power in Asia which for its own purposes is allied with Soviet Russia, but which in its own concepts and methods has become aggressively imperialistic with a lust for expansion and increased power normal to this type of imperialism. There is little of the ideological concept either one way or another in the Chinese make-up. The standard of living is so low and the capital accumulation has been so thoroughly dissipated by war that the masses are desperate and avid to follow any leadership which seems to promise the alleviation of local stringencies. I have from the beginning believed that the Chinese Communists' support of the North Koreans was the dominant one. Their interests are at present parallel to those of the Soviet, but I believe that the aggressiveness recently displayed not only in Korea, but also in Indochina and Tibet[8] and pointing potentially toward the south, reflects predominantly the same lust for the expansion of power which has animated every would-be conqueror since the beginning of time. [Applause.]

The Japanese people since the war have undergone the greatest reformation recorded in modern history. With a commendable will, eagerness to learn, and marked capacity to understand, they have,

---

[7] Chiang Kai-shek (1886–   ), Chinese general and statesman, has led the Chinese Nationalists since 1928, when he became Chairman of the Nationalist government and Commander in Chief of its armed forces. In 1949, under the pressure of the Communist forces, he retreated, with his troops, from the mainland of China to the island of Formosa (Taiwan), where the Nationalists maintain the Republic of China.

[8] Korea, in eastern Asia, is a peninsula divided since the Korean conflict into two separate powers, North Korea being under the influence of the Chinese Communists and South Korea receiving the support of the United States and the United Nations. Indochina encompasses a group of states in Southeast Asia, formerly under the domination of the French, adjacent to Thailand and Malaya. Recently separate sovereignties have been recognized as Cambodia, Laos, and North and South Vietnam. Tibet, central Asian territory bounded by China, India, and Nepal, has since 1720 maintained a somewhat ambiguous relationship with China.

from the ashes left in war's wake, erected in Japan an edifice dedicated to the primacy of individual liberty and personal dignity, and in the ensuing process there has been created a truly representative government committed to the advance of political morality, freedom of economic enterprise and social justice. [Applause.] Politically, economically and socially Japan is now abreast of many free nations of the earth and will not again fail the universal trust. That it may be counted upon to wield a profoundly beneficial influence over the course of events in Asia is attested by the magnificent manner in which the Japanese people have met the recent challenge of war, unrest, and confusion surrounding them from the outside, and checked communism within their own frontiers without the slightest slackening in their forward progress. I sent all four of our occupation divisions to the Korean battle front without the slightest qualms as to the effect of the resulting power vacuum upon Japan. The results fully justified my faith. [Applause.] I know of no nation more serene, orderly, and industrious—nor in which higher hopes can be entertained for future constructive service in the advance of the human race. [Applause.]

Of our former wards, the Philippines, we can look forward in confidence that the existing unrest will be corrected and a strong and healthy nation will grow in the longer aftermath of war's terrible destructiveness. We must be patient and understanding and never fail them, as in our hour of need they did not fail us. [Applause.] A Christian nation, the Philippines stand as a mighty bulwark of Christianity in the Far East, and its capacity for high moral leadership in Asia is unlimited.

On Formosa, the Government of the Republic of China has had the opportunity to refute by action much of the malicious gossip which so undermined the strength of its leadership on the Chinese mainland. [Applause.] The Formosan people are receiving a just and enlightened administration with majority representation on the organs of government; and politically, economically and socially they appear to be advancing along sound and constructive lines.

With this brief insight into the surrounding areas I now turn to the Korean conflict. While I was not consulted prior to the President's decision to intervene in support of the Republic of Korea, that decision, from a military standpoint, proved a sound one [applause] as we hurled back the invaders and decimated his forces. Our victory was complete and our objectives within reach when Red China intervened with numerically superior ground forces. This created a new war and an entirely new situation—a situation not contemplated when our forces were committed against the North Korean invaders—a situation which called for new decisions in the diplomatic sphere to permit the realistic adjustment of military strategy. Such decisions have not been forthcoming. [Applause.]

While no man in his right mind would advocate sending our ground forces into continental China and such was never given a thought, the new situation did urgently demand a drastic revision of strategic planning if our political aim was to defeat this new enemy as we had defeated the old. [Applause.]

Apart from the military need as I saw it to neutralize the sanctuary protection given the enemy north of the Yalu, I felt that military necessity in the conduct of the war made mandatory:

1. The intensification of our economic blockade against China;
2. The imposition of a naval blockade against the China coast;
3. Removal of restrictions on air reconnaissance of China's coast areas and of Manchuria [applause];
4. Removal of restrictions on the forces of the Republic of China on Formosa with logistical support to contribute to their effective operations against the common enemy. [Applause.]

For entertaining these views, all professionally designed to support our forces committed to Korea and bring hostilities to an end with the least possible delay and at a saving of countless American and Allied lives, I have been severely criticized in lay circles, principally abroad, despite my understanding that from a military standpoint the above views have been fully shared in the past by practically every military leader concerned with the Korean campaign, including our own Joint Chiefs of Staff. [Applause, the Members rising.]

I called for reinforcements, but was informed that reinforcements were not available. I made clear that if not permitted to destroy the build-up bases north of the Yalu;[9] if not permitted to utilize

⁹ The Yalu River in northeastern Asia flows into the Bay of Korea at Antung. For most

the friendly Chinese force of some 600,000 men on Formosa; if not permitted to blockade the China coast to prevent the Chinese Reds from getting succor from without; and if there were to be no hope of major reinforcements, the position of the command from the military standpoint forbade victory. We could hold in Korea by constant maneuver and at an approximate area where our supply line advantages were in balance with the supply line disadvantages of the enemy, but we could hope at best for only an indecisive campaign, with its terrible and constant attrition upon our forces if the enemy utilized his full military potential. I have constantly called for the new political decisions essential to a solution. Efforts have been made to distort my position. It has been said, in effect, that I am a warmonger. Nothing could be further from the truth. I know war as few other men now living know it, and nothing to me is more revolting. I have long advocated its complete abolition as its very destructiveness on both friend and foe has rendered it useless as a means of settling international disputes. Indeed, on the 2d of September 1945, just following the surrender of the Japanese Nation on the battleship *Missouri*, I formally cautioned as follows:

"Men since the beginning of time have sought peace. Various methods through the ages have been attempted to devise an international process to prevent or settle disputes between nations. From the very start, workable methods were found insofar as individual citizens were concerned, but the mechanics of an instrumentality of larger international scope have never been successful. Military alliances, balances of power, leagues of nations, all in turn failed, leaving the only path to be by way of the crucible of war. The utter destructiveness of war now blots out this alternative. We have had our last chance. If we will not devise some greater and more equitable system, Armageddon will be at our door. The problem basically is theological and involves a spiritual recrudescence and improvement of human character that will synchronize with our almost matchless advances in science, art, literature, and all material and cultural developments of the past 2,000 years. It must be of the spirit if we are to save the flesh." [Applause.]

---

of its course, the river forms the boundary between North Korea and Communist China.

But once war is forced upon us, there is no other alternative than to apply every available means to bring it to a swift end. War's very object is victory—not prolonged indecision. [Applause.] In war, indeed, there can be no substitute for victory. [Applause.]

There are some who for varying reasons would appease Red China. They are blind to history's clear lesson. For history teaches with unmistakable emphasis that appeasement but begets new and bloodier war. It points to no single instance where the end has justified that means—where appeasement has led to more than a sham peace. Like blackmail, it lays the basis for new and successively greater demands, until, as in blackmail, violence becomes the only other alternative. Why, my soldiers asked of me, surrender military advantages to an enemy in the field? I could not answer. [Applause.] Some may say to avoid spread of the conflict into an all-out war with China; others, to avoid Soviet intervention. Neither explanation seems valid. For China is already engaging with the maximum power it can commit and the Soviet will not necessarily mesh its actions with our moves. Like a cobra, any new enemy will more likely strike whenever it feels that the relativity in military or other potential is in its favor on a world-wide basis.

The tragedy of Korea is further heightened by the fact that as military action is confined to its territorial limits, it condemns that nation, which it is our purpose to save, to suffer the devastating impact of full naval and air bombardment, while the enemy's sanctuaries are fully protected from such attack and devastation. Of the nations of the world, Korea alone, up to now, is the sole one which has risked its all against communism. The magnificence of the courage and fortitude of the Korean people defies description. [Applause.] They have chosen to risk death rather than slavery. Their last words to me were "Don't scuttle the Pacific." [Applause.]

I have just left your fighting sons in Korea. They have met all tests there and I can report to you without reservation they are splendid in every way. [Applause.] It was my constant effort to preserve them and end this savage conflict honorably and with the least loss of time and a minimum sacrifice of life. Its growing bloodshed has caused me the deepest anguish and anxiety. Those gallant men will remain often in my thoughts and in my prayers always. [Applause.]

I am closing my 52 years of military service. [Applause.] When I joined the Army even before the turn of the century, it was the fulfillment of all my boyish hopes and dreams. The world has turned over many times since I took the oath on the plain at West Point, and the hopes and dreams have long since vanished.[10] But I still remember the refrain of one of the most popular barrack ballads of that day which proclaimed most proudly that—

"Old soldiers never die; they just fade away."

And like the old soldier of that ballad, I now close my military career and just fade away—an old soldier who tried to do his duty as God gave him the light to see that duty.

Good-by.

[10] Douglas MacArthur received his commission at West Point in 1903. He returned to West Point for a tour of duty as Superintendent in 1919–1922.

§ Critical Analysis

In his preface to *A Soldier Speaks*, Major Vorin E. Whan, Jr., observes: "It is often the case that a speech which sounds very impressive when delivered before a sympathetic audience loses in impact when read in the solitude of the library." Is this observation sound? Major Whan goes on to say, "Such is not the case with General MacArthur's public statements, for in each instance he had something substantive to say and the ability to say it skillfully." [1] As you read General MacArthur's "Old Soldiers Never Die," disregarding any difference of opinion you may have with the general's thesis, do you find that he did "have something substantive to say"? Did he say it skillfully?

§

In his critique of General MacArthur's speech, Professor Wilbur S. Howell declares that "Ethical ambiguities . . . tend also to weaken the effect he [MacArthur] wanted to have." [2] Can you find examples of the ambiguities, or even conflicts, that disturbed Professor Howell? On the other hand, Professor Herbert A. Wichelns observes that General MacArthur, like Demosthenes in dealing with similar problems, in the main "chose not to debate, in the sense of formulating proposals and defending them in full." Wichelns discovered the chief support for MacArthur's policy to be "neither logical argument nor emotional appeal, but the self-portrait of the speaker as conveyed by the speech." [3] Do you find MacArthur's chief reliance, as does Wichelns, in his ethos, or do you find strong support elsewhere? In your opinion, would MacArthur have strengthened or weakened his speech by citing authorities or evidence for his assertions concerning China's military commitment and the probable course of Russian policy? Did the general gain—or lose—credibility

[1] *A Soldier Speaks: Public Papers and Speeches of General of the Army Douglas MacArthur* (New York: Praeger, 1965), p. xviii.

[2] In Frederick W. Haberman, ed., "General MacArthur's Speech: A Symposium of Critical Comment," *The Quarterly Journal of Speech*, XXXVII, 3 (October 1951), 329.

[3] *Ibid.*, 328.

by relying on his own testimony as ample authority for his statements?

§

W. Norwood Brigance reported that the climax of the speech—"old soldiers never die"—was perhaps overdone for critics who heard the speech by radio. "Some," he says, "sneered at it as 'corn.'" Brigance goes on to say that "To those who saw it on television, however, it was emotionally effective, if not indeed spine-tingling and 'beyond the limits of ordinary present-day oratory.'"[4] Concerning the audience in the general's presence, Senator Wiley observed that "there was hardly a dry eye in the entire audience," and Senator Mundt declared that "no other speaker in our generation has moved strong men of politics to open tears."[5] What do the reports of the differing responses by the three audiences—those who witnessed the speech in the House chamber, those who heard it on the radio, and those who watched it on television—suggest concerning the problems of the orator today? If you add another audience—those who read the speech in the newspapers—does the orator's problem seem more or less complex?

§

Some critics of speechmaking have characterized General MacArthur's speech as "old-fashioned oratory," suggesting that it is not in keeping with the modern intimate, colloquial style demonstrated, for example, in the speeches of Adlai Stevenson and John F. Kennedy. Do you agree? Whether or not you agree, would you say that the American people should hear more of the MacArthurian kind of speechmaking?

§

Hubert H. Humphrey, who (as senator from Minnesota) heard General MacArthur's speech, had this to say:

"In my judgment, the basic issue involved in the controversy is one of civilian versus military control over our foreign policy."[6]

[4] *Ibid.*

[5] *Ibid.,* 324.

[6] Frederick W. Haberman, "General MacArthur's Speech: A Symposium of Critical Comment," *The Quarterly Journal of Speech,* XXXVII (October 1951), 323.

Do you agree with Humphrey's judgment concerning the basic issue?

§ SUGGESTIONS FOR FURTHER READING

The first book to read about General Douglas MacArthur is his *Reminiscences* (New York: McGraw-Hill, 1964). Completed not long before his death, it is MacArthur's own accounting for his life and actions. Hence, even though it reports the controversial as well as the noncontroversial episodes of his career and is written with laudable restraint, many persons will wish to read certain salient sections of the *Reminiscences* in conjunction with appropriate sections of other books, notably Harry S. Truman's *Memoirs* (Garden City, N.Y.: Doubleday, 1956).

The Roosevelt-MacArthur Conflict (Chambersburg, Pa.: Craft, 1950) describes in some detail MacArthur's troubles with President Franklin D. Roosevelt during World War II. MacArthur's *Revitalizing a Nation* (Chicago: Heritage Foundation, 1952), with captions by John M. Pratt and an introduction by Norman Vincent Peale, appears to be responsive to President Truman's action in relieving MacArthur of his command in Japan. John W. Spanier's *The Truman-MacArthur Controversy and the Korean War* (Cambridge: Harvard University Press, 1959) offers a scholarly analysis, largely favorable to the Truman administration, of events in Japan and Korea. It includes twenty-four pages of illustrations. *With MacArthur in Japan: A Personal History of the Occupation* (New York: Norton, 1965), by William J. Sebald with Russell Brines, is a personal account of the occupation and thus necessarily involves the policies of Douglas MacArthur, with whom Ambassador Sebald had a prolonged working relationship. MacArthur's views are of course recorded in various government documents and public papers.

Some of his speeches and public statements are presented systematically and conveniently in *A Soldier Speaks: Public Papers and Speeches of General of the Army Douglas MacArthur* (New York: Praeger, 1965) edited by Major Vorin E. Whan, Jr., with an introduction by General Carlos P. Romulo. An earlier compilation by Frank C. Waldrop, *MacArthur on War* (New York: Duell, Sloan and Pearce, 1942), includes some papers that do not appear in the later collection by Whan.

John Gunther, in *The Riddle of MacArthur* (New York: Harper &

Brothers, 1951), provides a highly readable account of some dramatic episodes in the career of General MacArthur, including his landing in Japan. Another part of the MacArthur story is related in John Hersey's *Men on Bataan* (New York: Knopf, 1942). Major General Charles A. Willoughby and John Chamberlain present events in somewhat greater perspective in *MacArthur: 1941–1951* (New York: McGraw-Hill, 1954). Major General Willoughby was General MacArthur's intelligence officer for many years. A critical analysis of MacArthur's address to the Congress of the United States may be found in "General MacArthur's Speech: A Symposium of Critical Comment," edited by Frederick W. Haberman, *The Quarterly Journal of Speech*, XXXVII, 3 (October 1951), 321–331.

In 1942 the Library of Congress accorded General MacArthur a recognition said not to have been given previously to a living person: the library published a bibliography of some 253 references to Douglas MacArthur. A dramatic and forceful personality, General MacArthur will be the subject of many other bibliographies and biographies in time to come, as the histories supplied by his staff to the Department of the Army and the mass of papers now in the archives of the MacArthur Memorial at Roanoke, Virginia, are exploited by historians and biographers.

John F. Kennedy

❧ | ☙

> "Let every nation know, whether it wishes us well or ill, that we shall pay any price, bear any burden, meet any hardship, support any friend, oppose any foe, in order to assure the survival of liberty." [1] —JOHN F. KENNEDY

BIOGRAPHICAL SKETCH

John Fitzgerald Kennedy, thirty-fifth President of the United States, was born in Brookline, Massachusetts, on May 29, 1917. He was the son of Ambassador Joseph P. Kennedy and Rose Fitzgerald Kennedy and the grandson of two Bostonians, Patrick Kennedy and John F. Fitzgerald. He attended the public schools of Brookline, the Canterbury School in New Milford, Connecticut, and the Choate School in Wallingford, Connecticut. Following a brief attendance at the London School of Economics, Princeton University, and Stanford University, he matriculated at Harvard University and was graduated *cum laude* in 1940. During World War II he served as a lieutenant in the United States Navy (September 1941 to April 1945). Injured in the line of duty, he was awarded the Purple Heart, as well as the Navy and Marine Corps Medal.

Kennedy was elected as a Democrat to the House of Representatives from the Eleventh Congressional District of Massachusetts and served in the Eightieth, Eighty-first, and Eighty-second Congresses. In 1952 he was elected to the Senate and served as senator from

NOTE: The observations presented here are based on the references cited in the section Suggestions for Further Reading, pp. 277–279, and on the personal responses of the editors who heard John F. Kennedy speak from the public platform and in broadcasts, notably by television in the Nixon-Kennedy debates.

[1] John F. Kennedy, "Inaugural Address, January 20, 1961," *Inaugural Addresses of the Presidents of the United States from George Washington 1789 to Lyndon Baines Johnson 1965*, 89th Congress, 1st Session, House Document No. 51 (Washington, D.C.: Government Printing Office, 1965), p. 268.

265

Massachusetts until he resigned on December 22, 1960, to assume the presidency of the United States on January 20, 1961. On September 12, 1953, he was married to Miss Jacqueline Lee Bouvier. To this union were born Caroline Bouvier (1957), John Fitzgerald, Jr. (1960), and Patrick Bouvier (deceased). President John F. Kennedy was assassinated in Dallas, Texas, on November 22, 1963. He is buried in the Arlington National Cemetery, Fort Myer, Virginia.

THE SPEAKER

John F. Kennedy reached the presidency of the United States before his forty-fourth birthday and died before his forty-seventh. Too young to be president, some people thought, and certainly too young to die, he left on the presidency and on his countrymen an impression not likely soon to be removed. His words and actions asserted the appeal of youth and vigor, of hope in a world troubled by nameless fears and violent confusions. By his example as by his precept, he brought again to the American people and to the world that ancient and indispensable virtue: courage.

By the time he came to the presidency, Kennedy was a veteran of many speeches, with many more to come not only in his own but also in other countries. Some of these presidential "speeches" he regarded merely as remarks or statements; but in his position as head of state of the most powerful nation in the world, whatever he said was noteworthy. His speeches, remarks, or statements were thus recorded, whether they were given from the public platform, or in a news release, or in a broadcast over radio or television. His views and his style are embodied in utterances as disparate as his New Year's greetings to leaders of the Soviet Union, his special message to the Congress on mental illness and mental retardation, his remarks at the anniversary luncheon of the Delta Sigma Theta Sorority, a colloquy at a meeting of the American Bankers' Association, an address of welcome to President Betancourt of Venezuela, an address to the United States Conference of Mayors in Honolulu, his remarks at a breakfast with Democratic State Committeewomen in Hollywood, and his commencement address at the State College, San Diego, California. In Germany he spoke in Bonn, in Berlin, in Cologne, in Bad Godesberg, in Wiesbaden, and in Hanau; in Ireland he spoke in Dublin, in Cork, in New Ross, in Wexford, in Galway, in Limerick, and at the Shannon airport on leaving for England, where he made more speeches before leaving for Italy and still more speeches in Naples and in Rome.[2]

The sheer number of Kennedy's recorded speeches suggests that the presidency of the United States is now a platform, that the office is a speaking post, and that the President should be articulate. A consecutive reading of the texts of Kennedy's speeches and the remembrance of his voice and presence in speaking suggest that he mastered the art of easy and disarming eloquence exemplified earlier by another Harvard man, Wendell Phillips. Kennedy's quick wit, his obvious rapport with his audience, his shrewd use of the timely topic and the immediate events indicate his instinct for finding common ground with his hearers.

With Kennedy, as with every other orator, particularly those of the present day, the question arises: Were his speeches his own? The answer is, "Yes, Kennedy's speeches were his own." The true test of the matter is not how much assistance the speaker had in the preparation of the speech; it is how intelligently and intelligibly he delivered it. By every test known to the rhetorician, Kennedy spoke with a full understanding of and concern for the content of his speeches at the very moment of delivery. Recognizing that presidential speeches are a matter of import, and that sometimes they make or declare policy, he wisely obtained all the assistance necessary in search and research, in preparing drafts, and in criticizing phrases. But Kennedy was always the man in charge not only in the delivery but in the preparation of his speeches. With no speech did he take more pains than with his Inaugural Address of January 20, 1961. He wanted his speech to be the shortest one in the twentieth

[2] A likely source for the texts of some of Kennedy's speeches, addresses, statements, and remarks is Harold W. Chase and Allen H. Lerman, eds., *Kennedy and the Press: The News Conferences* (New York: Crowell, 1965), an admirable reporting that demonstrates Kennedy's quick wit, lively imagination, and competent grasp of public questions.

century. "It's more effective that way," he said, "and I don't want people to think I'm a windbag." [3]

Strangely enough, John F. Kennedy seemed never to regard himself as an orator or even as a very effective speaker. He wished that he might have the mastery of inflection that he observed in the speeches of Adlai Stevenson.[4] It is no disparagement of Adlai Stevenson, who talked sense to the American people, to report that in adapting discourse to his hearers, in solving the problems that must be dealt with in speechmaking, John F. Kennedy at his best was the equal of Adlai Stevenson or any other American of his time.

THE SPEECH

Following the inauguration on January 20, 1961, *The New Yorker* published in "The Talk of the Town" an unusually discerning and discriminating piece of rhetorical criticism. It is here reproduced,[5] with the recommendation that it be studied along with the text of the Inaugural Address:

> As rhetoric has become an increasingly dispensable member of the liberal arts, people have abandoned the idea, held so firmly by the ancient Greeks and Romans, that eloquence is indispensable to politics. Perhaps President Kennedy's achievements in both spheres will revive a taste for good oratory—a taste that has been alternately frustrated by inarticulateness and dulled by bombast. There have been a few notable orators in our day— most recently, Adlai Stevenson—but they have been the exceptions, and it has taken Mr. Kennedy's success as a politician to suggest that the power to "enchant souls through words" (Socrates) may soon be at a premium once more. Whatever the im-

[3] Theodore C. Sorenson, *Kennedy* (New York: Harper & Row, 1965), p. 242. This book gives an account, fascinating for the rhetorician, of Kennedy's preparation of his Inaugural Address.

[4] Arthur Schlesinger, *A Thousand Days: John F. Kennedy in the White House* (Boston: Houghton Mifflin, 1965), p. 690.

[5] From "The Talk of the Town," *The New Yorker* (February 4, 1961), pp. 23–24. Reprinted by permission, © 1961, *The New Yorker Magazine*, Inc.

pact of the Inaugural Address on contemporary New Frontiers-men, we find it hard to believe that an Athenian or Roman citizen could have listened to it unmoved, or that Cicero, however jealous of his own reputation, would have found reason to object to it.

We are all familiar by now with the generally high praise the President received for his first speech, but before the responsibility for a final judgment is yielded to Time it would be a shame not to seek the opinion of a couple of true professionals. Both Aristotle and Cicero, the one a theorist and the other a theorizing orator, believed that rhetoric could be an art to the extent that the orator was, first, a logician and, second, a psychologist with an appreciation and understanding of words. Cicero felt, further, that the ideal orator was the thoroughly educated man. (He would be pleased by Mr. Kennedy's background, with its strong emphasis on affairs of state: the philosopher-orator-statesman.) Of the three types of oratory defined by the ancients—political, forensic, and display (in which audience participation was limited to a judgment of style)—the political was esteemed most highly, because it dealt with the loftiest of issues; namely, the fate of peoples, rather than of individuals. ("Now the trumpet summons us again . . . against the common enemies of man. . . .") The ideal speech was thought to be one in which three kinds of persuasion were used by the speaker: logical, to present the facts of the case and construct an argument based on them; emotional, to reach the audience psychologically; and "ethical," to appeal to the audience by establishing one's own integrity and sincerity. The Inaugural Address, being a variation on the single theme of man's rights and obligations, is not primarily logical, although it contains no illogic; it is an appeal to men's souls rather than to their minds. During the Presidential campaign, Mr. Kennedy tested and patented an exercise in American psychology that proved to be all the emotional appeal he required for the inaugural speech: "And so, my fellow-Americans, ask not what your country can do for you, ask what you can do for your country." His ethical persuasion, or indication of his personal probity, consisted of an extension of that appeal: ". . . ask of us here the same high standards of strength and sacrifice which we ask of you."

Aristotle recognized only one (good) style, while Cicero thought that there were three styles—the plain, the middle, and the grand. To Aristotle, who considered it sufficient for a style to be clear and appropriate, avoiding undue elevation (whence bombast) and excessive lowliness, it would have seemed that Mr. Kennedy had achieved the Golden Mean. The formality of the Inaugural Address ("To that world assembly of sovereign states, the United Nations . . .") is appropriate to the subject; the language ("In your hands, my fellow-citizens, more than mine, will rest the final success or failure of our course") is clear and direct. Cicero's ideal orator was able to speak in all three styles, in accordance with the demands of his subject, and in that respect Mr. Kennedy filled the role by speaking plainly on the practical ("All this will not be finished in the first one hundred days"), by speaking formally but directly on the purpose of national defense ("For only when our arms are sufficient beyond doubt can we be certain beyond doubt that they will never be employed"), and by speaking grandly on the potential accomplishments of the movement toward the New Frontier ("The energy, the faith, the devotion which we bring to this endeavor will light our country and all who serve it—and the glow from that fire can truly light the world").

The address, however, is largely in the grand style, which is characterized by Cicero as the ultimate source of emotional persuasion, through figures of speech and a certain degree of dignified periodic rhythm, not iambic ("The world is very different now. For man holds in his mortal hands the power to abolish all forms of human poverty, and all forms of human life"). The oration is so rich in figures of speech—the many metaphors include a torch, a beachhead, jungles, a trumpet, a tiger—that we can imagine students of the future studying it for examples of antithesis ("If a free society cannot help the many who are poor, it cannot save the few who are rich"), personification (". . . the hand of mankind's final war"), and anaphora ("Not as a call to bear arms, though arms we need; not as a call to battle, though embattled we are . . .”). “Battle” and “embattled”—an excellent example of paronomasia.

And so we leave the speech to the students of rhetoric, having invoked for Mr. Kennedy the blessings of Aristotle and Cicero, and for ourself the hope that he has reëstablished the tradition of political eloquence.

Inaugural Address

Mr. Chief Justice, President Eisenhower, Vice President Nixon, President Truman, reverend clergy, fellow citizens, we observe today not a victory of party, but a celebration of freedom—symbolizing an end, as well as a beginning—signifying renewal, as well as change. For I have sworn before you and Almighty God the same solemn oath our forebears prescribed nearly a century and three quarters ago.[1]

The world is very different now. For man holds in his mortal hands the power to abolish all forms of human poverty and all forms of human life. And yet the same revolutionary beliefs for which our forebears fought are still at issue around the globe—the belief that the rights of man come not from the generosity of the state, but from the hand of God.

We dare not forget today that we are the heirs of that first revolution. Let the word go forth from this time and place, to friend and foe alike, that the torch has been passed to a new generation of Americans—born in this century, tempered by war, disciplined by a hard and bitter peace, proud of our ancient heritage—and unwilling to witness or permit the slow undoing of those human rights to which this Nation has always been committed, and to which we are committed today at home and around the world.

Let every nation know, whether it wishes us well or ill, that we shall pay any price, bear any burden, meet any hardship, support any friend, oppose any foe, in order to assure the survival and the success of liberty.

This much we pledge—and more.

From *Inaugural Addresses of the Presidents of the United States from George Washington 1789 to Lyndon Baines Johnson 1965* (Washington, D.C.: Government Printing Office, 1965), pp. 267–270.

---

[1] The oath required of the Presidents of the United States is stated in Article II, Section 1, of the Constitution: "I do solemnly swear (or affirm) that I will faithfully execute the office of President of the United States, and will to the best of my ability, preserve, protect and defend the Constitution of the United States."

To those old allies whose cultural and spiritual origins we share, we pledge the loyalty of faithful friends. United, there is little we cannot do in a host of cooperative ventures. Divided, there is little we can do—for we dare not meet a powerful challenge at odds and split asunder.

To those new States whom we welcome to the ranks of the free, we pledge our words that one form of colonial control shall not have passed away merely to be replaced by a far greater iron tyranny. We shall not always expect to find them supporting our view. But we shall always hope to find them strongly supporting their own freedom—and to remember that, in the past, those who foolishly sought power by riding the back of the tiger ended up inside.

To those peoples in the huts and villages across the globe struggling to break the bonds of mass misery, we pledge our best efforts to help them help themselves, for whatever period is required—not because the Communists may be doing it, not because we seek their votes, but because it is right. If a free society cannot help the many who are poor, it cannot save the few who are rich.

To our sister republics south of our border, we offer a special pledge—to convert our good words into good deeds, in a new alliance for progress, to assist free men and free governments in casting off the chains of poverty. But this peaceful revolution of hope cannot become the prey of hostile powers. Let all our neighbors know that we shall join with them to oppose aggression or subversion anywhere in the Americas. And let every other power know that this hemisphere intends to remain the master of its own house.

To that world assembly of sovereign states, the United Nations, our last best hope in an age where the instruments of war have far outpaced the instruments of peace, we renew our pledge of support —to prevent it from becoming merely a forum for invective—to strengthen its shield of the new and the weak—and to enlarge the area in which its writ may run.

Finally, to those nations who would make themselves our adversary, we offer not a pledge but a request: that both sides begin anew the quest for peace, before the dark powers of destruction unleashed by science engulf all humanity in planned or accidental self-destruction.

273

We dare not tempt them with weakness. For only when our arms are sufficient beyond doubt can we be certain beyond doubt that they will never be employed.

But neither can two great and powerful groups of nations take comfort from our present course—both sides overburdened by the cost of modern weapons, both rightly alarmed by the steady spread of the deadly atom, yet both racing to alter that uncertain balance of terror that stays the hand of mankind's final war.

So let us begin anew—remembering on both sides that civility is not a sign of weakness, and sincerity is always subject to proof. *Let us never negotiate out of fear. But let us never fear to negotiate.*

Let both sides explore what problems unite us instead of laboring those problems which divide us.

Let both sides, for the first time, formulate serious and precise proposals for the inspection and control of arms—and bring the absolute power to destroy other nations under the absolute control of all nations.

Let both sides seek to invoke the wonders of science instead of its terrors. Together let us explore the stars, conquer the deserts, eradicate disease, tap the ocean depths, and encourage the arts and commerce.

Let both sides unite to heed in all corners of the earth the command of Isaiah—to "undo the heavy burdens and to let the oppressed go free."

And if a beachhead of cooperation may push back the jungle of suspicion, let both sides join in creating a new endeavor, not a new balance of power, but a new world of law, where the strong are just and the weak secure and the peace preserved.

All this will not be finished in the first 100 days. Nor will it be finished in the first 1,000 days, nor in the life of this administration, nor even perhaps in our lifetime on this planet. But let us begin.

In your hands, my fellow citizens, more than in mine, will rest the final success or failure of our course. Since this country was founded, each generation of Americans has been summoned to give testimony to its national loyalty. The graves of young Americans who answered the call to service surround the globe.

Now the trumpet summons us again—not as a call to bear arms, though arms we need; not as a call to battle, though embattled we are; but a call to bear the burden of a long twilight struggle, year in, and year out, "rejoicing in hope, patient in tribulation"—a struggle against the common enemies of man: tyranny, poverty, disease, and war itself.

Can we forge against these enemies a grand and global alliance, North and South, East and West, that can assure a more fruitful life for all mankind? Will you join in that historic effort?

In the long history of the world, only a few generations have been granted the role of defending freedom in its hour of maximum danger. I do not shrink from this responsibility—I welcome it. I do not believe that any of us would exchange places with any other people or any other generation. The energy, the faith, the devotion which we bring to this endeavor will light our country and all who serve it—and the glow from that fire can truly light the world.

And so, my fellow Americans, ask not what your country can do for you: Ask what you can do for your country.

My fellow citizens of the world: Ask not what America will do for you, but what together we can do for the freedom of man.

Finally, whether you are citizens of America or citizens of the world, ask of us the same high standards of strength and sacrifice which we ask of you. With a good conscience our only sure reward, with history the final judge of our deeds, let us go forth to lead the land we love, asking His blessing and His help, but knowing that here on earth God's work must truly be our own.

§ Critical Analysis

John F. Kennedy is said to have admired the oratory of Adlai Stevenson. As you compare their speeches, those within this volume and those to be found elsewhere, what observations can you make concerning the style of Kennedy and the style of Stevenson?

§

The New Yorker suggested that President Kennedy's achievements in eloquence and politics might revive a taste for good oratory. What evidence do you find that this hope was justified?

§

The New Yorker observes that the address is so rich in figures of speech that students in the future may study it for examples of antithesis, personification, anaphora, and paronomasia. What examples do you find of these and other figures of speech?

§

At 3:50 P.M. on Monday, November 25, 1963, Harold Macmillan, former Prime Minister of Great Britain, rose in the House of Commons to pay a quietly eloquent and moving tribute to the late President Kennedy. He said, "We mourn a world statesman, to whose leadership, in these critical but inspiring days, all the peoples of the world, of whatever race, creed, or colour, looked with confidence and hope." [1] What evidence do you find within President Kennedy's Inaugural Address to support Macmillan's statement?

§

Pierre Salinger reports[2] that the late Marguerite Higgins asked Mr. Kennedy, then President-elect, if he had a good Inaugural speech, whereupon he replied with a smile, "It's a smash." Do you agree or disagree with President Kennedy's estimate of his Inaugural Address?

---

[1] *Parliamentary Debates: House of Commons Official Report*, Session 1963–64, Fifth Series, Vol. 685: Comprising Period from 25th November–6th December, 1963.
[2] *With Kennedy* (Garden City, N.Y.: Doubleday & Company, 1964), pp. 108–109.

§ SUGGESTIONS FOR FURTHER READING

If from the current offering concerning the late President John F. Kennedy one were to recommend a single book, that book would surely be Theodore C. Sorenson's *Kennedy* (New York: Harper & Row, 1965). Sorenson, who was special counsel to Kennedy, obviously undertook his work as a labor of love; yet the book reveals its author as both percipient and remarkably objective. Written in the true elegance of simplicity, it could have come only from a man who had free access not only to the facts of Kennedy's career but also to some of the privacies of his mind and spirit. Since one of Sorenson's primary tasks was the drafting of Kennedy's speeches, the book is especially useful to students of speechmaking. See, for example, Sorenson's account (pp. 240–248) of the Inaugural Address. Although Sorenson's is a major biography, as an early one it will doubtless be followed by many others. Meanwhile it is indispensable, and it is unlikely that it will soon be supplanted.

Of the spate of recent books and articles about President John F. Kennedy and the Kennedy family, the following may be mentioned: Hugh Sidey's *John F. Kennedy: President* (New York: Atheneum, 1963) is a reporter's account of the Kennedy years in the White House. As the author says (p. vii), it deals mostly with crises and, with few exceptions, is based on his observation of the administration. Pierre Salinger's *With Kennedy* (Garden City, N.Y.: Doubleday, 1966) is also a reporter's account, but Salinger's obligations as press secretary were so specific and his relation to President Kennedy so close that the book has a special value. Frank L. Kluckhohn's *America Listen!* (Derby, Conn.: Monarch, 1961) concerns the "threat to our survival" as well as the Kennedy family.

Helen Fuller's *Year of Trial: Kennedy's Crucial Decisions* (New York: Harcourt, Brace & World, 1962) describes President Kennedy's decisions and the circumstances in which he made them, beginning with the fateful choice of Lyndon B. Johnson as his running mate. Jim Bishop's *A Day in the Life of President Kennedy* (New York: Random House, 1964) is the work of "the last writer to work with President Kennedy on an exclusive story." *The Kennedy Circle* (Washington, D.C.: Luce, 1961), edited by Lester Tanzer with an introduction by David Brinkley, consists of twelve chapters by thirteen Washington reporters concerning nineteen men who were close to President Kennedy.

James MacGregor Burns' *John Kennedy: A Political Profile* (New York: Harcourt, Brace & World, 1961) is perhaps unique for although it was written while John F. Kennedy was an active aspirant for the presidency (the preface is dated "November, 1959"), it seems to fulfill its claim not to be a campaign biography; or, if it is one, it is unusual in its objectivity and in its avoidance of the partisan clichés. *John F. Kennedy on Education* (New York: Teachers College Press, Columbia University, 1966), edited by William T. O'Hara, is a convenient source for Kennedy's views on education.

President Kennedy characteristically relied on task forces to provide him with the information he required before making major decisions. The texts of the task force reports presented to him prior to 1962, with a foreword by M. B. Schnapper, are readily available in *New Frontiers of the Kennedy Administration* (Washington, D.C.: Public Affairs, 1961). Arthur Schlesinger's *A Thousand Days: John F. Kennedy in the White House* (Boston: Houghton Mifflin, 1965) is useful as a personal account of Kennedy's presidency. *The Kennedy Years* (New York: Viking, 1964) provides some charming photography with a text prepared under the direction of Harold Faber of *The New York Times*.

With few exceptions the flood of print that followed the assassination of Kennedy may be ignored by those interested chiefly in his speechmaking. One of the exceptions is *Memorial Addresses in the Congress of the United States and Tributes in Eulogy of John Fitzgerald Kennedy Late a President of the United States* (Washington, D.C.: Government Printing Office, 1964). This official volume of more than 900 pages, including the memorial addresses delivered in the United States Senate and House of Representatives as well as editorials from the newspapers and tributes from other nations, will suggest Kennedy's ethos. Another exception is *Tribute to John F. Kennedy: President of the United States of America,* a brochure containing the texts of addresses delivered on November 25, 1963, during the session of the European Parliament (Publications Department of the European Communities, 1963); and still another is *A Tribute to John Fitzgerald Kennedy Originally Presented in England on the BBC Television Program* (New York: National Broadcasting Company, 1963).

John F. Kennedy, who was once briefly a newspaperman, wrote a good many ephemeral pieces. At least three works from his pen, however, deserve more than passing notice: *Why England Slept* (New York: W. Funk, 1940); *A Nation of Immigrants,* with an introduction by Robert F. Kennedy (New York: Popular Library, 1964); and *Profiles in Courage* (New York: Harper & Brothers, 1956). Many of Kennedy's speeches, in addition to the inaugural address, are easily available, both in print and on tape. The obvious source for the texts is in government documents, as for example John F. Kennedy, *Public Papers of the President of the United States Containing the Public Messages, Speeches, and Statements of the President* (Washington, D.C.: Government Printing Office, 1962, 1963, 1964). The 1964 volume contains the text of his famous remarks in the Rudolph Wilde Platz in Berlin on June 26, 1963 (pp. 524–525), including the well-known *Ich bin ein Berliner*—"I am a Berliner"—and of his "Address Before the Irish Parliament" in Dublin on June 28, 1963 (pp. 534–539).

Some of Kennedy's speeches on foreign policy were first published in England under the title *The Strategy of Peace* (London: Hamish Hamilton, 1960). A selection of his speeches delivered from the time of his election through the 1961 adjournment of Congress was edited by John W. Gardner and published with a foreword by Carl Sandburg and an introduction by President Kennedy under the title *To Turn the Tide* (New York: Harper & Brothers, 1962). The texts of the Kennedy-Nixon debates, with eighteen chapters of critical analysis and comment, are available in Sidney Kraus, ed., *The Great Debates: Background, Perspective, Effects* (Bloomington: Indiana University Press, 1962). For the student of speech-making, as well as for students of journalism and of politics, President Kennedy's news conferences revealed a mind actively at work under pressure. They are reported in *Kennedy and the Press: The News Conferences* (New York: Crowell, 1965), edited and annotated by Harold W. Chase and Allen H. Lerman, with an introduction by Pierre Salinger.

Adlai E. Stevenson

> "We travel together, passengers on a little space ship, dependent on its vulnerable reserves of air and soil; all committed for our safety to its security and peace; preserved from annihilation only by the care, the work, and, I will say, the love we give our fragile craft." [1] —ADLAI E. STEVENSON

BIOGRAPHICAL SKETCH

Adlai Ewing Stevenson was born in Los Angeles on February 5, 1900, and died in London on July 14, 1965. Named for his grandfather, who was Vice-President of the United States during the second administration of Grover Cleveland, Stevenson was active in politics and civic affairs during most of his adult life. He spent his childhood in the family home at Bloomington, Illinois, attended Choate School and Princeton University, served two years in the Navy during World War I, completed his law studies at Northwestern University, and was admitted to the Illinois bar in 1926. He practiced law in Chicago until 1941, when he became special assistant to Frank Knox, Secretary of the Navy. Subsequently he served as assistant to Edward R. Stettinius and later to James F. Byrnes, in the Department of State. He served as adviser to the United States delegation at the San Francisco conference on world organization (1945), as senior adviser to the United States delegation at the first session of the United Nations General Assembly in London (1946), and as an alternate delegate to the General As-

NOTE: The sources for this essay will be found in the section Suggestions for Further Reading, pp. 303–304. The editors heard Adlai Stevenson speak, both in person and on television, and have discussed the Stevenson rhetoric with numerous professional and lay persons.

---

[1] Adlai E. Stevenson, "Strengthening the International Development Institutions," *Department of State Bulletin*, Vol. LIII, No. 1361 (July 26, 1965), p. 151.

semblies of 1946 and 1947, in New York. In 1948 by an unprecedented majority, Stevenson was elected Governor of Illinois. In 1952 he was a somewhat reluctant candidate for the presidency. On the election of General Eisenhower, Stevenson returned to the practice of law, with time out, however, for a world tour designed to enhance his knowledge of world affairs. In 1956 he was again a candidate for the presidency, was again defeated by Eisenhower, and again returned to the practice of law. During the presidential campaign of 1960, he served as adviser on foreign affairs to John F. Kennedy and on Kennedy's election was named United States Ambassador to the United Nations, a post he held with great distinction until his death.

The Speaker

On July 14, 1965, Adlai Stevenson's sudden death on a London street closed his notable career as parliamentarian, diplomat, statesman, and public orator. During his sixty-five years Stevenson had amply justified the encomium Oxford University conferred on him May 24, 1957, with the honorary degree of Doctor of Civil Law:

> I present to you Adlai Stevenson, amid the strains and stresses of national and international politics the champion of humanism in word and deed, and himself the source.

Superbly educated, Stevenson had been taught not only by Princeton but also, as Pericles said of the Athenians, "by life itself to reason and to judge." In "Strengthening the International Development Institutions," posterity has recorded the last formal address Stevenson delivered in person, although, as could happen only in this scientific age, a speech of his was broadcast electronically not long after he died.

As a practiced orator, Stevenson could and did speak on many different occasions, to many kinds of audiences, for various purposes, on diverse subjects. He is perhaps best known and best remembered for his gentle, self-deprecating humor and for his folk stories somehow akin to those of Abraham Lincoln, who was the object of Stevenson's profound regard. Stevenson's collection of Lincolniana occupied a prominent place in his library. Indeed the comparison between Lincoln and Stevenson—two sons of the Illinois prairie—can hardly escape the thoughtful student. To be sure, Lincoln did not have the advantage—and possible political disadvantage—of an Ivy League schooling, but he and Stevenson shared the Periclean ability to learn from life itself. Like Lincoln, Stevenson had a troubled marriage, and like Lincoln he had sons who were a joy to him. Lincoln's son, to his father's manifest sorrow, died in boyhood. Stevenson's son experienced injury in a calamity that brought grief to the father. Stevenson, as did Lincoln, witnessed in youth a tragic death that may have fixed a sadness beneath the outward humor that both found necessary for survival. Both men were sometimes thought to be indecisive. Yet Lincoln and Stevenson, in their several administrations, were capable of strong opinions and firm decisions when these were required. Perhaps the most striking comparison between the two Illinoisians will be found in their style, in their use of language to promote ends desirable for mankind. For although the Stevenson style is not Lincolnian in the minutiae, in the larger elements it is. In its humanity, in its compassion, in its sometimes homely humor, in its demonstration of the wish of the speaker to talk sense to the American people and the people of the world, the Stevenson language is the language of the Lincoln whom he regarded as his exemplar. It is doubtless no accident that when in 1952 Stevenson sought a way to explain his feelings following his overwhelming defeat by General Eisenhower, he referred to Abraham Lincoln:

> Someone asked me, as I came down the street, how I felt, and I was reminded of a story that a fellow townsman of ours used to tell—Abraham Lincoln. They asked him how he felt once after an unsuccessful election. He said he felt like a little boy who had stubbed his toe in the dark. He said that he was too old to cry, but it hurt too much to laugh.[2]

THE OCCASION AND THE AUDIENCE

"Strengthening the International Development Institutions" was delivered before the Economic and Social Development Council of

[2] Kenneth S. Davis, *A Prophet in IIis Own Country: The Triumphs and Defeats of Adlai E. Stevenson* (Garden City, N.Y.: Doubleday, 1957), p. 428.

the United Nations meeting in Geneva, Switzerland, on July 9, 1965. Soon thereafter it was published by the Department of State as a document available to all who wished to read it. The years 1960–1970 had been designated by the United Nations as the "Decade of Development" and the year 1965 as the "Year of International Cooperation." Stevenson employs these facts in presenting his program.

THE SPEECH

Adlai Stevenson's last speech was chosen for this anthology not because it is typical of Stevenson's speeches, for he delivered too many kinds of speeches for any one of them to typify the whole of his discourse. Nor does the speech provide the humor that made Stevenson a legend in his own day. It does exemplify, however, as well as any other, his sober discourse—as equally notable as his humor although less well known. This speech, like many of those he gave before the United Nations and elsewhere, is one that "does work." Not all speeches are or should be designed to entertain, to amuse, or even to persuade in the limited sense. The highest function of oratory is to deliberate a program to which the wise and the just can repair. It is precisely such a program that Stevenson sets forth here.

Strengthening International Development Institutions

❦

We meet here in Geneva at the midpoint of the Year of International Cooperation and the midpoint of the Decade of Development.[1] Let us be neither cynical nor despondent about the gap between these brave titles and the fact that at the moment our world community is in fact chiefly notable for minimal cooperation and very lopsided development. Our aspirations are there to spur us on, to incite us to better efforts. They are emphatically not there as a blind or a cover or as rhetoric to suggest that we are really doing very well.

I take as the understood premise of everything I say that as a world community we are not developing as we should and that our record of cooperation is inadequate, to say the least. But I believe—I hope—we can do better and that the nations meeting in 1970 will say: "Ah, yes, 1965 was a kind of turning point. That was the moment at which we began to realize how much better our performance has to be."

How much better can best be registered by a glance at where we are now.

We launched the Decade of Development because we realized, as a world community, that while our wealth was growing, its distribution had become increasingly unbalanced. I need hardly repeat the figures—the developed market economies and the developed centrally planned economies make up about a quarter of the world's population and account for three-quarters of the world's trade, production, and investment.

From *Department of State Bulletin*, Vol. LIII, No. 1361, Publication 7927 (July 26, 1965), pp. 142–151. Asterisked footnotes appeared in this issue of the *Department of State Bulletin*.

---

[1] Made before the 39th session of the U.N. Economic and Social Council at Geneva, Switzerland, on July 9, 1965 (Press Release 170).

By the chances of history and geography, these developed nations are largely to be found to the north of the Tropic of Cancer. Ideology makes no difference here. Soviet Russia belongs by income and growth to the developed "north," Ghana to the developing "south" in our new economic geography.

These facts we knew in 1960. In the last 5 years the contrasts have grown more vivid. The developed nations with per capita incomes of above $700 a year have grown—the index I use is gross national product per head of population—by not less than 3 percent a year.

Below them a smaller group of nations, which are in the range of $200 to $700 per capita, have grown even more rapidly—by 4 to 8 percent a year.

But at the bottom of the scale at a figure of $200 per head and less, comprising over a hundred nations making up over two-thirds of humanity, the rate of per capita growth has in many instances been less than the average of 2.3 percent of the developing countries as a whole. Population growth has swallowed up their margins, and per capita growth hovers around zero.

THE HIDDEN MISERIES

This is the statistical picture which emerges from the present data about world development. But how bare and uninformative such numbers really are. They tell us nothing about the rates of child mortality—10 times higher among poor than rich. They give us no picture of the homeless migrant living without water or shelter on the fringe of Asian or Latin American cities. We get no feel from them of the dull ache of hunger or the debility that comes from diets without enough protein and vitamins.

These are the hidden miseries about which we talk with our figures of per capita gross national product, our statistical comparisons, our impersonal percentages. We are talking about pain and grief and hunger and despair, and we are talking about the lot of half the human race.

EXPANSION IN THE DEVELOPED SOCIETIES

But we are also talking about another phenomenon—the extraordinary increase in resources available to human society taken as a whole. These 3- or 4-percent increases in the national growth of developed societies mean an unparalleled expansion of new resources.

Under steady and responsible economic management, we cannot see, and we certainly do not want, any end to this process of expansion. Out of the research that is connected with weaponry, with space, and with the whole wide range of needs of our civilian economy, we are constantly making new breakthroughs—new methods, new products, new sources of food or energy or medical relief that increase our capacity to reproduce wealth still further. We have harnessed energy to take us into outer space and to convert saline waters into drink for the thirsty. The isotopes which grow from nuclear experiments can revolutionize medical and agricultural research. And we know not what new, still undiscovered sources of abundance lie ahead.

We have to begin to grasp and digest this new, astonishing liberation of our industrial resources, for only after such an understanding can we hope to act on the scale and with the audacity that our profound problems of poverty and hopelessness and obstruction demand. We shall conquer, no doubt, the dark face of the moon. But I would hope we can with equal confidence conquer the dark face of poverty and give men and women new life, new hope, new space on this planet.

Let's face it: We are nowhere near conquering world poverty. None of us—neither the weak nor the strong, the poor nor the rich, the new nations nor the old—have yet taken seriously enough the contrast between the abundance of our opportunities and the scarcity of our actions to grasp them. It is good that the rich are getting richer—that is what economic development is for. But it is bad that, despite our considerable efforts in the first half of this decade, the poor are still poor—and progressing more slowly than present-day society can tolerate.

What shall we do to improve the trend during the next 5 years? There is something for everybody to do. There are tasks for all of us, and it won't help the poor countries for us to sit around this table blaming the state of the world on each other. There are clear and present tasks for the developing countries in doing what they know is necessary to their own economic growth and social progress. There are tasks, equally clear and equally present, for the industrialized countries. And there are tasks—a growing number of much larger tasks—for U.N. organizations themselves.

I think each of us should come to this table vowing to bring proposals that his nation can—and intends to—do something about. In that spirit I will not rehearse here my views on how the developing nations can better help themselves but will suggest what the wealthier countries can do to help and how the U.N. itself can do more about development and do it better.

A Convergent Strategy

Let me suggest first the sense of a convergent strategy for the industrialized nations. Its aim should be to see to it that more of the wealth and purchasing power of our expanding world economy will be used to stimulate economic growth in the developing nations.

We can accomplish this aim only by the coordinate use of a variety of means: by the direct transfer of resources from developed nations to developing nations through effective aid programs; next, by assuring the developing countries greater access to the expanding markets of the world; next, by working to reduce fluctuations in the export earnings of the developing countries; next, by working harder, doing more specific research, on what the more developed countries can do to help the less developed create more wealth faster; next, by helping to slow down the vertiginous growth in the numbers of people which the still fragile developing economies have to support. A steady, overall, 4-percent rate of growth in national income is in itself a difficult achievement. Its effects are tragically nullified if the rate of population growth is 3 percent or even more.

These five strands of a convergent strategy contain no mysteries. We have discussed them over and over again. What has been lacking has been an adequate urgency of purpose and decision and a real determination to face the full costs.

There is no doubt that we can afford whatever direct transfer of resources can really be put to effective use. There are so many manmade obstacles in the developing process that there is a kind of natural limit to the transfer of resources from the richer countries to the poorer countries.

In my judgment, we are in no danger at all of harming our own healthy economies by maximizing our efforts to promote international development. Our problem, rather, is to step up the training of people, the surveying of resources, and the investigation of opportunities—in a word, the preinvestment work—which still sets the ceiling on direct investment, public and private, in the economic growth of most developing countries.

With my next point—improved trading opportunities for the developing countries—I come to all the issues at stake in the continuing work of the new U.N. Trade and Development Board and its committees, and of the GATT [General Agreement on Tariffs and Trade]. These are some of the problems we must face together. Primary prices are unstable, and many have tended downward in the last decade. The tariff structures in the industrial countries hit harder at the processed and manufactured goods than at raw materials. Internal taxes discourage the consumption of tropical products. And finally, there is need for greater effort to improve production and efficiency in the export industries of the developing countries.

Many of the developing countries suffer enormous uncertainties and interruptions of trade, with their unstable, fluctuating export earnings. The world has already put into effect some means of providing compensatory finance and balance-of-payments support to help the developing countries deal with such difficulties. Perhaps we will never find an ideal solution, but I think we have by no means reached the end of the road in dealing with these problems. We must continue to do everything practicable to provide to developing countries resources that are effectively related to the fluctuations in their export trade.

When I say we need a concerted attack on these obstacles, I do not mean a great debate in which the attack is concerted against the governments of the wealthier countries. Complaints about other countries' policies have their place in international politics—they seldom change what the other nations actually do, but they help make the complainant a hero to his own countrymen—and that has its place in politics too.

But when it comes to trade between the world's "north" and the world's "south," we need not a general debate about general principles but concrete proposals, direct negotiations, specific nose-to-nose confrontations about particular ways the developing countries can increase their exports and how the rest of us can really help, commodity by commodity.

RESEARCH ON CAUSE AND CURES OF POVERTY

Another vital contribution the industrialized nations can make to development is to expand their own research into the cause and cures of poverty. Partly this is a matter of putting extra emphasis on those fields of science that are especially relevant to the needs and possibilities of the developing countries. We stand here in the presence of exciting breakthroughs in nutrition, in farming, in water use, in meteorology, in energy. All these are vital, and it is particularly gratifying that the United Nations Advisory Group of Scientists have put the development of water resources and the evolution of new high-protein diets at the top of their list of points needing special attack.

Mr. President, while I am on this subject, I should like to say a special word about the work of the Advisory Committee on the Application of Science and Technology to Development. My Government will make known in due course its detailed views with respect to the specific proposals made by this group in the report which is before us.[*] As to the report itself, I would only say at this time that it is clear, precise, and professional—high testimony to the quality of work that can be done in our international community. On behalf of my delegation, I should like to congratulate all members of the Advisory Committee, the many experts of the

[*] U.N. doc. E/4026.

specialized agencies who contributed to it, and the members of the United Nations Secretariat under whose supervision the work went forward.

But I have more in mind than the merits of the recommendations put forward and the quality of the report as a whole. I have in mind the background of this report and the process by which these proposals have taken shape for our consideration.

The background of the report, as we all know, is the Conference on the Application of Science and Technology to Problems of the Developing Areas, held here in Geneva in early 1963.* That conference was criticized by superficial observers. They said that the whole thing was much too big—too many people, too many subjects, too many papers, too much talk to do any good. They said that the whole thing was much too vague—too general, too unfocused, too disparate—and perhaps there was something in some of this criticism.

But it was a start. And the big thing is that we did not let it die. We maintained the momentum generated at that conference. We went on to the next step. Within a few months after the close of that conference, this Council recommended the establishment of an expert committee of advisers to carry on—to pick up where the conference left off—to sort the important from what is merely useful.

I have no doubt, Mr. President, that what followed was a difficult and tedious exercise for the committee of advisers. But they went about it systematically. They consulted and took evidence. They worked steadily and quietly. And out of thousands of things that might be good to do, they have derived a few dozen of things which it is urgent and necessary to do—which, in fact, it would be outrageous not to do. They have resisted dreams of tomorrow's science and thought hard about today's technology. They have refrained from proposing yet another agency and come to grips instead with existing agencies—what more they might do, what we know they can do better, with foreseeable resources.

So what began as a seemingly unmanageable project has been tamed, mastered, and transmitted into a sensible list of specific

* For background, see Bulletin of Feb. 4, 1963, p. 188, and Feb. 25, 1963, p. 302.

proposals of priority value and manageable proportion. This is no small accomplishment in so short a time. And we can all take heart from this exercise. It bodes well for the work of the Council and of the U.N. system at large.

RESEARCH ON URBANIZATION

The Advisory Committee focused of course on science and technology—that is what it was asked to do. But we need research and inquiry fully as much in great areas of social confusion and uncertainty.

I must be content with one vital example. All through the developing world we face an increasing crisis of accelerated and uncontrolled urbanization. Men and women and children are streaming into the great cities, generally the capital cities, from the monotony and all too often the misery of rural life, and they are moving, bag and baggage, long before farming can afford to lose their labor or the city is ready to put them to work and accommodate them properly.

This rootless, hopeless, workless urban poverty is the greatest single cause of misery in the world. Can we lessen or redirect this flow? Can we prepare the urban world better to receive it? Or improve the rural world enough to diminish the flood? We don't know, because we have not sought seriously to find out.

We lack adequate policies, because we have so few facts and so few people trained to develop and implement programs. For too long we have proceeded on the false assumption that people would really rather live in villages than anywhere and that it is better for society if they did. The trouble is they don't—even when the village is modernized and sanitized and electrified, people move into larger towns and cities.

Some countries have in fact recognized that the problem is not less urbanization but more urban areas—not just one or two in each country. Some are experimenting with regional development programs—and here I mean regions within countries—in an effort to create new urban centers which will not only deflect migration headed for already overcrowded capital cities but will have an impact on the surrounding countryside and improve rural living in a wide area around the new cities. But the process of decentralization is difficult and complex, and failures—temporary or permanent— are as common as successes.

This is the background against which we helped launch the unanimous decision of the Social Commission to recommend a research training program in regional development, using as a laboratory the current efforts being made in a variety of different lands, political systems, and cultures to deal with the problems of urban in-migration.

With some systematic research perhaps some usable conclusions can be drawn about how best to encourage an appropriate pattern of urban development which will avoid the blight and misery so visible in so many cities throughout the world. This is precisely the kind of research we need if the full weight of modern discovery and modern resources is to be brought to bear on the social as well as the technical problems of the developing world.

POPULATION CONTROL

In this same context—of science applied to an explosive human and social problem—we have to make a wholly new attack upon what President Johnson has called "the multiplying problems of our multiplying populations." * It is perhaps only in the last 5 years that we have come fully to realize on what scale they are proliferating. Since 1960, under United Nations auspices, censuses have been held in scores of countries, in nine of them for the first time. They have all underlined the same fact—that population is increasing more rapidly than had previously been imagined and that this accelerating growth, in all developing lands, is eating into the pitiful margins needed to give bread and hope to those already born. We have to find the ways of social, moral, and physical control adequate to stem the rising, drowning flood of people. We need more knowledge, we need more cooperative effort. In fact, much that we do elsewhere will be undone unless we can act in this vital field.

* Ibid., July 19, 1965, p. 98.

Aid, trade, research, population control—in all these fields we can mount a convergent attack upon the great gap between rich and poor. But we must also mount it together. And that brings me to some quite concrete suggestions about international organizations in the development field—in what direction they should be going and how fast they should be growing.

MERITS OF FUNCTIONAL ORGANIZATIONS

The organizations of the U.N. family perform a rich variety of useful labors. At a moment when one of the central political organs in the U.N. is temporarily hung up on a constitutional hook, it is worth reflecting on the success and growth of the specialized agencies and of the central funds which provide a growing fraction—more than half in some cases—of the resources they apply to the business of development. These agencies are an illustration, and a good one, of the proposition that international politics is not a game in which an inch gained by our player must mean an inch lost by another.

The reality is that international agreements can be reached, and international organizations can be formed, and international common law can be elaborated, on subjects which draw nations together even as they continue to quarrel about the frontiers and friends and ideological frenzies which keep them apart.

So let's look for a moment at the political merits of functional organizations—the kind that work at peace through health, or food, or education, or labor, or communications, or meteorology, or culture, or postal service, or children, or money, or economic growth, or the exploration of outer space—organizations, that is, for the pursuit of some specific and definable task beyond the frontiers of one nation, a task for which the technology is already conceived or conceivable, for which a common interest is mutually recognized, for which institutions can—and therefore must—be designed.

Organizations like these begin by taking the world as it is. No fundamental political reforms are needed; no value systems have to be altered; no ideologies have to be seriously compromised. These organizations start from where we are and then take the next step. And that, as the ancient Chinese guessed long ago, is the only way to get from here to there.

These organizations tackle jobs that can be managed through imperfect institutions by fallible men and women. Omniscience is not a prerequisite; the peace of the world does not stand or fall on the success of any one organization; mistakes need not be fatal.

These limited-purpose organizations bypass the obstacle of sovereignty. National independence is not infringed when a nation voluntarily accepts in its own interest the restraints imposed by cooperation with others. Nobody has to play who doesn't want to play, but for those who do play, there are door prizes for all.

All these special characteristics of the functional agencies are important to their survival value and growth potential. The best example is also momentarily the most dramatic. In the midst of the military, political, and diplomatic turmoil of Southeast Asia, the governments which are working together to promote the regional development of the Lower Mekong Basin have continued to work there in surprising and encouraging harmony.

POLITICAL DISPUTES IN TECHNICAL AGENCIES

But a certain shadow hangs over the affairs of the technical agencies —a shadow which threatens to compromise the very virtues we have just been discussing. That shadow is political controversy, and it has no place on the agenda of the technical agencies.

I shall not attempt to draw sharp lines along the sometimes murky borders between the politicoideological and the functional fields—between just what is doctrinal and just what is technical. The important distinctions are clear enough. The difference between appropriate content for the general debate in the General Assembly and appropriate content for debates on international labor or world literacy or world health does not need much elaboration. We can all recognize that the remaining problems of colonialism have practically nothing to do with the problem of adult literacy—and vice versa. We have organizational arrangements for dealing with both. We have times and places set aside, we have agenda prepared and representatives assigned, for dealing in separate and orderly ways with these and other subjects.

Yet we cannot overlook a disturbing tendency to dilute the proceedings of the technical agencies with ideological dispute—and to steal time, energy, and resources needed to help the developing countries, and divert it instead to extraneous issues calculated to stir everybody's emotions without raising anybody's per capita income.

This limits the value, inhibits the growth, hurts the prestige, and crimps the resources of the technical agencies. It is a wasteful and moreover a futile exercise. It is only to be hoped that these diversionary tactics will fade from our forums so we may get along more promptly with the practical, useful, technical tasks which lie before us in such profusion.

The great spurt in useful activity by the U.N. specialized and affiliated agencies has come about through the good sense of the members, expressed in a series of actions by the Economic and Social Council and in the General Assembly, and designed to provide new resources to break down the main obstacles to development.

Through the Expanded Program of Technical Assistance and the U.N. Special Fund the members have already provided close to $1 billion to help the developing countries organize the use of knowledge and to get ready to make effective use of large capital investments. Now these two programs, on the recommendation of the Council, are to be merged in the 20th General Assembly to become the U.N. Development Program.

We are reaching this year, for the first time, the target of $150 million a year for that program. My Government believes that this has been a useful and efficient way to provide technical assistance and preinvestment capital. The target should now be raised. For our part, we would be glad to see the target set substantially higher.

We also think that the use for development of noncommercial exports of food from some of the surplus producing countries has been promising. At a meeting in Rome last week we have already indicated that we would be glad to see the World Food Program continued, with a target for the next 3-year period almost triple that of the 3-year experimental period which is just now coming to an end. We hope that other nations which foresee noncommercial surpluses in their agricultural horoscope will join in expanding the World Food Program as another way to transfer needed resources for the benefit of the developing countries.

We are also pleased with the progress of industrial development. The establishment of the Center for Industrial Development in the U.N. Secretariat has clearly proved itself a sound and progressive move. We think the time has come to move further along this line and find much promise in the suggestions made by the distinguished representative of the United Kingdom on this subject. We strongly agree that it will be necessary to secure additional resources for the promotion of industrialization. We believe, however, that rather than to establish yet another special voluntary fund, such resources could best be made available by special arrangements within the framework of the new U.N. Development Program.

INTERNATIONAL DEVELOPMENT PROGRAMS

Beyond raising the target for the Development Program, and expanding the World Food Program, and giving a special push to the work of industrialization, I would foresee another kind of development activity to which I believe every government should accord a very high priority indeed. This is the field which might be called truly international development programs.

So far we have needed to define the word "development" to encompass only the elements of an individual country's economic growth and social progress. Some regional projects have gained favor as well, but clearly visible now on the horizon are programs and projects in which the operating agency will not be a national government or a private company or even a small group of governments in a region—but rather one of the U.N.'s own family of worldwide organizations.

The best example—one that is already requiring our attention—is the World Weather Watch now being planned by the WMO [World Meteorological Organization]. In the preliminary design work already underway, it is proposed, for example, to:

—probe into atmosphere from satellites in orbit;

—establish ground stations to read out what the satellites have to say and to process and communicate weather information throughout continental regions;

—establish floating weather stations to give more coverage to vast oceanic areas, particularly in the Southern Hemisphere;

—possibly even launch balloons from international sites which will travel around the world at a constant level making weather observations as they go.

The major components of the World Weather Watch must continue to be the national facilities, operated primarily for national purposes and also contributing to the needs of the world. But we are speaking here of additional facilities, some of which may need to be internationally operated and perhaps internationally owned and which may be very costly even at the start. Money would have to be raised on a voluntary basis and placed in the hands of an international agency—the WMO, perhaps, or some new operating facility.

Here, then, is a new kind of problem for us to think about before it overtakes us. Here is a great big development project, involving activity inherently international which will have to be financed internationally. We would propose that the U.N. Development Program start experimenting with this kind of development activity, modifying as necessary the rules and procedures that were drafted with national development projects in mind.

Maybe such large projects will have to be financed in some special way. But for a start we would like to see the new U.N. Development Program, with its rich experience in financing various kinds of development, work on this subject and present to its own board, and to this Council, an analysis of the problem of meeting the costs of global international operations.

If all these suggestions for raising our sights—yes, and our contributions—give the impression that the United States believes in the strengthening of international development institutions, you may be sure that that impression is correct. Most of these institutions need to be strengthened to meet, within their respective areas, the challenge of the requirements and aspirations of the developing countries. Equally, and perhaps even more important, their policies and actions need to be harmonized, for there is no room left in this world for narrow parochialism. The various aspects and problems of economic and social development—modernization of agriculture and industrial growth, health and production, education and social welfare, trade and transportation, human rights and individual freedom —have become so closely interrelated as to call for interlocking measures and programs.

These basic conditions in the contemporary world give meaning and urgency to the review and reappraisal of the Economic and Social Council's role and functions which U Thant proposed in this chamber a year ago. The position of my Government is set forth in our submission to the Secretary-General reproduced in document E/4052/Add.2 and needs no further explanation.

But there are just a few points I want to stress:

With the U.N. system as envisaged in and established by the charter, the General Assembly and ECOSOC [2] are the two principal intergovernmental organs with overall responsibilities for U.N. policies and activities in the economic and social field, their orderly development and effective implementation.

Whatever the record of the Council in the past—and we believe that it is a good record—it has become evident that the Council faces ever-increasing difficulties in the discharge of its functions due to the ever-widening scope of the United Nations and the multiplication of machinery.

To make the Council fully representative of the total enlarged membership of the U.N., its size will soon be increased by the necessary ratifications of the charter amendment.

We believe that the role of the Council as a preparatory body for the General Assembly, and acting under its authority, needs to be clarified and strengthened. It should make a significant contribution to the work of the General Assembly by drawing its attention

[2] Economic and Social Council.

to major issues confronting the world economy; by formulating proposals for relevant action; by providing supporting documentation; and in preparing and reviewing programs with a sense of financial responsibilities—and thus assisting in the preparation of budget estimates by the Secretary-General for appropriate action by the committees of the General Assembly.

In stressing the coordination function of ECOSOC every care needs to be taken to encourage rather than to hinder the work of functional and regional economic and social bodies and the activities of the specialized agencies and other related organizations. The role of these functional organizations in achieving coordination within their areas of competence needs to be more fully recognized.

The review and reappraisal proposed by the Secretary-General is a difficult task and adequate time must be allowed for it. Many of the constructive suggestions he made yesterday regarding research, documentation, and sound budgeting are directly related to the work of the Council and deserve most careful thought. It is our hope that the Council at the present session will make the necessary arrangements to facilitate and assure such study in depth and full consideration.

We assume the review will go through several stages, including consideration by both the Council and the General Assembly. The Council will have to undertake thorough preparatory work in order to enable the General Assembly and its Committees II [Economic and Financial], III [Social, Humanitarian and Cultural], and V [Administrative and Budgetary] to reach informed conclusions and to take the necessary actions.

Last but not least, and this I cannot stress strongly enough, the review will require the closest possible cooperation between all members of the Council representing developed and developing countries. The Council will wither away, whatever conclusions are reached by the review, unless there is a will among all of us to make it succeed. And succeed it must as an indispensable organ of the United Nations for the achievement, beyond anything we have experienced to date, of constructive international cooperation in the economic and social fields and as a powerful aid to the promotion of economic development.

Finally, let me say that the need for joint action in the wide field of development is obvious. Whether we are talking about aid, or trade, or research, or urban development, or industrialization—whether we are talking about scientific discovery or about institution building—we hold that there are no monopolies of trained minds and disciplined imaginations in any of our countries.

Joint action is, after all, the final significance of all we do in our international policies today. But we are still held back by our old parochial nationalisms. We are still beset with dark prejudices. We are still divided by angry, conflicting ideologies. Yet all around us our science, our instruments, our technologies, our interests, and indeed our deepest aspirations draw us more and more closely into a single neighborhood.

This must be the context of our thinking—the context of human interdependence in the face of the vast new dimensions of our science and our discovery. Just as Europe could never again be the old closed-in community after the voyages of Columbus, we can never again be a squabbling band of nations before the awful majesty of outer space.

We travel together, passengers on a little space ship, dependent on its vulnerable reserves of air and soil; all committed for our safety to its security and peace; preserved from annihilation only by the care, the work, and, I will say, the love we give our fragile craft. We cannot maintain it half fortunate, half miserable, half confident, half despairing, half slave—to the ancient enemies of man—half free in a liberation of resources undreamed of until this day. No craft, no crew can travel safely with such vast contradictions. On their resolution depends the survival of us all.

§ Critical Analysis

A speech designed to "do work" normally has a central thesis, an overall proposition to which the discourse, even with possible digressions, must conform. Can you find such a thesis in Stevenson's last speech? In an article published in *Foreign Affairs* and reprinted in his book *Putting First Things First*, Stevenson opens with the statement, "Peace is the most imperative business in the world today." [1] In what way and to what extent may this statement be regarded as the unstated thesis of Stevenson's last speech?

§

In the tradition of American, as of British, politics, a reputation for humor is thought to be detrimental to a candidate. Americans, so it is said, want their politicians to be pleasant, bland, and dull. For example, an Arkansas Democrat was heard to say while following a television broadcast of one of Stevenson's campaign speeches, "Hmph! Still jokin'." He did not vote for Stevenson. What is your judgment concerning Stevenson's use of humor, off and on the platform? Did it help or hinder him in speechmaking, in his campaigns, in his career? Do you find any example of humor in "Strengthening the International Development Institutions"?

§

Stevenson asserts: "A steady, overall, 4-percent rate of growth in national income is in itself a difficult achievement. Its effects are tragically nullified if the rate of population growth is 3 percent or even more." What assumptions are hidden in this assertion?

§

What do you conceive to be the function intended for the following language? "We shall conquer, no doubt, the dark face of the moon. But I would hope we can with equal confidence conquer the dark face of poverty and give men and women new life, new hope, new space on this planet." How well do you think it fulfills that function?

[1] "Putting First Things First," *Foreign Affairs*, 38 (January 1960), 191; *Putting First Things First: A Democratic View* (New York: Random House, 1960), p. 3.

§

In his exciting anthology of speeches Houston Peterson asks two questions concerning Adlai Stevenson: "Why did this man win such a large following overnight in this country as well as in Europe? Why did so many people turn to him simply after hearing one or two speeches on the radio?" [2] How would you answer Professor Peterson?

§ SUGGESTIONS FOR FURTHER READING

There is as yet no adequate biography of Adlai Stevenson. Doubtless one will be forthcoming in due course. Meanwhile two thoughtful books by Stuart Gerry Brown may be relied on: *Conscience in Politics: Adlai E. Stevenson in the 1950's* (Syracuse, N.Y.: Syracuse University Press, 1961) and *Adlai E. Stevenson: A Short Biography: The Conscience of the Country* (Woodbury, N. Y.: Barron's Woodbury Press, 1965).

Tributes of his friends, partial reports by those who knew him in some phase of his active life, and campaign biographies obviously designed with an eye toward 1952 or 1956, even though limited for one reason or another, may serve a useful purpose. Among these books the following may be mentioned: *As We Knew Adlai: The Stevenson Story by Twenty-Two Friends*, edited and with a preface by Edward P. Doyle and a foreword by Adlai E. Stevenson III (New York: Harper & Row, 1966); Richard N. Goodwin, with a eulogy by President Lyndon B. Johnson, *The Sower's Seed: A Tribute to Adlai E. Stevenson* (New York: New American Library, 1965); Lillian Ross, *Adlai Stevenson* (Philadelphia: Lippincott, 1966); Alden Whitman and *The New York Times, Portrait: Adlai E. Stevenson: Politician, Diplomat, Friend* (New York: Harper & Row, 1965); Kenneth S. Davis, *A Prophet in His Own Country: The Triumphs and Defeats of Adlai E. Stevenson* (Garden City, N.Y.: Doubleday, 1957); Noel F. Busch, *Adlai E. Stevenson of Illinois: A Portrait* (Farrar, Straus and Young, 1952); John Bartlow Martin, *Adlai Stevenson* (New York: Harper & Brothers, 1952); Bessie R. James and Mary Waterstreet, ed., *Adlai's Almanac: The Wit and Wisdom of Stevenson of Illinois* (New York: Henry Schuman, 1952); Elizabeth Stevenson Ives and Hildegarde Dolson, *My Brother Adlai* (New York: Morrow, 1956).

[2] *A Treasury of the World's Great Speeches* (New York: Simon and Schuster, 1954), p. 822.

Perhaps the best way to become acquainted with the life and thought of Adlai Stevenson is through his speeches, on which he lavished care and in which he took a pardonable pride. Fortunately, although there is no definitive edition of his speeches, the texts of many of them have been published and should be available in any well-furnished library. Others, buried in the reports of the United Nations or the files of the Department of State, may be found by willing searchers; and anyone truly interested in Stevenson and his speechmaking may seek recordings that, better than any printed text, demonstrate Stevenson's grace and power as a speaker. The scholarly and quasi-scholarly studies of his discourse now coming from the graduate schools will intrigue students of rhetoric; and Americans generally look forward to the eventual publication of Stevenson's papers now being edited at the University of Hawaii by Walter Johnson and Carol Evans under the sponsorship of a distinguished Advisory Committee.

Among the sources for the printed texts of Stevenson's speeches, the following should be mentioned as an example: *Major Campaign Speeches of Adlai E. Stevenson: 1952* (New York: Random House, 1953) includes an introduction by Stevenson, with the texts of some fifty speeches, notably his welcoming address and his speech of acceptance at the Democratic Convention in Chicago in 1952. Another readily available collection —*Putting First Things First: A Democratic View* (New York: Random House, 1960)—includes the texts of speeches delivered at Harvard University, McGill University, and elsewhere. *Looking Outward* (New York: Harper & Row, 1963), edited with commentary by Robert L. and Selma Schiffer, has an introduction by Adlai Stevenson and a preface by the late President John F. Kennedy. Among the texts of the speeches provided in it are the eulogies for Dag Hammarskjold and Eleanor Roosevelt and the arraignment of the Soviet Union (October 25, 1962) for the building of sites for nuclear weapons in Cuba. *Call to Greatness* (New York: Harper & Brothers, 1954) is taken from the Godkin Lectures delivered by Stevenson at Harvard University in March 1954.

Stevenson made many work-a-day speeches, characteristically with lucidity and reason, at the United Nations and elsewhere. Not all of them by any means have been collected. One may be cited as an example: *Major Accomplishments of the U.N. General Assembly*, Department of State Publication 7505 (Washington, D.C.: Government Printing Office, 1963). This pamphlet provides the text of a statement made by Ambassador Stevenson at a press conference at the United Nations, December 21, 1962.

Index